Israel, Land of
God's Promise

"Murray Dixon has been teaching on God's purposes for the nation of Israel and the Jewish people for nearly thirty years. It is nearly twenty years since the publication of the widely acclaimed *The Rebirth and Restoration of Israel*, which has since become one of the classic books written about this subject. Murray skillfully demonstrates from the Scriptures the relationship between the Gentile Church and God's purposes for the Jewish people, and he explains the historic severance of the Church from its Jewish and biblical roots, which has left us all the poorer.

This book is a compelling 'must-read' for every Christian. It is firmly based upon the Holy Scriptures and helps us to understand the purposes of the God of history. He helps us understand that the destiny of the world today, including the Church, and the destiny of Israel are closely woven together."

Hugh Kitson
Author and documentary film-maker
(*Jerusalem, The Covenant City; Lest We Forget; The Forsaken Promise*)

Israel, Land of God's Promise

Murray Dixon

Sovereign World

Sovereign World Ltd
PO Box 784
Ellel
Lancaster LA1 9DA
England

ISBN–10: 1 85240 442 6
ISBN–13: 978 1 85240 442 0

Typeset by CRB Associates, Reepham, Norfolk
Cover design by CCD, www.ccdgroup.co.uk
Printed in Malta

Contents

Dedication

To Rosemary, my encouraging wife; Rowan, Jeremy and Ruth, my family who share the burden; and to the host of unknown intercessors for Israel.

This is what the LORD says:

"Sing for joy for Jacob;
    shout for the foremost of the nations.
Make your praises heard, and say,
    'O LORD, save your people,
    the remnant of Israel.'"

(Jeremiah 31:7)

Acknowledgments

The material for this book has built up over a period of many years, during which time I have avidly read and listened to teaching concerning Jewish–Christian relations and the inheritance God has prepared for his covenant peoples. My thinking has, therefore, been influenced by many people, not all of whom I am able to name. However, I particularly want to acknowledge my heartfelt gratitude to the late Dr Derek Prince, Mr Lance Lambert and the Reverend David Pawson, who provided an oasis at a time when I was very thirsty.

During my first visit to Israel, a Jewish woman who confessed Yeshua as Messiah challenged me, "If you Christians don't pray for the Jews, who will?" Not only have I never been able to forget her heart-cry, but I was also reminded of Jesus' words: "From the one who has been entrusted with much, much more will be asked" (Luke 12:48). I owe much to this daughter of Zion who ensured I was involved in Israel's restoration.

My understanding developed initially over twenty years of visits to Israel. Then, during the past six years I have lived in the region. This was firstly on Mount Carmel, near where Elijah challenged the god of the Baals, then in the town of Mary Magdalene known today as Migdal on the shore of Lake Galilee, and now in Jerusalem, the city of the great King. There I am Rector of Christ Church, the first Protestant church in the Middle East.

The questions posed to me by pilgrims in the various groups we have led to Israel, and members of the many congregations with whom I have been privileged to speak, have stimulated deeper thinking and research. Meanwhile the various opportunities of living with Israeli families have deepened my awareness of how little I have learned and understood. To all these people I am indebted.

I am extremely thankful to Ken Burnett for his friendship, his encouragement, and for his patience and wisdom as he read through my script making those needful suggestions for correction and improvement. To the late Alison Bartlett for proofreading and suggestions that have also sharpened the text. I hope that my family who have borne inconvenience are rewarded with the fulfillment I have received in pursuing this burning concern within me.

Foreword by Lance Lambert

I have known Murray Dixon for some twenty years, and it is a pleasure for me to write this foreword. Not a few servants of the Lord begin in the Spirit and end in the flesh. It is however not so with Murray. From a life of spiritual vision and understanding he has written this book. I can personally attest to his faithfulness to the Lord and to the calling that he has received.

In this present era Israel has been considerably and consistently misrepresented by the world media. This fact in itself is dangerous because it has given rise to a growing anti-Semitism in the Western and developed nations, and is now masquerading in its new guise as anti-Israelism. It is sad that so many Christian believers and Church leaders have been influenced not by the Word of God but by the media of a fallen world.

Yet it is clear that it is not merely the Old Testament which speaks authoritatively concerning the salvation of Israel and the Jewish people but also the New Testament. The apostle Paul prophesies,

> If their fall is the riches of the world, and their loss the riches of the Gentiles; how much more their fullness?
>
> (Romans 11:12 asv)

And again,

> If the casting away of them is the reconciling of the world, what shall the receiving of them be, but life from the dead?
>
> (Romans 11:15 asv)

Paul then asserts by the Spirit of God,

> As touching the gospel, they [the Jewish people] are enemies for your sake: but as touching the election, they are beloved for the fathers' [patriarchs'] sake. For the gifts and the calling of God are not repented of [are irrevocable].
>
> (Romans 11:28–29 asv)

No amount of theological acrobatics can undo the reality of these words.

Murray Dixon has done the true believing church in the world today a great service in updating and expanding this book. May the Lord use it to bring light and illumination to many, and where necessary a deliverance from the spirit of anti-Semitism which lurks in so much of Western society and not least in many Christians. It would be wonderful if many Christians were to begin to understand the mystery of Israel and to see the whole drama of redemption in its fullness.

Lance Lambert

Foreword by Reuven Berger

I was deeply touched by *Israel, Land of God's Promise* because of the depth of the heart understanding expressed by Mr Dixon in relation to God's plan for Israel and the Church. Though many books have been written and are now being written on this subject, few have penetrated the mystery of the drama of Israel, the Church and the nations with the clarity of perception that is revealed in this book. *Israel, Land of God's Promise* gives the reader a solid foundational theological explanation of Israel's present physical and spiritual restoration which is backed up by much historical evidence confirming the prophetic Scripture. The approach that the author takes in his presentation of this restoration will require a major shift in the understanding held by many Christians, even many who claim to be great friends of Israel. The author brings us back to the essence of the identity of Yeshua, the Messiah of Israel, His Jewishness, His deep connection to His people Israel, and to the very essence of the nature of the New Covenant people of God, as seen in relation to the holy messianic remnant in Israel.

For many readers, this book will present a clear challenge to repent of many of the historical and generational sins of the Church against the people of Israel, sins which the author describes in detail and with uncompromising clarity. This book will also shed fresh light upon Scripture and will be instrumental to correct much of the historical deviations which took place in Christian theology, by unfolding the one continuous plan of the God of Israel who has remained forever faithful to Israel and to His promises and covenants with her. The holy remnant of Israel remains forever the cultivated Olive Tree into which the believing Gentiles are grafted making them part of the greater Commonwealth of Israel. This reality makes us better understand the importance of the Messianic Body which God is restoring today amongst His Jewish people, throughout the world but especially in Israel and in Jerusalem. The author presents the Church in a light that helps her to relate properly to the whole nation of Israel and most particularly to the holy remnant in Israel so that being properly related and joined both to the tree and to the Root, Yeshua the Jew, the Church receives both her true messianic identity and finds the way back to true unity.

Mr Dixon's book is both revelatory in the way the author expounds Scripture and factual in the way he supplies abundant historical information related to the history of the Jewish people and the Church. The book is comprehensive in the way it traces the development of the wrong attitudes and theological understanding of the fathers of the Church which eventually led to massive persecution of the Jews throughout the centuries. It provides much relevant historical information which explains the path which the Church pursued leading to its tragic decline because of its twisted relationship to God's Word and the Jewish people and the horrific consequences which followed from nation to nation. Even though Mr Dixon holds the Church and the nations responsible before God for their grievous deviations and cruel persecution of the Jews, he also shows how through the sins of the nations, Scripture was being fulfilled in relation to the judgments proclaimed upon Israel for her disobedience. The author does not escape facing the paradox of God's dealings in this mystery of His relationship to Israel. Israel is being judged through the horrendous sins of the nations and yet she is led as the scapegoat of the nations on a parallel course with her suffering Messiah King, identifying deeply with Him while still blinded to His identity.

Israel, Land of God's Promise also explains in detail the historical reality behind the physical and spiritual restoration of Israel, enumerating many relevant facts that most readers will not have known before. This information helps to make the reality of the miracle of Israel's restoration even much greater than what was formally understood. Here again, the abundance of historical details concerning early Christian support and vision for the restoration of Zion, the various *aliyot* from the different nations, the restoration of the Hebrew language etc. cause the reader to be deeply strengthened in faith and in thanksgiving to the God of Israel who has performed such great wonders. The book also covers in a meticulous way the very pressing threat of the battle which faces Israel today in relation to the present revival of fundamentalist Islam in the Arab and Moslem world. This threat is not just Israel's personal challenge, but a reality that that confronts the entire world.

Israel, Land of God's Promise is written with a sincere love of the truth and though it presents much of the hard reality of the past, present and future in a clear, non-diplomatic and uncompromising language, in no way is the book prejudiced nor hostile to any part of the Church nor to any people group. The underlying reality that pervades the narrative is God's love and the promise and hope of His redemption for all mankind. Though the book presents the contemporary picture of the Middle East in its full impending gloomy reality, it leaves the reader not with a sense of despair but one of hope rooted in the fulfillment of God's wonderful plan and promises. As one who has lived in this part of the world for many years, both amongst the Jews and the Arabs, Mr Dixon has succeeded in communicating both a prophetic trumpet sound of alarm and a comforting message about the God who is faithful to keep His Word despite man's sin and continuous unfaithfulness. This book will greatly enrich all those who read it with an open and sincere heart. I would encourage both those who are believers from all different Church backgrounds and those who do not profess to be believers to read this book and give it your full attention. It can surely help to give you a new vantage point that could change your whole perspective of God, His Word and plan, our times, and God's relationship to Israel, the Church and the nations.

Reuven Berger
Pastor, Congregation of the Lamb on Mount Zion
(which meets at Christ Church, Jerusalem)

Preface to First Edition

My reading of Jewish history during the time of the Church has resulted in considerable inner anguish and even weeping as I have discovered the depths of inhuman treatment vented upon this ancient people. Accompanying this sense of anguish is my shame for the horrific treatment we Christians have been guilty of perpetrating in the lives of Jewish people for generations and the wider ramifications this influence has exerted.

So deeply entrenched is anti-Semitism that we use many phrases, terms of reference and jokes destructive to Jewish people. They are often used unwittingly, but nevertheless find roots in anti-Semitism. We often hear a hard-hearted moneylender or unscrupulous businessman referred to as a "Shylock," a reminder of Shakespeare's caricature of the Jew as a monstrous, bloodthirsty usurer.

How frequently do we participate in a rousing cheer: "Hip! Hip! Hooray!"? Originally this was *"Hep! Hep!"* – a derogatory rallying cry against the Jewish people. It is said to have been the Crusaders' rallying cry and was certainly used in the anti-Jewish riots of Germany. The term derives from the initials of *Hierosolyma est perdita* – "Jerusalem is lost!" – the rejoicing cry of many in Greece at the misfortunes of Jerusalem in the first century.

Even our censuring judgment on behavior which we describe as "beyond the pale," originates from the unjust confinement of Jews in settlements in Poland.

I have often heard preachers refer to the Israelites in order to illustrate blindness and hardness of heart but rarely refer to their examples of faithfulness and obedience. And so I could continue, but the point is made.

It has been a shocking awakening to me, as I suspect it will be to many Christians, to realize the extent of unbiblical teaching concerning the Jewish people within the Church. The resulting wicked behaviors ensuing from that teaching, climaxing in the infamous attempt to destroy all Jews in the Holocaust, has been something even harder, perhaps impossible for me to fully grasp.

Therein, surmounting the centuries of erroneous teaching, we have seen the crucifixion of the Jews, from which by God's overruling we have also witnessed their physical resurrection. I have endeavored to trace the roots and development of anti-Semitism in the hope that their exposure will lead to a better understanding of the truth.

If we are going to make sense of history and understand the complete function of the Church, there are fundamental things we need to understand. These include the Church's Jewish roots, the place God has determined for Israel in history, the relationship of the Church with Israel, and the responsibility of the Church to Israel. I have begun this book by demonstrating the Jewishness of Jesus and the significance of his Jewishness.

I will reflect on the revelation Paul received of the mystery of the Church and the inheritances promised to Israel and the Church. Within three centuries of Paul's writing, the Church leaders separated the Church from the Jews and the Bible from its Jewishness. The extent of this error is witnessed in the record of the compounding tragedies suffered by both the Jewish people and the Church in the centuries which followed.

During the Evangelical revival of the nineteenth century, the return to the Bible stimulated a change of heart towards the Jewish people. Not only was there expression of concern for the restoration of the Jewish homeland but there emerged a genuine compassion for the Jewish people. Many Jewish people were touched by this authentic concern for them, some then recognizing Jesus as their Redeemer.

Coinciding with this turning point was the emergence of the Zionist movement and plans for the restoration of their ancient homeland. As the twentieth century progressed, we saw evidence of the fulfillment of the promises to Israel. Parallel to this was restoration of the Church due to the renewed work of the Holy Spirit.

Before us lies the challenge to make up for the years of inexpressible but repairable damage that we Christians have been responsible for to the Jewish people. We do need to understand the past in order to act in accordance with God's will and purpose for the future. It is my prayer that you will be challenged into action, as I personally have felt the need to be.

Murray Dixon
Rosh Hashanah 1987

Preface to Second Edition

Nearly two decades have passed since this book was first published, a period marked by two extraordinary events that changed the Middle East region and particularly Israel: the collapse of the Soviet Union that ended the Cold War, and the Gulf War of 1991. The collapse of the Soviet Union ended the financial and military support enjoyed by both Egypt and Syria as proxies since the 1960s, in the Soviet Union's attempts to destroy Israel which was supported by the other superpower, the United States of America.

The power vacuum thereby created enabled Iran, currently working towards nuclear weapon capability, to establish the foothold it required in its drive to dominate the region and destroy Israel. Using the Hizb'allah [the party of allah] as a proxy militia in Lebanon, Iran with the Syrians had undermined Lebanon's political stability, and instigated a war with Israel on 12 July 2006, that lasted until a cease-fire on 14 August.

During the Gulf War, Israel received thirty-nine missile attacks from Iraq but did not retaliate. Miraculously only one Israeli was directly killed although over four thousand buildings were damaged. The unfinished business of the Gulf War, when Iraq invaded Kuwait, was continued in March 2003 with "Operation Iraqi Freedom" initiated by the US. Saddam Hussein, Iraq's president, was captured and his regime destroyed. The US seized the opportunity to establish a democratic government, causing widespread bloodshed among the Muslim factions and the foreign military presence that continues to this day.

The 1990s opened with Russian Jews, now free to immigrate, flooding to Israel: over that decade 1,000,000 became Israelis. In 1991 "Operation Solomon," a daring undercover airlift, rescued 15,000 Jews from Ethiopia. A greater contrast could not be imagined. Into twentieth-century Israel came Russian engineers, mathematicians, surgeons, dentists, physicists and professional musicians, alongside Ethiopians transported from a twelfth-century lifestyle: all Jews immigrating to the land of the patriarchs. Together they struggled to adapt to Israeli culture and to communicate in the Hebrew language; together they added their unique contributions to this ancient, once dispersed and now regathered people, in the land of promise.

An attempt at a peaceful resolution to the Israeli–Palestinian conflict, which began in Oslo in September 2003, drew traumatic responses from both Palestinians and Israelis. Following the Israeli Prime Minister, Yitzak Rabin's assassination by a religious Jew at a peace rally in November 1995, waves of kamikaze Palestinians blew themselves up in buses, cafés, malls, hotels and other public places. Representatives from the United States, the European Union, the United Nations, and Russia formed "The Quartet," which began to shape international policy toward resolution of this conflict: the "road map," as it came to be known.

In May 1996 the Palestinian Authority was established, and in January 2004 Hamas, a fundamentalist Islamic party allied with Iran, was elected the dominant power of government. Since Israel had withdrawn its army and Jewish population from Gaza in August 2005, Hamas was now fighting Islamic Jihad in Gaza. This soon developed into war with Israel. Israel was now fighting a war on two fronts: in the south and the north.

Fundamentalist Islam is grasping to exert its authority by destroying Israel and reclaiming territory it lost with the collapse of the Ottoman Empire. Israel is the eye of the Islamic storm that is intent upon taking the world for allah. These groups will use any means, usually violent, at their disposal, particularly by instilling fear into the nations. The Psalmist expressed it clearly:

> "Come," they say, "let us destroy them as a nation,
>   that the name of Israel be remembered no more."
>
> (Psalm 83:4)

Israel, Land of God's Promise testifies to the covenants of Israel's God becoming historical facts – His Story – as he continues restoring Israel in the land of promise until that day when Israel is redeemed. Then God's *shekinah* glory will radiate from this chosen nation to all the nations of the earth.

Murray Dixon
Jerusalem, 14 August 2006
(The day of the Israeli-Hizb'allah ceasefire)

"The Truth Will Set You Free" (John 8:32)

> Forgive us for crucifying Thee a second time in their flesh. For, O Lord, we know not what we did.

These words conclude a prayer of repentance uttered by Pope John XXIII, for actions by Christians towards the Jewish people. It is a prayer which needs to flow from the hearts of Christians worldwide.

Not until we are familiar with the Church's behavior for nineteen hundred years towards the Jewish people do we understand the deep significance of this prayer. Nor do we realize, until we have opened the history books, how deeply seated is the anti-Semitic teaching in the Church that even today influences biblical interpretation and Christian action. The Church has been so involved in accusing the Jews of "deicide" – the killing of God – that we Christians stand accountable to the charge of "genocide."

The horrific facts of the Nazi Holocaust in Second World War Europe mark the end of a period of history. Not only does the Holocaust represent a calculated attempt at the genocide of the Jewish people but it also marks the lowest ebb of man's inhumanity to man, sanctioned by the Church by her interlude of silence.

A Jewish theologian, Dr Jakob Jocz, made an astute observation in his book *The Jewish People and Jesus Christ after Auschwitz*:

> Auschwitz is a landmark ranking high in the scale of tragic events in the history of the Jewish people, equal to, if not surpassing, the tragedy of the Fall of Jerusalem in AD 70. Auschwitz is not only a tragedy for Jews; it is a tragedy for mankind.

After Auschwitz marks the possibility of a new beginning for the Jewish people, for the Church, for the world. In regard to Jewish–Christian relationships two events are of outstanding importance: the creation of the State of Israel and Vatican II. Both these events will have far-reaching consequences for the future.[1]

Second thoughts

Declarations from the Roman Catholic Church's Vatican Council of 1962–1965, Vatican II – the legislative body of the Church – not only reflect a careful analysis of both Scripture and Church history regarding the Jewish people, but also make statements reversing their entire theological perception.[2]

The traumatic event of the Holocaust and the startling rebirth of Israel have caused many Christian teachers to pause. They have had to rethink biblical exegesis which claims that God has concluded his dealings with Israel and the Jewish people and now the Church can exclusively claim their promises as her own. The rebirth of Israel within her promised borders on 14 May 1948, and the fact that her multitudinous enemies have not succeeded in destroying her over fifty-eight years, have caused some within the Church to reconsider their own position.

Repentance means a change of heart

John Stott, the evangelical theologian says,

> We need to get the failures of the Church on our conscience, to feel the offence to Christ and the world which these failures are, to weep over the credibility gap between the Church's talk and the Church's walk, to repent of our readiness to excuse and even condone our failures, and to determine to do something about it.[3]

Nowhere is this more applicable than in our history and relationship with the Jewish people. Worldwide there is evidence of a change of heart among many Christians, a repentance that sometimes seems sentimental, but for others is very practical.

Discovery of our Jewish roots as Christians is persuading Gentile Christians to re-read the Bible with new understanding of the

Jewish emphasis. As increasing numbers of Jewish people are finding the fulfillment of their faith in the New Testament, they are providing the Church with a new dimension of teaching and understanding. This not only brings Christians and Jews together, but shatters long-standing prejudices and provides the Church with a fresh vision.

In our reading of Scripture, we have often failed to recognize the identity of both the writer and those for whom it was primarily meant. We have been guilty of appropriating what suits us without due respect to those to whom the promises, statements, commandments, blessings and curses were addressed. We even have evidence of alterations by translators to suit their own purposes.[4]

Restored truth

As Israel is being restored, archaeological discoveries are upholding the authenticity of Scripture and refuting the confusion raised by modernists. The discovery of the Dead Sea Scrolls at Qumran in 1947 was the most significant find to date.

Some teachers claimed that Isaiah chapters 52 and 53, prophesying the details of Jesus' death, were altered after his death to correct the scriptural record. This clearly undermined the prophetic aspect of the word. Since the texts formerly used by our translators only date back to the sixth century AD, the argument could not be disproved. However, with the Qumran discovery we now have a text of Isaiah dating back to one hundred years before Jesus' crucifixion. This text corresponds with the later texts, thereby proving the authority of the prophetic writing.

The restoration of the Hebrew language, which had not been used as an everyday language since the final dispersion of the Jewish people from their land in the second century, has provided a key to biblical understanding. Some eminent biblical scholars working in Israel are convinced that the first language of the New Testament was Hebrew – not Aramaic as has long been held.

Dr Robert Lindsey described his discovery, when translating the Gospel of Mark into Hebrew, of a strong Hebraism in the Gospels of Matthew, Mark and Luke. His attention was caught by the very Hebraic word order of the Greek text of Mark.

Dr David Bivin and Dr Roy Blizzard, in their book, *Understanding*

the Difficult Words of Jesus, explain that our modern translations of
the New Testament are translated from a Greek text that derives
from an earlier Greek text, originally taken from a Hebrew "Life
of Jesus." The writings of the early Church Fathers refer to the
Gospels in Hebrew although no such evidence has yet been
unearthed. From their studies, they deduce that 91% of the original
entire Bible was written in Hebrew.

The root of the problem lies in trying to translate Hebrew words
and idioms into Greek which became meaningless and even more
mystifying when translated into English. An example is the unusual
word *ochloi* that occurs frequently in the Gospels and has been translated "multitudes" which does not fit the text. It has been discovered
that the rabbis used the word *ochloism* which is plural for "the people
of the locality." Not only does this meaning satisfy the context but it
clarifies the meaning.

Although no Hebrew text has yet been discovered these scholars
have demonstrated that difficult scriptural phrases translated from
the Greek, which have puzzled Bible scholars for generations, are
given clear meaning when translated back into Hebrew.

Bivin and Blizzard state,

> Many scholars in Israel are now convinced that the spoken and
> written language of the Jews in the Land of Israel at the time of
> Jesus was indeed Hebrew: and that the Synoptic Gospels were
> derived from original Hebrew sources.[5]

William Albright, the expert archaeologist on the ancient Middle
East, supports these claims. After the discovery of the Dead Sea
Scrolls, he spoke of the Jewishness of the Bible not only being
confirmed but being, in fact, more pronounced than previously
thought. "It was written entirely by Jews, with a spiritual and
literary background in the Bible and the proto-rabbinic culture. So it
remains a Jewish work ... " Albright emphasized the importance of
the Dead Sea discovery concluding "it becomes more Jewish than
we had thought – as truly Jewish as the Old Testament is Israelite."[6]

The Psalmist spoke prophetically,

> But you, O LORD, sit enthroned forever;
>   your renown endures through all generations.

You will arise and have compassion on Zion,
    for it is time to show favor to her;
    the appointed time has come.

                                      (Psalm 102:12–13)

The late Dr Derek Prince, while explaining that today God is restoring both Israel and the Church, comments on these verses from Psalm 102 and their association with Acts 3:20–21, noting the distinction between Israel and the Church:

> Here we have a clear reference to the same period and the same purposes of God. When we read "Zion" in the Bible I think we should understand it in part at least, as the assembly of God's people. As I understand it, "Zion" is a word that is used for all who are related to God as his people by a covenant. It is really the one word that covers Israel and the Church. I do not believe the Church is ever called Israel or that Israel is ever called the Church, but this word "Zion" does cover both God's people: the natural people, Israel, and the spiritual people, the Church...
>
> So, in the New Testament and the Old alike, we have this clear prediction of a time of restoration, a time of rebuilding when God is going to intervene in sovereign grace and in mercy on behalf of his people, to restore them and to build them up. This is the period when we may confidently look for the return of the Lord Jesus Christ, his appearance in glory.[7]

The restoration of Zion – the Church and Israel – is not only a parallel restoration but also a restoration where each is dependent upon the other. God's eternal purpose expressed in the prophets to restore his people to the Land, and the Land to his people, seems to have largely been ignored by both the Jews and the Church. It has taken overwhelming tragedy to achieve this plan and to cause the Church to take another look at the Scriptures in order to understand what God is doing in our time. As the Church begins to perceive how her destiny and that of Israel are interwoven, she will earnestly desire to respond to what the Holy Spirit is saying to the Church.

Isaiah 42:19 is the voice of the Spirit to both Israel and the Church:

> "Who is blind but my servant,
>   and deaf like the messenger I send?
> Who is blind like the one committed to me,
>   blind like the servant of the LORD?"

The fig tree and the vine

Whether we Christians look backwards or forwards, we should see our inseparable relationship with Israel. Our Jewish past is reflected in our treasured Scriptures written by Jewish hands concerning a Jewish Messiah, Jewish apostles, Jewish prophets, and Jewish patriarchs all in the Jewish language.

But the Jewish contribution does not stop at the close of the biblical period. Although our surviving records of the Church's history reflect large gaps, they do bear rich testimony to the Jewish contribution. In the words of one writer:

> Limitations of space prevent the inclusion of many Jewish Christians[8] who have worthily contributed to the growth and glory of the Church ... Suffice it to say that Hebrew Christians are legion, and are to be found in all walks of life."[9]

Although not always recognized, Jewish Christians made significant contributions to the Reformation and to the Evangelical Revival of the nineteenth century. Both Martin Luther and John Wycliffe were profoundly influenced by the fourteenth-century noted biblical scholar and writer, Nicholas of Lyra.[10]

Emmanuel Tremellius made an important contribution to the Reformation as a theologian and an outstanding expert on the Hebrew language. He was looked upon as one of the most learned scholars in oriental languages of his time and celebrated for his Latin translation of the Bible. Tremellius was invited to England by Thomas Cranmer to help frame the Thirty-Nine Articles and the compilation of the Book of Common Prayer. It is not widely understood that a Jew played such a significant role in the doctrinal and liturgical constitution of the Church of England.[11]

Jewish Christian Bible translators, theologians, writers and historians countered the destructive inroads of rationalism into the nineteenth-century European Church, and these contributions are reported in chapter 10.

Our promised future, described in both the Old and the New Testaments, tells of an awesome revival in Israel as the Holy Spirit brings alive the faith of the Jewish people to reveal the glory of the God of Israel to the non-Jewish world:

> For if their rejection is the reconciliation of the world, what will their acceptance be but life from the dead?
>
> (Romans 11:15)

We look forward to a future where the long-awaited Jewish King will rule the earth from Jerusalem, whose gates are to be inscribed with the names of the twelve tribes of Israel and the foundations of whose walls are to be inscribed with the names of the twelve Jewish apostles – and there all the nations shall gather (see Jeremiah 3:17; Zechariah 14:16; Revelation 21).

As the Bible frequently links the fig tree and the vine, the symbols of Israel and the Church, so our destinies are intertwined. While neither can bear the fruit of the other, both are promised fruitfulness – fruit that is now coming to maturity.

> The trees are bearing their fruit;
>> the fig-tree and the vine yield their riches.
> Be glad, O people of Zion,
>> rejoice in the LORD your God,
> for he has given you
>> the teacher for righteousness.
>
> (Joel 2:22–23)

The Jewishness of Jesus

> I've been a Christian for over thirty years and I've never realized the importance of Jesus being a Jew. Of course I've always known he is Jewish but I didn't know its significance.

This was the statement of a man after seeing the Gospels in a new light. His comment highlights the blindness in the Church concerning God's purposes for Israel and the Jewish people. Let us research the history of the Church and note her attitude towards the Jewish people.

Consider first Jesus the Jew.

Born to be King

A Jewish man once said to me, "I struggled and struggled with the idea that Jesus is the Messiah. I had heard of Jesus and I thought he was for the Catholics, but I am Jewish, so I was convinced he was not for me. One day I read in the New Testament the book by Matthew. I discovered that Jesus is Jewish! Jesus is totally Jewish! He did all the things that a Jew does."

Matthew opens his Gospel with Jesus' genealogy. He begins with Abraham, showing the line through King David. We see that Jesus is not only Jewish but that he is also of royal descent. Luke likewise shows that Jesus is of the royal line. In chapter 2, where he describes Jesus' birth at the time of the census, Mary and Joseph have to travel from Galilee to Bethlehem, "the town of David, because he [Joseph] belonged to the house and line of David" (Luke 2:4).

Jesus' royal birth was also acclaimed by non-Jews. Magi had

traveled from the distant east to Jerusalem asking the question, "Where is the one who has been born king of the Jews?" (Matthew 2:2).

At his crucifixion a sign was placed over his head declaring in Hebrew, Latin and Greek, "This is Jesus, the King of the Jews." Ensuring that everybody from all nations would know that Jesus is King, this was written in the three common languages of the time. It is not just that Jesus is King. Jesus is the *Jewish* King.

Each Gospel writer makes it very plain that Jesus totally participated in Jewish life and faith.

> On the eighth day, when it was time to circumcise him, he was named Jesus, the name the angel had given him before he had been conceived.
>
> (Luke 2:21)

Luke explains from the books of the Law (see Leviticus 12:3) that God ordered this consecration to the Lord of a first-born male. This had been practiced by the Jewish people ever since the command was given through Moses (Exodus 13:2) and this is exactly what the scripture records.

> The parents brought in the child Jesus to do for him what the custom of the Law required.
>
> (Luke 2:27)

This is known as Jesus' *brit mila* or "covenant of cutting" which every Jewish boy experienced. To be sure that we realize that everything Jewish had been completed before leaving Jerusalem, Luke adds,

> When Joseph and Mary had done everything required by the Law of the Lord, they returned to Galilee ... "
>
> (Luke 2:39)

The only other detailed event we know about Jesus' childhood is his visit to Jerusalem, which Luke specifically states was at the age of twelve years, although Luke explains that Jesus' parents participated in Passover each year in Jerusalem – presumably with Jesus.

Every year his parents went to Jerusalem for the Feast of
the Passover. When he was twelve years old, they went up to the
Feast, according to the custom. After the Feast was over, while his
parents were returning home, the boy Jesus stayed behind in
Jerusalem, but they were unaware of it ... they found him in the
temple courts, sitting among the teachers, listening to them and
asking them questions. Everyone who heard him was amazed at
his understanding and his answers. When his parents saw him, they
were astonished.

(Luke 2:41–43, 46–48)

Why has Luke carefully noted Jesus' age? The Jewish scholar
Dr Pinchas Lapide believes that during this Passover visit to
Jerusalem Jesus underwent his *bar mitzvah*.[1] This is the time when
a young Jewish man "attains religious and legal maturity," when he
commits himself to the responsibilities of a member of the
community of faith.

Jesus' subsequent ability to engage the Jewish elders and doctors
of the Law in discussion to the astonishment of others, including
Joseph and Mary, not only indicated this to be an important
occasion in Jesus' life but again emphasizes his Jewishness.

Lapide makes the following summary:

> Jesus' parents were devout Jews who probably had a *mezuzah* (a
> roll of parchment containing some Hebrew scriptures known as
> the *"shema"*) on the doorpost of their modest home in Nazareth
> and kept a kosher kitchen. Aron (the Jewish author, Robert Aron)
> believes that Mary probably put *tzitzit*, or fringes, on the child's
> coat in obedience to an injunction in Deuteronomy 22:12, and that
> Joseph taught him the carpenter's trade. "Just as it is necessary to
> feed one's son," says the Talmud, "so it is necessary to teach him a
> manual trade."
>
> Jesus' parents undoubtedly brought him up to recite the bene-
> dictions and prayers prescribed for certain hours of the Hebrew
> day, and sent him to the synagogue for the study of Hebrew and
> the Law. Perhaps it was at the family's Passover Seder, when an
> empty chair is placed at the table in case the prophet Elijah should
> return, that Jesus first learned about the Messiah.
>
> Much of the Lord's Prayer paraphrases the old Aramaic prayer,

the Kaddish, which Jesus must have learned and absorbed as a youth. Even the beatitudes in the Sermon on the Mount are a direct reflection of common Jewish beliefs that Jesus could have heard from the rabbis at the Nazareth synagogue . . .

What emerges from the Gospel account, therefore, is the figure of a humble Jewish carpenter, born, circumcised and reared as a Jew, who spent all his earthly life amongst Jews of what today would be called "the working classes," living and preaching ethical precepts which were imbued with the Torah of Moses and the teachings of Israel's prophets.[2]

As his custom was

Years later, after his baptism and his victory over the devil in the wilderness Jesus traveled north.

> He went to Nazareth, where he had been brought up, and on the Sabbath day he went into the synagogue, as was his custom. And he stood up to read.
>
> (Luke 4:16)

We are told it was usual for Jesus to attend the synagogue in Nazareth. As with all Jewish boys he had been taken along to synagogue every Sabbath by Joseph and the other sons of the family since his infancy. This was the Jewish practice.

However, on this particular occasion he did something very significant. He came forward and read from the scrolls. Jesus had the right to do this only because he had undertaken the responsibility of entering the community of the faithful, otherwise he would not have been permitted that privilege. Jesus is totally Jewish.

If any man thirst

Jesus traveled to Jerusalem to celebrate the Feast of *Succot*, or Tabernacles, as described in John chapter 7. This feast is prescribed in Leviticus 23:33–43. It is a thanksgiving at the conclusion of the fruit and vegetable harvest and it is a time to pray for rain in readiness for the planting of the next crops. It would normally not have rained since Passover, six months earlier; the ground would be extremely dry after the hot summer and now very warm autumn.

Rain in season in the Middle East is always regarded as a sign of blessing. When rain comes, the people dance for joy! An eighth day is added after the last day of this celebration, which the scripture describes as "the last and greatest day of the Feast." On the seventh day the priests carried gold jugs of water up to the altar in the Temple and while the prayers for rain ascended the priests poured the water upon the altar until it spilled down the steps. While this was happening Jesus stood up and said,

> "If a man is thirsty, let him come to me and drink. Whoever believes in me, as the Scripture has said, streams of living water will flow from within him."
>
> (John 7:37–38)

About two months after this occasion we see Jesus again traveling to Jerusalem. It is now winter, the month of December. He has come to celebrate the Feast of Dedication as recorded in John 10:22. This feast, unlike Passover and Tabernacles, is not prescribed by the Law. It is a celebration by the Jewish people of the Dedication of the Temple. It had been instituted by Judas Maccabeus in 164 BC when the Temple, which had been desecrated by Antiochus Epiphanes, was cleansed and re-dedicated to the service of God.

When the Temple services were restored by Judas Maccabeus, the oil was found to have been desecrated. Only one phial of pure oil was discovered. The supply was sufficient to feed the large seven-branch candlestick for one day only. By a miracle the phial lasted for eight days, till a fresh supply could be obtained. In memory of this, it was ordered the following year, that the Temple be illuminated for eight days on the anniversary of its Dedication. This feast, which the Jews still celebrate, is called *Hanukkah*.

The hem of his garment

Luke records an event, the significance of which even some Bible translators miss, concerning the action of the woman who had suffered from hemorrhaging for twelve years, she "came up behind

Him and touched the tassel of His garment; and immediately her
flow of blood ceased" (Luke 8:44, AMP).

Jesus was wearing clothing as prescribed by the Law:

> "Throughout the generations to come you are to make tassels on
> the corners of your garments, with a blue cord on each tassel. You
> will have these tassels to look at and so you will remember all the
> commands of the LORD."
>
> (Numbers 15:38–39)

The woman seeking healing reached through the crowd to touch
the tassels or *tzitzit* as they are known in Hebrew. At present the
tzitzit are worn as a special under-garment or on the prayer shawl
(*tallith* in Hebrew) but in ancient time they seem to have been
worn on the outer garment itself. When this desperate woman
thrust her hand through the crowd towards Jesus she deliberately
reached to grasp the *tzitzit*, knowing the touch of God could heal
her instantly.

Jesus, the Messiah in the Jewish Scriptures

Jesus' Jewishness is even further demonstrated as we read the
Jewish Scriptures. As far back as Eden, God foretold his plan of
redemption through the promised Messiah:

> "I will put enmity between you [Satan] and the woman
>   [Mary – who mothered Jesus],
>   and between your seed and her seed;
> he shall bruise your head,
>   and you shall bruise his heel."
>
> (Genesis 3:15, RSV)

Jacob, the Jewish patriarch, prophesied of the promised Messiah's
victory as a king returning from battle, ruling the nations:

> "You are a lion's cub, O Judah;
>   you return from the prey, my son ...
> The scepter will not depart from Judah,
>   nor the ruler's staff from between his feet,

> until he comes to whom it belongs,
>   and the obedience of the nations is his."
>
> (Genesis 49:9–10)

Israel's God explains that the only way of atonement is by shedding blood:

> "For the life of a creature is in the blood, and I have given it to you to make atonement for yourselves on the altar; it is the blood that makes atonement for one's life."
>
> (Leviticus 17:11)

Moses speaks of his own ministry as being a foreshadowing of Messiah's ministry, adding that Messiah will be Jewish – and describes him as a *"brother"*:

> The Lord your God will raise up for you a prophet like me from among your own brothers. You must listen to him.
>
> (Deuteronomy 18:15)

Centuries later God began to reveal details of Messiah – who he would be, where he would come from, what he would accomplish, how he would accomplish his work.

Following on from Genesis 3:15, we find that the *"seed"* would come through a Jewish woman and that the birth would be a *"sign."* Just as the unusual nature of Isaac's birth had been a sign to Abraham of God's keeping his covenant in bringing to birth the Jewish nation, so the unique nature of this *"virgin"* birth would be a sign to the Jewish people. Contained in this child's name is the revelation of a mystery – *Immanuel* – God with us. In the Messiah of Israel God would be present.

> Therefore the Lord himself will give you a sign: The virgin will be with child and will give birth to a son, and will call him Immanuel.
>
> (Isaiah 7:14)

Jacob had revealed that the Messiah would rule over the nations. Isaiah prophesied that he would rule eternally from the Jewish throne of David in peace and justice:

For to us a child is born,
    to us a Son is given,
    and the government will be on his shoulders.
And he will be called
    Wonderful Counselor, Mighty God,
    Everlasting Father, Prince of Peace.
Of the increase of his government and peace
    there will be no end.
He will reign on David's throne
    and over his kingdom,
establishing and upholding it
    with justice and righteousness
    from that time on and for ever.

                                              (Isaiah 9:6–7)

Micah, the Jewish prophet, predicted the birthplace of Israel's eternal Ruler:

    "But you, Bethlehem Ephrathah,
        though you are small among the clans of Judah,
    out of you will come for me
        one who will be ruler over Israel,
    whose origins are from of old,
        from ancient times."

                                              (Micah 5:2)

That the Messiah would come through the House of David is confirmed – he would be of the stock of Jesse, David's father. A detailed description of the nature of the Messiah's rule and life during that reign is revealed in Isaiah 11:1–10:

    A shoot will come up from the stump of Jesse;
        from his roots a Branch will bear fruit . . .

With great emphasis, Isaiah focuses upon the atoning work of the Messiah as the seed of the woman. He will make atonement with his own blood, becoming the sacrifice himself. It is God's will that the Messiah is the sacrifice. We need to notice that the phrase *"my people"* refers to the Jewish people.

He grew up before him like a tender shoot,
    and like a root out of dry ground.
He had no beauty or majesty to attract us to him,
    nothing in his appearance that we should desire him.
He was despised and rejected by men,
    a man of sorrows, and familiar with suffering...
Surely he took up our infirmities
    and carried our sorrows,
yet we considered him stricken by God,
    smitten by him, and afflicted.
But he was pierced for our transgressions,
    he was crushed for our iniquities;
the punishment that brought us peace was upon him,
    and by his wounds we are healed...
For he was cut off from the land of the living;
    for the transgression of *my people* he was stricken.
He was assigned a grave with the wicked,
    and with the rich in his death,
though he had done no violence,
    nor was any deceit in his mouth.
Yet it was the Lord's will to crush him
      and cause him to suffer,
    and though the Lord makes his life a guilt offering,
he will see his offspring and prolong his days,
    and the will of the Lord will prosper in his hand...
For he bore the sin of many,
    and made intercession for the transgressors.

           (Isaiah 53:2–5, 8–10, 12, emphasis added)

In contrast to this description of the Messiah's suffering seen from the observer's viewpoint, David is given insight into the Messiah's suffering from the Messiah's viewpoint:

My God, my God, why have you forsaken me?
    Why are you so far from saving me?...
All who see me mock me;
    they hurl insults, shaking their heads:
"He trusts in the Lord;
    let the Lord rescue him"...

Many bulls surround me;
    strong bulls of Bashan encircle me.
Roaring lions tearing their prey
    open their mouths wide against me.
I am poured out like water,
    and all my bones are out of joint.
My heart has turned to wax;
    it has melted away within me.
My strength is dried up like a potsherd,
    and my tongue sticks to the roof of my mouth . . .
    they have pierced my hands and my feet.
I can count all my bones;
    people stare and gloat over me.
They divide my garments among them
    and cast lots for my clothing . . .

(Psalm 22:1, 7–8, 12–18)

Seeing but not seeing – hearing but not hearing

As Christians of Gentile origin we are apt to become over-familiar with these portions of Scripture without recognizing their full and initial significance. Many of us have two blind spots. Firstly, we see the Old Testament with hindsight and so we lack understanding of the struggles, the unbelief, the testings and the victories at each particular stage of revelations and growth.

It is like hearing the life-testimony of a man that God has used in a remarkable manner. The audience is aware of the great faith of this man but as he recalls his conversion experience years ago and recounts the details of stages in his growth – the early steps of faith, the feeling of uncertainty, the incidents of doubt and unbelief, the searching for God and crying out to him when seemingly he didn't hear, his failures and his sin – somehow the reality of those details do not register because the audience has only known him as a great man of God.

We have not always read Scripture noting to whom it was addressed and by whom it was written, realizing that its content applied to the particular audience and that promises made applied only to the party with whom they were made. We are blinded to the full truth of Scripture if we fail to recognize these two important points. Failure to do so has resulted in serious error in the Church, as we will demonstrate.

Secondly, we often fail to understand not only that each stage of revelation was given to the Jewish people, but also we fail to grasp what the significance of each stage of the revelation meant to the discerning Jew. As a result we have identified these passages with Jesus our Savior and Lord but wrested Jesus from his Jewishness and seen him as a Gentile. This in turn has made it easier to reject the Jewish people.

This weakness has also rendered ineffective through the centuries much Christian witness to the Jewish people, separating Christians and Jews rather than uniting them. We need to hear and understand Jesus' statement: "salvation is from the Jews" (John 4:22).

Awaiting the Jewish King

Failing to recognize Jesus' Jewishness also affects our understanding of God's purposes both today and in the future.

We have discovered that Jesus was born to be king, and to rule from the throne of David. Both Isaiah (11:2–10) and Jeremiah (23:5–6) describe the age in which Jesus will reign, when there is both peace and justice of an order that neither we nor the world have ever experienced.

In the book of Revelation, he is described as "the ruler of the kings of the earth" (1:5) and "Lord of lords and King of kings" (17:14; 19:16). He is also named "the Lamb" (17:14) identifying him as the One who atoned for sin. In other words, this king is Jewish.

It is important for us to notice that on the occasion when the apostles questioned the risen Jesus about when he was going to restore the kingdom to Israel (Acts 1:6), Jesus did not correct their thinking. He rather explained that this was *not the time* for such a restored Jewish kingdom. He then instructed them as to what they should be doing in the meantime.

Those Jews recognized Jesus as their king. On the occasion of Jesus' circumcision in the Temple, the elderly Simeon recognized him as destined to be Israel's ruler. At the same time, the prophetess, Anna, recognized Jesus to be Israel's Redeemer (Luke 2:29–32, 34–35). Philip knew Jesus to be the one "Moses wrote about in the Law" (John 1:45), and then Nathanael confessed to

Jesus, "You are the King of Israel" (John 1:49). The large Jewish crowd that gathered in Jerusalem for Passover shouted to Jesus, "Blessed is the King of Israel!" (John 12:13). Paul, in writing to Timothy, referred to Jesus as the "only Ruler, the King of kings and the Lord of lords" (1 Timothy 6:15).

Not only Jews but also Gentiles recognized Jesus to be Israel's king. Wise men traveled a considerable distance from the east to worship the Jewish King (Matthew 2:2). Pilate was so convinced of Jesus' kingship that he ordered it to be written over his head upon the Cross – "Jesus of Nazareth, the King of the Jews" (John 19:19), and to be sure all could read it he had it written in Hebrew, Latin and Greek!

Jesus' response to Pilate's questioning seals the truth:

> "My kingdom is not of this world ... But now my kingdom is from another place."
>
> "You are a king, then!" said Pilate.
>
> Jesus answered, "You are right in saying I am a king. In fact, for this reason I was born, and for this I came into the world, to testify to the truth. Everyone on the side of truth listens to me."
>
> (John 18:36–37)

Zechariah tells us that King Jesus will return to the Mount of Olives:

> Then the LORD will go out and fight against those nations, as he fights in the day of battle. On that day his feet will stand on the Mount of Olives, east of Jerusalem, and the Mount of Olives will be split in two from east to west, forming a great valley, with half of the mountain moving north and half moving south.
>
> (Zechariah 14:3–4)

Zechariah also tells us how the Gentile nations will acknowledge the king of the Jews:

> Then the survivors from all the nations that have attacked Jerusalem will go up year after year to worship the King, the LORD Almighty, and to celebrate the Feast of Tabernacles. If any of the peoples of the earth do not go up to Jerusalem to worship the King, the LORD Almighty, they will have no rain ...
>
> (Zechariah 14:16–17)

Jesus even tells us that the Jewish people will be ready to greet their king with the Jewish greeting, "Blessed is he who comes in the name of the Lord" (Matthew 23:39; cf. Psalm 118:26).

Rich roots

Many Christians are not aware that the roots of their faith are Jewish. An understanding of the gospel is shallow if it disregards this fact with all that God had prepared for the coming of the Redeemer – Jesus.

When a seed begins to grow it first puts down its unseen root. The root grows down into the soil establishing itself unnoticed. Only then does the stem develop upward where we can see its growth. But the health of that stem depends totally upon the sound, well-established root system. Only this principle can produce a sturdy tree.

Jesus appeared on earth as a tree of sound root structure:

> "As the terebinth and oak
>   leave stumps when they are cut down,
>   so the holy seed will be the stump in the land . . . "

> A shoot will come up from the stump of Jesse;
>   from his roots a Branch will bear fruit.
> The Spirit of the LORD will rest on him . . .

> (Isaiah 6:13; 11:1)

We must be very careful not to see Jesus as separate from the "tree" of which he is, humanly speaking, a part. Paul's statements concerning the root further stress its importance: "if the root is holy, so are the branches" (Romans 11:16); conversely the branches can only be holy if the root is holy: "the nourishing sap comes from the olive root" (Romans 11:17), which means that the entire tree is dependent upon the quality of food which the root provides.

To an observant Jew, Paul's statement is clear. God had commanded the Jewish people,

> When you come into the land into which I bring you, then it shall be, that, when you eat of the bread of the land, you shall offer up a

gift to the LORD. You shall offer up a cake of the first of your dough for a gift: as you do the gift of the threshing floor, so shall you set it apart.

(Numbers 15:19–20, JB)

Even today an orthodox Jewish woman takes a portion of the bread she has prepared and puts it in her oven where she burns it to a cinder. That is God's portion and represents the portion that the ancient Jewish woman took to the Temple priest. The whole loaf is made holy as a result of giving to God his portion.

In addressing the Gentiles Paul uses this practice to illustrate their dependence upon their Jewish roots, especially pointing out that their holiness is totally dependent upon their relationship with Jesus:

If the part of the dough offered as firstfruits is holy, then the whole batch is holy; if the root is holy, so are the branches.

(Romans 11:16)

Members of the Commonwealth of Israel

"Christ is the head of the church, his body, of which he is the Savior," wrote the Apostle Paul (Ephesians 5:23).

Can we claim to belong to the Head without identifying with the Jewish nature of the Head? Today that is essentially what the Church has done. We have reached a point where we claim a rich inheritance through our privileged relationship with the Head, but usurp the rights of those who are Jewish.

It is true most will say, "The Jews may accept salvation just as we do." The history of the Church has shown this to mean that the Jew is required to renounce his Jewishness in order to become a Gentile Christian. Is that in line with the teaching of Scripture?

Paul writes about this very problem to the young church in Ephesus reminding them of their past:

> Remember that you were at that time separated from Christ, alienated from the commonwealth of Israel, and strangers to the covenants of promise, having no hope and without God in the world. But now in Christ Jesus you who once were far off have been brought near in the blood of Christ.
>
> (Ephesians 2:12–13, RSV)

Paul is clearly stating that the Gentiles, before they knew Christ, were "alienated from the commonwealth of Israel."

As a New Zealander I am a member of the British Commonwealth. The word "commonwealth" can be broken up into its parts: "common" – shared ownership; and "wealth" – that which is owned. It speaks, then, of possessions commonly owned. We have enjoyed trade privileges with Britain, freedom of movement and the opportunity to work in Britain, while still retaining our New Zealand independence.

Before going further we have to identify the *"Israel"* of the commonwealth of which we have become members. Paul makes the statement:

> Not all who are descended from Israel are Israel. Nor because they are his descendants are they all Abraham's children.
>
> (Romans 9:6–7)

Being able to trace back natural lineage to Abraham does not, in itself, qualify a person to be regarded as of *"Israel."* The qualification is restricted to those who are "the children of promise who are regarded as Abraham's offspring" (Romans 9:8). Those qualifying for this group are obviously fewer in number than the group who simply are natural descendants of Abraham.

Later, Paul refers to Elijah's experience when he thought he was the only faithful Israelite remaining. Although God had reserved for himself 7,000 faithful Israelites, it is apparent that this was only a small group compared to the total population of Israel.

These smaller groups of Jewish people are described in Scripture as "the remnant" (see Romans 11:2–5). In Elijah's day the remnant must have been inconspicuous, judging from his ignorance of their existence. This quietness, which is characteristic of the remnant, is not indicative of a poor quality – reflecting indifference, but rather a quiet, steady confidence in their God: it is a sign of their strength.

Peter, whose ministry was as an apostle to the Jews (Galatians 2:8) wrote to the Jews, "the elect exiles of the dispersion" (1 Peter 1:1, AMP), that the nation as a whole failed but the elect within the nation did not fail – these are the remnant (1 Peter 2:4–8).

Paul is in agreement: "So too, at the present time there is a remnant chosen by grace" (Romans 11:5) – the true Israel.

Gentiles: foreigners and aliens

It is very important for us to understand the extent of the Gentiles' separation. "Gentile" is the Greek equivalent of the Hebrew *goyim*, meaning "the people of the nations," that is, anybody who is not Jewish. We will study Scripture and then Jewish writing to grasp the totality of this separation.

Jeremiah, in declaring the word of the Lord, rebukes Israel for changing their God,

> "Has a nation ever changed its gods?
>   (Yet they are not gods at all.)
> But my people have exchanged their Glory
>   for worthless idols.
> Be appalled at this, O heavens,
>   and shudder with great horror,"
>   declares the LORD.
>
> (Jeremiah 2:11–12)

The point is absolutely clear – only those belonging to Israel knew God while everybody else (the Gentiles) were idol-worshiping pagans. "The nations" and "the heathen" were interchangeable terms.

Nehemiah reflects the Jewish attitude towards the Gentiles:

> Should you not walk in the fear of our God because of the reproach of the nations, our enemies?
>
> (Nehemiah 5:9, NASB)

The Psalmist presents to us the confusion and helplessness of the Gentile nations in their opposition to God:

> Why are the nations in an uproar,
> And the peoples devising a vain thing?
> The kings of the earth take their stand
> And the rulers take counsel together
> Against the LORD and against his Anointed, saying,
> "Let us tear their fetters apart
> And cast away their cords from us!"
>
> (Psalm 2:1–3, NASB)

> The nations have sunk down in the pit which they have made;
> In the net which they hid, their own foot has been caught...

The wicked will return to Sheol,
Even all the nations who forget God.

(Psalm 9:15, 17, NASB)

Ezra described "the impurity of the nations of the land" (Ezra 6:21, NASB). Joshua reports God's command to kill all the heathen in Canaan rather than to allow their survival in Israel's Promised Land – only then was peace and prosperity promised Israel. Moses forbade intermarriage with the heathen peoples (Deuteronomy 7:1–3).

Constantly throughout the Old Testament, the nation of Israel is contrasted with the Gentile nations to emphasize God's unique purpose for Israel, and to offer hope to the Gentile nations through Israel. God's initial call to Abraham promised,

"In you all the families of the earth will be blessed."

(Genesis 12:3, NASB)

Human prejudice

Dr Alfred Edersheim, the Jewish author, in his monumental study, *The Life and Times of Jesus the Messiah,* summarizes ancient Jewish writings concerning Jewish attitudes towards Gentiles during the New Testament period:

> In truth the bitter hatred which the Jew bore to the Gentile can only be explained from the estimate entertained of his character. The most vile, and even unnatural crimes were imputed to them. It was not safe to leave cattle in their charge, to allow their women to nurse infants, or their physicians to attend the sick, nor to walk in their company, without taking precautions against sudden and unprovoked attacks. They should, as far as possible, be altogether avoided, except in cases of necessity or for the sake of business.
>
> They and theirs were defiled; their houses unclean, as containing idols or things dedicated to them; their feasts, their joyous occasions, their very contact, was polluted by idolatry. And there was no security: if a heathen were left alone in a room, that he might not, in wantonness or by carelessness, defile the wine or meat on the table, or the oil and wheat in the store. Under such

circumstances, therefore, everything must be regarded as having been rendered unclean.

Three days before a heathen festival (according to some, also three days after) every business transaction with them was prohibited, for fear of giving either help or pleasure. Jews were to avoid passing through a city where there was an idolatrous feast – nay, they were not even to sit down within the shadow of a tree dedicated to idol-worship. Its wood was polluted; if used in baking, the bread was unclean; if a shuttle had been made of it, not only was all cloth woven on it forbidden, but if such had been inadvertently mixed with other pieces of cloth, or a garment made from it placed with other garments, the whole became unclean.

Jewish workmen were not to assist in building basilicas, nor stadia, nor places where judicial sentences were pronounced by the heathen. Of course, it was not lawful to let houses or fields, not to sell cattle to them. Milk drawn by a heathen, if a Jew had not been present to watch it, together with bread and oil prepared by them, were unlawful. Their wine was wholly interdicted – the mere touch of a heathen polluted a whole cask; nay, even to put one's nose to heathen wine was strictly prohibited![1]

We find in the New Testament examples of Gentile awareness of these Jewish attitudes towards them.

In the case of the centurion who desired Jesus to heal his servant, he sent Jewish elders rather than Gentile messengers to Jesus. Secondly, when Jesus came near his house the centurion did not expect Jesus to enter his Gentile home (Luke 7:1–8).

A Canaanite woman approached Jesus on her daughter's behalf, seeking deliverance. Her persistence attracted Jesus' attention. Jesus' reply, "It is not right to take the children's bread and toss it to their dogs," is a recognition that she, a Gentile woman is seeking something that belongs to the Jewish people (Matthew 15:21–28).

Peter was shown all the unclean animals which are used to symbolize the Gentiles, and his reluctance to obey the Lord's command to eat of them revealed his desire to be obedient to the Law of Moses (Acts 10:9–23). He had yet to understand how the promise of Abraham was to be fulfilled.

Paul's description of a Gentile as a "foreigner" and an "alien" before becoming a member of the commonwealth of Israel is therefore not surprising. A "foreigner" belongs to another people of different thinking and culture. Today "alien" often refers to one from a different world or planet, stressing his difference from us as absolutely different in every conceivable way, to the point of unfriendliness.

This is how the Jewish people looked upon Gentiles, as totally different and inferior in their manner of life, morals, gods, language and attitudes.

No partiality with God

God's purpose with Israel had always been that they, who were called out of the world, would reflect God's glory and so influence the nations for God.

Significant examples of Gentiles who have been drawn to the God of Israel are: Rahab of Jericho, who protected the Jewish spies in the land and so was blessed by becoming a member of the commonwealth of Israel, and Ruth, the Moabitess, who accepted as her own Naomi's people and Naomi's God and later married Boaz the Jew. Both Rahab and Ruth are included in the royal line of David (Matthew 1:5).

There is ample evidence of widespread conversion of Gentiles to Judaism during the Old Testament period, including members of the royal families of Greece and Rome. Isaiah bears witness to the fact that not only are these Gentiles "joined to the LORD" but that God guarantees them their security:

> Let no foreigner who has bound himself to the LORD say,
>> "The LORD will surely exclude me from his people."
> And let not any eunuch complain,
>> "I am only a dry tree."

For this is what the LORD says:

> "To the eunuchs who keep my Sabbaths,
>> who choose what pleases me
>> and hold fast to my covenant –
> to them I will give within my temple and its walls
>> a memorial and a name
>> better than sons and daughters;

I will give them an everlasting name
 that will not be cut off.
And foreigners who bind themselves to the LORD
 to serve him,
to love the name of the LORD,
 and to worship him,
all who keep the Sabbath without desecrating it
 and who hold fast to my covenant –
these I will bring to my holy mountain
 and give them joy in my house of prayer.
Their burnt offerings and sacrifices
 will be accepted on my altar;
for my house will be called
 a house of prayer for all nations."

(Isaiah 56:3–7)

Change of status

A glorious change takes place in our lives when we accept the redeeming work of Jesus at Calvary, when we are united with Christ – we have changed our status in God's eyes. Our status changes from being an "alien from the commonwealth of Israel" to being included in that commonwealth! When we were aliens we were "foreigners to the covenants of the promise, without hope." But through our acceptance of Christ we share in the inheritance of the covenants of promise which were given to Israel!

The covenants of promise

Having established that our Gentile inheritance lies in our relationship with Israel's remnant and there is a distinction between Jews and non-Jews within God's purposes, Paul presents the inheritance of the Jewish people:

> Theirs is the adoption as sons; theirs the divine glory, the covenants, the receiving of the law, the temple worship and the promises. Theirs are the patriarchs, and from them is traced the human ancestry of Christ, who is God over all, forever praised!

(Romans 9:4–5)

It is essential that we now understand the content of the covenants to know what is promised the Jewish people, and what is promised to Gentiles who are members of the commonwealth of Israel.

In order to do this we need to go back to God's covenant with Abraham:

> The LORD had said to Abram, "Leave your country, your people and your father's household and go to the land I will show you.
>
> "I will make you into a great nation
>   and I will bless you;
> I will make your name great,
>   and you will be a blessing.
> I will bless those who bless you,
>   and whoever curses you I will curse;
> and all peoples on earth
>   will be blessed through you."
>
> (Genesis 12:1–3)

> The LORD appeared to Abram and said, "To your offspring I will give this land."
>
> (Genesis 12:7)

> The LORD said to Abram after Lot had parted from him, "Lift up your eyes from where you are and look north and south, east and west. All the land that you see I will give to you and your offspring forever. I will make your offspring like the dust of the earth, so that if anyone could count the dust, then your offspring could be counted. Go, walk through the length and breadth of the land, for I am giving it to you."
>
> (Genesis 13:14–17)

God promised blessings to Abraham, to his offspring and to the Gentiles.

Abraham would be the father of a great nation who would possess the land God allocated them. This land allocation is obviously very important for God repeats "to you and your offspring I will give this land." Abraham's offspring is the nation of Israel who are promised an enormous population that will fill the full extent of the territory Abraham looked upon but which Israel has never yet totally possessed – even under Solomon's reign. God is giving Israel the title deeds to the land. To the Gentiles, spiritual blessing is promised.

So important is this covenant that God ensures that we have a complete description of his signing the covenant and sealing the covenant with Abraham. The report of the signing of the covenant, recorded in Genesis chapter 15, follows Abraham's request for a sign to confirm that God meant business in his real estate promise.

Acting upon God's command Abraham prepared the covenant sacrifice. Then God did an extraordinary thing. After putting Abraham to sleep, he revealed the future of Abraham's descendants and appeared in *Shekinah* glory to sign the covenant. This is an unconditional covenant, where God was the sole signatory. Its fulfillment rests on God's faithfulness alone.

God's signed covenant now has to be sealed. Recorded in Genesis chapter 17, Abram ("exalted father") is renamed Abraham ("father of many [nations]") and God confirmed the promise of a populous, fruitful nation which would live in the land formerly promised. An everlasting covenant between God, Abraham and his descendants and sealed by circumcision, the God-given sign of the covenant people.

The importance of the covenant is further emphasized when later, God confirms these promises to Isaac, Abraham's promised son (Genesis 26:2–5, 24) and years later to Jacob, Isaac's son (Genesis 28:13–15).

Returning to Paul's writing:

> Theirs are the patriarchs, and from them is traced the human ancestry of Christ, who is God over all.
>
> (Romans 9:5)

And writing of God's election of the Jewish people:

> As far as election is concerned, they are loved on account of the patriarchs.
>
> (Romans 11:28)

The apostle is referring to the promises contained in the covenants God made with Abraham, Isaac and Jacob – the patriarchs.

During the centuries that followed, God built on the Abrahamic covenant with four other covenants.

The Mosaic covenant or the Law of Moses, recorded in Exodus 20:1 through Deuteronomy 27:26, is the only conditional covenant. Blessings follow obedience to the Law and cursings follow disobedience. Unlike the other covenants this is not an eternal covenant. The key element of this covenant is the blood sacrifice (Leviticus 17:11) preparing the way for an eternal covenant. Its purpose was to make sin obvious.

God reaffirmed the territorial promise of his Abrahamic covenant in the land covenant in Deuteronomy chapters 28 and 30. Attention was focused upon the consequences of disobedience – calamities and dispersion from the land. Repentance would result in restoration of the land. Whereas in the covenant with Abraham God gave Israel the "title deeds" to the land, here God is declaring that Israel's right of residency in the land is dependent upon their obedience to his Law.

The seed aspect of the Abrahamic covenant is developed in the covenant which God made with David, who represents the house of David. This covenant singled out one family from whose seed the Messiah would come. In 2 Samuel 7:11-17 God promised David that his son would establish David's kingdom, build a house or dynasty for God's name, and that the throne of this son's kingdom would be established forever. God also promised to be a father to David's son whom God will discipline when he strays. At first reading it appears that 1 Chronicles 17:10-15 is just a repetition of this passage.

But, while God makes the same promises of an eternal kingdom, house or dynasty and throne there is a sharp contrast on two points:

1. The son spoken of by Samuel will have to be disciplined, while there is no mention of disciplining the son referred to by the Chronicler.
2. Of this son God promises, "I will set him over my house and my kingdom forever; his throne will be established forever" (1 Chronicles 17:14).

The promises recorded by Samuel refer to a descendant of David establishing an earthly kingdom, throne and house which will be established forever. However, the Chronicler records God's promise of his son who will rule from the throne over God's house and kingdom *forever*. There is a clear distinction between two of God's sons who will be involved in establishing a throne, building a house, and ruling over a kingdom. History has shown us that

Solomon, who had to be disciplined, fulfilled the first function and the second will be fulfilled by Israel's Messiah.

In the fifth covenant – the New Covenant – God and Israel are involved (Jeremiah 31:31–34). This is amplification of the spiritual blessing of the Abrahamic covenant which is made with the houses of Israel and Judah. It is distinct from the Mosaic covenant in which God demanded righteousness from the Jewish people but never gave them the power to keep it. This unconditional covenant replaces that temporary conditional covenant, promising the nation spiritual regeneration, the forgiveness of sin, and a relationship where all in Israel will know God.

Through this covenant the Gentiles receive the spiritual blessings promised in the Abrahamic covenant and it is to this covenant that Jesus refers:

> "This is my blood of the covenant [or, "the new covenant"], which is poured out for many for the forgiveness of sins."
>
> (Matthew 26:28)

While the Mosaic covenant served to keep the Jewish people distinct by controlling their food, clothing and working habits, it also functioned as a barrier or "dividing wall of hostility" separating the Gentiles from the privileges of the Jewish spiritual blessings.

As we have seen, throughout the Old Testament period the only way a Gentile could receive the spiritual blessings provided by the Jewish covenants was to become a proselyte to Judaism. This involved submission to the Law, circumcision and living according to Jewish requirements. Paul is saying that with this "dividing wall of hostility" destroyed (Ephesians 2:14), Gentiles can now enjoy the spiritual blessings on the basis of faith.

We dare not underestimate the importance God places on these covenants and must heed his faithfulness to them:

> He remembers his covenant forever,
>> the word he commanded, for a thousand generations,
> the covenant he made with Abraham,
>> the oath he swore to Isaac.
> He confirmed it to Jacob as a decree,
>> to Israel as an everlasting covenant:

"To you I will give the land of Canaan
as the portion you will inherit." . . .
He allowed no one to oppress them;
for their sake he rebuked kings:
"Do not touch my anointed ones;
do my prophets no harm."

(Psalm 105:8–11, 14–15)

A new creation, one new man

When the Gentile, or the non-Jew, finds peace in Jesus, he is made "one" with Israel's remnant:

> For He Himself is our peace, who made both groups into one and broke down the barrier of the dividing wall . . .
>
> (Ephesians 2:14, NASB)

What does this oneness mean? Often unity in the Church has been interpreted as a bland all-togetherness, all looking the same.

School boards have instituted the system of pupils wearing uniforms to avoid obvious discrimination between the rich and the poor. They try to make all the pupils look the same. The Church seems to expect a similar uniformity. Such thinking is taken to the extreme where Jews have been expected to become Gentiles – in character and thinking. This is not scriptural unity as with the relationship of Jews and Gentiles.

When we return to the Hebrew word for "one" the difficulty of understanding is immediately overcome. This is the scripture spoken daily by every orthodox Jew:

> *Shema Israel Adonai Elohenu Adonai Ehad.*
> [Hear, O Israel: The Lord our God, the Lord is one.]
>
> (Deuteronomy 6:4)

The word *Elohenu* is plural, meaning "Gods" – as in the "royal we." Consequently the word "one," *ehad*, is also plural. This word *ehad* is used ninety times in the Old Testament as a composite unity. In Genesis 2:24 we read of a man and his wife becoming "one flesh" (*basar ehad*). From Canaan they brought "a single cluster of grapes" (*eshcol ehad*) (Numbers 13:23). We read of Israel "together and united as one man against the city" (*ish ehad*) (Judges 20:11).

In Ephesians 5, Paul writes about this composite unity regarding the marriage relationship. The husband is given a certain nature and the wife has a complementary nature. Marriage is a close relationship where the two partners are one and the relationship is enriched by what each contributes. Then at the conclusion of the passage Paul states,

> This is a profound mystery – but I am talking about Christ and the Church.
>
> (Ephesians 5:32)

The marriage relationship typifies the relationship between Christ and his Church, and similarly applies to the relationships within the Church. So that when Paul speaks of the new relationship between the Gentile believer and Israel he says, concerning Jesus:

> His purpose was to create in himself one new man out of the two.
>
> (Ephesians 2:15)

Members of the household

Paul continues his explanation:

> Consequently, you are no longer foreigners and aliens, but fellow-citizens with God's people and members of God's household, built on the foundation of the apostles and prophets, with Christ Jesus himself as the chief cornerstone. In him the whole building is joined together and rises to become a holy temple in the Lord. And in him you too are being built together to become a dwelling in which God lives by his Spirit.
>
> (Ephesians 2:19–22)

Previously Paul had said that by reconciliation with Christ a Gentile becomes a member of the commonwealth of Israel. Here he is saying that as part of the commonwealth of Israel we become "members of God's household." The relationship with Israel is even more intimate.

In a household the members are closely knit together. When one joins a household one is joining a body of people that already exists and is already knit together. Membership in such a body brings privilege with it, and requires adjustment to the life of that established household. A new member cannot come in and expect to change all that is established according to his whims and fancies. Rather he adapts to fit into the household, and in doing so the newcomer shares in all the advantages and security that have developed before his admission.

Jewish foundations

Paul teaches us that the Gentiles who are "fellow citizens" with "God's people" the Jews are "built on the foundation of the apostles and prophets with Christ Jesus himself as the chief cornerstone." He had said previously that Gentile believers are changed in status from "foreigners and aliens" to members of the commonwealth of Israel. He goes on to describe Israel's solid foundation.

This foundation is composed firstly of the apostles. Each one of them was a devout Jew who had come under a dynamic power that drew thousands of Jews into an understanding of faith in the resurrected Jesus of Nazareth that absolutely transformed their world.

Secondly, the foundation is made up of the prophets. These Jewish men of God have over the centuries fearlessly spoken forth God's will and purpose, calling Jewish people to deepen their relationship with God. They define purity, offer hope, foretell events of the ages to come and make known the Messiah of Israel.

Thirdly, the Messiah[2] is the chief cornerstone through whom all is created, in whom everything is held together, by whom all knowledge is given, and without whom nothing can exist.

These three make up the mighty foundation of the commonwealth of Israel of which we Gentiles are privileged to become citizens. Paul says:

> God raised us up with Christ and seated us with him in the heavenly realms in Christ Jesus, in order that in the coming ages he might show the incomparable riches of his grace, expressed in his kindness to us in Christ Jesus."
>
> (Ephesians 2:6–7)

Mysteries Revealed

This mystery is that through the gospel the Gentiles are heirs together with Israel.

(Ephesians 3:6)

Although God had said many times to the Jewish people that they would be a light to the Gentile nations, he kept secret from his people details of his provision for the Gentiles, and the future relationship of his chosen people with them. The great challenge Paul faced was that God had selected him to reveal mysteries never before made known to man.

When Paul revealed what was shown to him, many did not believe or understand him. Today there are many of us who still do not believe or understand some of those same truths which Paul labors to explain:

In reading this, then, you will be able to understand my insight into the mystery of Christ, which was not made known to men in other generations as it has now been revealed by the Spirit to God's holy apostles and prophets. This mystery is that through the gospel the Gentiles are heirs together with Israel, members together of one body, and sharers together in the promise in Christ Jesus.

... to make plain to everyone the administration of this mystery, which for ages past was kept hidden in God, who created all things. His intent was that now, through the church, the manifold wisdom of God should be made known to the rulers and authorities in the heavenly realms, according to his eternal purpose which he accomplished in Christ Jesus our Lord. In him and through faith in him we may approach God with freedom and confidence.

(Ephesians 3:4–6, 9–12)

As we have discovered, God prepared a way for the coming of Jesus into the world, through Israel, of which he is a part. At the same time, God prepared a way through the work of Jesus for non-Jewish people, Gentiles, to become a part of Israel.

This does not make Gentiles Jewish any more than it makes Jews into Gentiles. When the two become "one man" we see an expression of spiritual unity where all that has separated them has been removed. They become members of "one body," the Church, each making his distinct contribution.

In order to see clearly the purpose of the Church we need to look back to our origin. God reminded Israel of this:

"Listen to me, you who pursue righteousness,
Who seek the Lord:
Look to the rock from which you were hewn
And to the quarry from which you were dug."

(Isaiah 51:1, NASB)

Israel needed to be reminded then, and the Church needs to be reminded now, that Abraham, the man separated unto God, fore-shadows a people separated unto God. Both the man and the people by faith and obedience will inherit the promise. The covenant with Abraham is not yet fulfilled but it will reach total fulfillment when that new man inherits the Kingdom of God.

Paul's intense anguish for his brothers

Paul, who described himself as "advancing in Judaism beyond many Jews of my own age" (Galatians 1:14), writes out of great anguish for his Jewish brethren:

I have great sorrow and unceasing anguish in my heart. For I could wish that I myself were cursed and cut off from Christ for the sake of my brothers, those of my own race, the people of Israel.

(Romans 9:2–4)

Paul's anguish comes from the state of his brothers:

> It is not as though God's word had failed. For not all who are
> descended from Israel are Israel. Nor because they are his descend-
> ants are they all Abraham's children . . . Israel who pursued a law of
> righteousness, has not attained it . . . Because they pursued it not by
> faith but as if it were by works.
>
> (Romans 9:6–7, 31–32)

The Apostle is writing to a confused church composed of Christian
Jews and Christian Gentiles, each group claiming advantages over
the other. Throughout this letter Paul is travailing to explain that all
men are sinful and in need of redemption. The Jewish people cannot
simply claim superiority because God has favored them by giving
them the covenants of promise. Furthermore the Gentiles need to
recognize their own indebtedness to Israel and also that God has not
yet fulfilled his purpose in the Jewish people:

> I ask then: Did God reject his people? By no means! . . . Again I ask:
> Did they stumble so as to fall beyond recover? Not at all!
>
> (Romans 11:1, 11)

Paul directs the attention of both Israel and the Church to the great
hope revealed by God that lies ahead in the one man in the one
body. That hope will be fully realized when both Israel and the
Church have appropriated the fullness of the covenants of promise.
Meantime a season of "hardening in part" is upon Israel.

Israel hardened in part

Paul reveals the reason for Israel's partial response to Jesus as
Messiah:

> What Israel is seeking, it has not obtained, but those who were
> chosen obtained it, and the rest were hardened . . . I do not want
> you, brethren, to be uninformed of this mystery – so that you will
> not be wise in your own estimation – that a partial hardening has
> happened to Israel until the fullness of the Gentiles has come in;
> and so all Israel will be saved.
>
> (Romans 11:7, 25–26, NASB)

We learn from this that there is to be a period in history when God is going to provide opportunities for the Gentiles to come into fullness of faith. But in revealing this truth Paul cautions the Gentiles about becoming conceited now that they are receiving God's rich blessings.

Paul, deeply aware of human nature and the proud arrogance that Gentiles are already displaying in their attitude towards Israel, goes out of his way to emphasize that this opportunity for the Gentiles is only for a restricted period of time, and even gives the reason why God has permitted the Gentiles this privilege of salvation:

> Because of their transgression, salvation has come to the Gentiles to make Israel envious. But if their transgression means riches for the world, and their loss means riches for the Gentiles, how much greater riches will their fullness bring!
>
> (Romans 11:11–12)

Not only has God graciously offered this special opportunity to the Gentiles but he declares his purpose is that Gentiles are to make Israel *envious* of their redemption privilege. We Gentiles should be so blessed by our acceptance into the commonwealth of Israel, being made heirs of the covenants of promise given to Israel, that we not only recognize God's special place for Israel, but we also want to embrace Israel, and to encourage her into her God-ordained inheritance.

God also tells us that there will be a time when Israel will come into the fullness of her inheritance and bring rich blessing to the world and final fulfillment of God's promise to Abraham.

Paul goes even further in making his point, addressed to the Gentiles, concerning the inheritance of Israel and the Gentiles:

> As far as the gospel is concerned, they are enemies on your account; but as far as election is concerned, they are loved on account of the patriarchs, for God's gifts and his call are irrevocable.
>
> (Romans 11:28–29)

God's covenant with the patriarchs still stands no matter what man does – God is always faithful! God will bring Israel into the inheritance he has purposed for them and no man or circumstance will thwart God's purpose.

We are soberly reminded of God's graciousness towards us without which we would be nothing:

> Just as you who were at one time disobedient to God have now received mercy as a result of their disobedience, so they too have now become disobedient in order that they too may now receive mercy as a result of God's mercy to you. For God has bound all men over to disobedience so that he may have mercy on them all.
>
> (Romans 11:30–32)

God's sovereignty

Before revealing the truth of these mysteries Paul carefully prefaces the section with the fact of God's sovereignty which he illustrates with God's choice of Jacob in preference to Esau:

> Rebecca's children had one and the same father, our father Isaac. Yet, before the twins were born or had done anything good or bad – in order that God's purpose in election might stand: not by works but by him who calls – she was told, "The older will serve the younger." Just as it is written: Jacob I loved, but Esau I hated."
>
> (Romans 9:10–13)

Anyone who knows Middle-Eastern culture realizes that a younger son never takes precedence over an older son – it just does not happen! But God has done just that and his decision was made before the boys' birth. Paul concludes:

> It does not, therefore, depend on man's desire or effort, but on God's mercy ... Therefore God has mercy on whom he wants to have mercy, and he hardens whom he wants to harden.
>
> (Romans 9:16, 18)

Prior to entering the Promised Land, Moses strengthens Israel's faith by reminding them of God's sovereignty in their lives and his faithfulness to his covenants:

"The LORD did not set His love on you nor choose you because you were more in number than any of the peoples, for you were the fewest of all peoples, but because the LORD loved you and kept the oath which He swore to your forefathers, the LORD brought you out by a mighty hand, and redeemed you from the house of slavery, from the hand of Pharaoh king of Egypt. Know therefore, that the LORD your God, He is God, the faithful God, who keeps His covenant and His lovingkindness to a thousandth generation with those who love Him and keep His commandments; but repays those who hate Him to their faces, to destroy them . . . "

(Deuteronomy 7:7–10, NASB)

Paul, like Moses before him, is striving to bring understanding of God's purpose for his people.

The rich root of the olive tree

At the climax of his teaching Paul uses the olive tree as a symbol. This tree common to all Middle-East countries is significant for its persistent life – it does not die! This stresses the certainty of God's purposes with his people.

Some of the olive branches have been broken off; these represent Israelites who have not received the promise. Wild olive shoots have been grafted in among natural olive branches. These grafted-in wild olive shoots represent Gentiles who have accepted the promises of God, and they are receiving their nourishment from the root of the olive tree.

Gentiles are warned against boasting about being grafted in because nourishment comes from the roots, not the branches. It is important that the Gentiles recognize that the natural branches are broken off because of unbelief. Because the Gentiles are grafted in by faith, they do well to learn the lesson from the breaking off of the natural branches in case their arrogance in turn results in their own removal.

I am talking to you Gentiles ... if the root is holy, so are the branches. If some of the branches have been broken off, and you, though a wild olive shoot, have been grafted in among the others and now share in the nourishing sap from the olive root, do not boast over those branches. If you do, consider this: You do not support the root, but the root supports you. You will say then, "Branches were broken off so that I could be grafted in." Granted. But they were broken off because of unbelief, and you stand by faith. Do not be arrogant, but be afraid. For if God did not spare the natural branches, he will not spare you either. Consider therefore the kindness and sternness of God: sternness to those who fell, but kindness to you, provided that you continue in his kindness. Otherwise, you also will be cut off.

(Romans 11:13, 16–22)

Grafting is an excitingly creative activity. Successful grafting is carried out when the sap is flowing in the tree. A small, tender shoot is taken, its stem sharpened until the growth cells under the bark are exposed and the microscopic cells that convey the food to the plant are clean and exposed. This shoot is then gently fitted into a cut-away branch on the tree, where the natural branch has been removed, so that the layer of growing cells are matched and the food-conveying cells are matched. This join is bound up so that air and water cannot reach it. The grafted-in shoot is fragile, needing protection against knocks, and is totally dependent upon the natural tree for its sustenance.

When I was a child my father grafted into a sturmer apple tree shoots from a granny-smith and a golden delicious apple tree. In time, these grew – producing three varieties of apple, each in its own season, on the one tree. We were picking sturmers, granny-smiths and golden delicious off the same tree! The granny-smiths and the golden delicious were only branches and they were totally dependent upon the sturmer trunk and roots which in turn provided the nourishment they depended upon. And each variety of apple had its own characteristic color, flavor, shape and time for maturing.

This is exactly what Paul is saying. The shoot and its subsequent fruit, which appears in its own season, is dependent upon the trunk and roots for nourishment. The Gentiles, grafted in, are totally dependent upon the Israel of promise, and it is Israelites of whom Paul speaks:

Theirs is the adoption as sons; theirs the divine glory, the coven-ants, the receiving of the law, the temple worship and the promises. Theirs are the patriarchs, and from them is traced the human ancestry of Christ, who is God over all, forever praised!

(Romans 9:4–5)

In the Gospels we read of a Roman centurion who came to Jesus for healing on behalf of his servant. Jewish elders approached Jesus giving the centurion a reference: "This man deserves to have you do this, because he loves our nation and has built our synagogue" (Luke 7:4–5). Commentators believe this is the same centurion recorded in Acts 10 where he is named as Cornelius. He and his household were the first Gentiles to be grafted into the olive tree. An important characteristic of Cornelius' faith was his love for Israel.

An exciting future lies ahead:

And if they do not persist in unbelief, they will be grafted in, for God is able to graft them in again. After all, if you were cut out of an olive tree that is wild by nature, and contrary to nature were grafted into a cultivated olive tree, how much more readily will these, the natural branches, be grafted into their own olive tree!

(Romans 11:23–24)

As we witness the power of Christ at work among the Gentile members of his Church, as thousands are today being grafted into the olive tree, we must remember we are seeing him graft contrary to nature, wild olive branches into a natural tree that is flourishing. How much easier it will be for God to graft back the natural branches into the natural tree and how much more will that olive tree flourish!

It is not surprising that when I have met Jewish people who have worshiped the God of Israel and later come to receive the promise God offers them in Jesus Christ, I have observed in them a depth of understanding that is not found in most Gentile believers. Of course it should be so, for they are the natural olive branches.

A future event in Scripture shows how the Gentiles will ultimately recognize and be drawn to Jews who have received the promises of God:

This is what the LORD Almighty says: "In those days ten men from all languages and nations will take firm hold of one Jew by the hem of his robe and say, 'Let us go with you, because we have heard that God is with you.'"

(Zechariah 8:23)

The Synagogue and the Church

It is generally believed that the Church was born (or revealed) on the glorious day of Pentecost recorded in Acts chapter 2. God graciously visited the Jewish people as they gathered from the extremities of the Roman Empire, in the Temple in Jerusalem, to offer thanks for his provision of the gathered-in wheat harvest. The dynamic of faith released within these faithful Jews created a growing body of believers who were soon accused of "turning the world upside down"!

The 120 Jews, whose lives had been transformed by Jesus of Nazareth, were immediately joined by another 3,000, and then by another 5,000 Jewish men. Within a few years a large number of priests from the Temple believed. Later still there were many thousands, or "myriads" as the New King James Version puts it (Acts 2:41; 4:4; 6:7; 21:20). Other records state that within twenty years, by AD 50, there were over 50,000 Jewish believers in Jesus in Jerusalem alone! By the end of the first century there were more than 1,000,000 Jewish followers of Jesus the Messiah, according to August Neander the nineteenth-century Jewish historian.[1]

Paul, who "to the Jews ... became like a Jew, to win the Jews" (1 Corinthians 9:20) states:

> I am not ashamed of the gospel, because it is the power of God for the salvation of everyone who believes: first for the Jew, then for the Gentile.
>
> (Romans 1:16)

We must note two very important facts. These were Jewish people who had received the fullness of the promises of God with the visitation of the Holy Spirit. They did not separate themselves into a new body leaving the synagogue and Temple, cutting themselves off from other Jews to build a church, but saw the new dimension of their faith as a fulfillment of all they had been promised in the Law, the Prophets and the Psalms.

From the synagogue emerges the Church

The origins of the New Testament Church can be understood only in relation to the structure and function of the synagogue. It has been suggested by many New Testament commentators and Church historians that the young church emerged as a totally new organization. This is not correct, as we shall demonstrate.

The total destruction of the Temple, and the Jewish exile in Babylon for seventy years (commencing in 586 BC), caused a dramatic upheaval in Jewish life. The sacrifices and oblations, around which their whole life had centered, ceased. The religious leaders developed a religious institution that remains in Judaism until today.

The synagogue, which is Greek for "assembly," is known in Hebrew as *bet knesset*, "the house of the assembly." While it is organized primarily as an institution for teaching, the synagogue tends to be the center for all Jewish community life and has been responsible for holding Judaism together through the centuries of dispersion among the many nations. The structure which emerged in Babylon is clearly the synagogue of the New Testament period.

The synagogue structure

Overseeing the functioning of the synagogue is the *nasi,* or president, whose role is primarily administrative. He acts as the administrator of the congregation.

The *skanaim,* derived from the Hebrew word *zaken,* meaning "old" or "elder," are a group of men who act as elders, a role not dependent upon their age but their spiritual maturity. These men are really the spiritual leaders of the synagogue and congregation.

Another group, whose function is to teach, derives its name from the Hebrew word for "man of leisure" – the *batlahmim.* Ideally, each synagogue has ten of these men who usually have independent

THE SEPARATION OF CHURCH FROM SYNAGOGUE

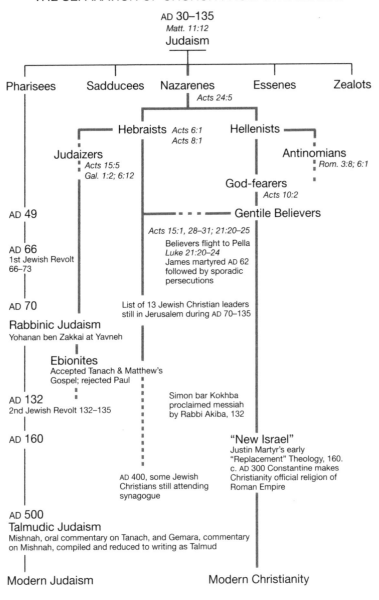

Key:

——— Judaism – Modern Judaism
━━━ Judaism – Modern Christianity

financial means and can therefore devote themselves to constant study and to teaching the congregation.

There is another group of men known in Hebrew as the *gabet zdaka*, which means "those who undertake acts of righteousness." Their task is to minister to the everyday needs of the community, especially to the widows, orphans and to other special needs.

The *schlakim*, those who were sent forth from the synagogue oversight as public announcers, communicated messages to other synagogues and individuals.

The *bet din*, which means "house of judgment," was the court of law in the synagogue before whom offenders appeared for judgment. The *kazan*, who today functions as the cantor, was the one who dealt the punishment after judgment was passed. Each synagogue was an autonomous body with its own government and court. Jesus clearly referred to this:

> "When you are brought before synagogues, rulers and authorities, do not worry about how you will defend yourselves or what you will say, for the Holy Spirit will teach you at that time what you should say."
>
> (Luke 12:11–12)

Jesus was referring to the *bet din*. We can also see here the background to New Testament teaching regarding disagreements among believers:

> "If your brother sins against you, go and show him his fault, just between the two of you. If he listens to you, you have won your brother over. But if he will not listen, take one or two others along, so that 'every matter may be established by the testimony of two or three witnesses.' If he refuses to listen to them, tell it to the church."
>
> (Matthew 18:15–17)

The *meturganaim* were the interpreters. When the Jewish people were dispersed to the nations they always worshiped in Hebrew so that when the Bible was read it had to be translated into the local language.

The *mahgeed*, men gifted in public speaking, traveled among the synagogues – stimulating congregations with their inspiring messages at the president's request. They were not necessarily associated with one particular synagogue. We find occasions in the Gospels when Jesus was invited to speak to the congregation – it was in this capacity.

A *rabbi* could be shared among several small congregations or in the case of a large synagogue there could be several rabbis. We have seen that there are already several spiritual leaders so the rabbi was not the only one fulfilling that role. His wisdom was sought after in matters of the Law and he was needed to supervise conversions. In the synagogue service all the Jewish members are equal as ministers and all can take part.

New dimensions

Following the day of Pentecost, Luke describes the activities of these Jewish believers in Jesus:

> They devoted themselves to the apostles' teaching and to the fellowship, to the breaking of bread and to prayer. Everyone was filled with awe, and many wonders and miraculous signs were done by the apostles. All the believers were together and had everything in common. Selling their possessions and goods, they gave to anyone as he had need. Every day they continued to meet together in the temple courts. They broke bread in their homes and ate together with glad and sincere hearts, praising God and enjoying the favor of all the people. And the Lord added to their number daily those who were being saved.
>
> (Acts 2:42–47)

These were Jews who saw in their new dimension of faith the fulfillment of the Messianic covenants God had made with Abraham, Isaac and Jacob and they continued their involvement in the Temple and synagogue.

As their numbers grew rapidly the leadership gifts to which they had been accustomed in the synagogue emerged in the embryonic church. We read of this in Paul's letters:

> And in the church God has appointed first of all apostles, second prophets, third teachers, then workers of miracles, also those

having gifts of healing, those able to help others, those with gifts of administration, and those speaking in different kinds of tongues.

(1 Corinthians 12:28)

An apostle is one who is sent (from the Greek word *apostolos*). We see the young church sending out men, *schlakim*, commissioned by the believers to communicate with other groups of believers. Just as the "sent-out ones" were responsible to the synagogue, the apostles were responsible to Jesus on whose behalf they were commissioned.

Teachers are equivalent to "the men of leisure," *batlahmim*, who spent their time studying the Scriptures in readiness to impart their knowledge. The evangelist corresponds to the *mahgeed*, an able public speaker who visited the synagogues with an inspiring message.

The role of pastor is that of an elder, *skanim*. We use the term pastor in quite a loose sense today where his function is not always clearly defined; often the pastor, as we see him today, fulfils the function of the biblical role of deacon. Deacon comes from the Greek *diakonia*, first mentioned in Acts 6 when needs of believers were being overlooked. Those appointed to care for these needs were called deacons, modeled on the office of the *gabet zdaka* in the synagogue and are a helping ministry.

For centuries there have been rabbis who have visited the sick, laying on hands and anointing with oil.

Justin Martyr, one of the notable leaders of the Church during the late first century and early second century (the period following soon after the New Testament period) described the Church worship of his day. In this description we can clearly see the pattern of the synagogue:

On Sunday a meeting is held of all who live in the cities and villages and a section is read from the memoirs of the apostles and the writings of the prophets as long as time permits. When the reading is finished, the president, in a discourse, gives the admonition and the exhortation to imitate these noble things. After this we all arise and offer a common prayer and at the close of the prayer, as we have before described, bread and wine and thanks for them are offered, and the congregation answers "Amen."

Then the consecrated elements are distributed to each one and partaken of and are then carried by the deacons to the houses of the absent.

The wealthy and the willing then give contributions according to their free will and this collection is deposited with the president who therewith supplies orphans, widows, prisoners, strangers and all who are in want.[2]

Born anew

We have seen in chapter 3 the state of the Gentiles, totally separated from God without hope or promise, and the opportunity for them to come close to the God of Israel as proselytes. The process of becoming a proselyte involved baptism, which again demonstrates to us an activity of the synagogue adopted by the church and given a new dimension of meaning.

There were four categories of proselytes to Judaism but "the proselytes of righteousness" were those who fully embraced the God of Israel – they were also referred to as "perfect Israelites" which means they were Israelites in every respect both as regards duties and privileges. Three things were required for the admission of such proselytes; circumcision (*mila*), baptism (*tebhila*), and a sacrifice (*corban*).

These proselytes are frequently mentioned in the New Testament – in the Authorized Version they are referred to as those who "fear God," who are "religious," "devout," and who "worship God" (Acts 13:16, 26, 43, 50; 17:4, 17; 16:14; 18:7).

It was considered a great thing when a non-Jew "sought shelter under the wings of the Shekinah" and his change of condition was complete. When the proselyte stepped out of the waters of baptism he was considered as "born anew." The rabbis described it as if he were "a little child just born" and in another place as "a child of one day."

This new birth was not "a birth from above" in the sense of moral or spiritual change, but only as implying a new relationship to God, to Israel, and to his own past, present and future. He was then instructed in the difficulties of his "new citizenship," particularly regarding his changed status and his past. As a new man, his country, habits, friends and relations were separated from him; the old – with its defilements – was buried in the waters of baptism.

Clearly Jesus had this in mind when replying to Rabbi Nicodemus:

> "No one can see the kingdom of God unless he is born again."
>
> (John 3:3)

Paul also had this in mind when he spoke on baptism:

> What shall we say, then? Shall we go on sinning, so that grace may increase? By no means! We died to sin; how can we live in it any longer? Or don't you know that all of us who were baptized into Christ Jesus were baptized into his death? We were therefore buried with him through baptism into death in order that, just as Christ was raised from the dead through the glory of the Father, we too may live a new life ... For we know that our old self was crucified with him so that the body of sin might be rendered powerless, that we should no longer be slaves to sin – because anyone who has died has been freed from sin ... Therefore do not let sin reign in your mortal body so that you obey its evil desires.
>
> (Romans 6:1–4, 6–7, 12)

Passover or Easter?

Today many Christians do not realize that the death and resurrection of Jesus was a precise and accurate fulfillment of the Jewish Passover, a practice commanded by God through Moses and recorded in Exodus 12 and Numbers 9.

Easter was not instituted until the fourth century, when the anti-Jewish thinking among the leaders of the Church led them to make two detrimental changes. They separated the date for celebrating Jesus' death and resurrection from the time Jewish people observed Passover, which was biblical, and attached it instead to the date of a pagan festival. The influence of pagan practices and understanding replaced the Jewish, biblical purpose of the event. This marks an ongoing, determined attempt to remove Jewishness from the Church.

It is very significant that the Jewish believers in Jesus continued to celebrate his death and resurrection at Passover as did many non-Jewish believers in Jesus even after the Church leaders separated the observance from the Jewish date.

The instructions in the Law of Moses and the Gospel accounts were written for Jews and must be understood as they would have understood them. This principle is fundamental to a right understanding of Scripture and would shed light on many scriptures obscure to the Gentile mind but very clear to the Jews.

A Jewish scholar, Arnold Fruchtenbaum, highlights a vital truth when he explains that the Church lacks depth of understanding because of its disregard of the Jewish perspective:

> If this had been the pattern followed by the Church throughout the centuries, it could have saved itself a great amount of doctrinal error. For no Jew would have remained in the local church and allowed anyone to challenge the authority of the Scriptures or to deny the Virgin Birth and the Resurrection. The church has lost much in failing to bring the gospel to the Jew.[3]

The scholar James Parkes also recognizes the important place Jewish members of the Church played in its stability and the weakness it suffered as a result of their being cut off. But that is not all; he records for us a determined effort by the Gentile Christians to continue the Jewish biblical practice after Church leaders had legislated otherwise:

> Though there is no evidence of Christianity adopting any practices of post-Christian Judaism, yet relations with contemporary Jews were continual, and are shown by the number of centuries it took to separate the Jewish Passover from the Christian Easter. It was not until the time of Constantine that a formal decision was taken, and even in later centuries councils had frequently to prohibit Gentile Christians from celebrating Easter on the same day as the Jews celebrated the Passover.
>
> In other matters also it is evident that many, apart from Christians of Jewish birth, were powerfully influenced by the teaching and practice of the Synagogue. Though this provoked the furious denunciation of such bishops as Chrysostom, it is significant that he has no definite moral charges to bring against the Christians who were involved, and it seems to have been fear of Jewish influence which caused his violence more than anything else.[4]

The Separation of the Synagogue and the Church

"The Jews killed Jesus!" This has been the accusing cry of many Christians down the ages. Such a torrent of vengeance and bloodshed has followed this accusation that a deep stain has marred church history.

Sadly, little attention has been paid to Paul's warnings against the arrogance and pride of Gentiles who despised the Jewish people. Although there is some evidence of Christian concern for the Jewish people, the policy has been generally hostile, bringing persecution and intense suffering.

A theology concerning the Jewish people has been built upon their statement at the time of Jesus' trial:

> All the people answered, "Let his blood be on us and on our children!"
>
> (Matthew 27:25)

A doctrine of hate has been built upon this one verse which ignores all the teaching of Paul and even the words of Jesus, just hours after this trial scene, when he prayed from the cross for these very people who were crucifying him:

> Jesus said, "Father, forgive them, for they do not know what they are doing."
>
> (Luke 23:34)

Whose responsibility?

The responsibility for Jesus' crucifixion is apportioned very carefully by Peter:

Indeed Herod and Pontius Pilate met together with the Gentiles and the people of Israel in this city to conspire against your holy servant Jesus, whom you anointed. They did what your power and will had decided beforehand should happen.

(Acts 4:27–28)

The responsibility is clearly apportioned:

1. Some Jewish people were responsible for Jesus' crucifixion.
2. Herod, Pontius Pilate and other Gentiles were responsible for Jesus' crucifixion.
3. Almighty God foreordained this one and only means of salvation for mankind. In the book of the Revelation we read of "the Lamb that was slain from the creation of the world" (13:8). Clearly the sacrificial death of Jesus was in the mind of God before the world was created.
4. Jesus said of his life, "No one takes it from me, but I lay it down of my own accord. I have authority to lay it down and authority to take it up again. This command I received from my Father" (John 10:18).
5. We who are believers need to consider our own personal involvement insofar as Scripture teaches, "He was pierced for *our* transgressions, he was crushed for our iniquities" (Isaiah 53:5).

Parting of the ways

Many Christians know the early Church only from the pages of the New Testament. Often it comes as a surprise to find that the secular authorities did not distinguish between the Jews within Judaism and the Jews who believed in Jesus.

The main body of the believers was all Jews: 3,000 in Acts 2:41 and 5,000 men in Acts 4:4. Many were being added daily to their number until there were thousands, even "myriads" recorded in Acts 21:20 (NKJV). These were all Jews receiving salvation, being baptized, and sharing their faith with fellow Jews. We see further in Acts that Gentiles were added and so the Gentile numbers grew. The Apostle Paul's ministry is evidence that Gentiles were ripe for harvest.

As time progressed the believers became more dispersed throughout the Roman Empire. It became evident that they were separate from the Jews of Judaism, although they were initially seen as a sect of Judaism.

Judaism was more accepted within the Roman Empire than was early Christianity. While it is true that some emperors were harsh towards Jewish people, they intensely persecuted Christians. The religion of the Jews enjoyed a privileged place within the Roman Empire generally. Jewish people were able to worship and live according to their Law, provided they did not conflict with Roman requirements.

You will remember the occasion when the Pharisees tried to trap Jesus by asking about paying tax to Caesar and his famous reply, "Give to Caesar what is Caesar's and to God what is God's" (Matthew 22:21). The Jewish leaders had always protected their privileged position and they feared Jesus might be responsible for their losing it. This is an important part of the reason why the leaders in Jerusalem wanted Jesus removed.

Church growth was phenomenal. If tradition is correct, the apostles had reached as far as India in the east and Britain in the north. It was evident that the Church was distinct from Judaism and it was harshly treated by the Roman authorities. We see clear evidence of persecution even in the New Testament. This is the reason for John's exile on Patmos Island. The Church operated underground, and it grew because of persecution.

The growing tensions that we see in the Gospels between Jesus and the Jewish religious leaders were inherited by the young Church. Christianity had been protected as long as it was seen to be part of Judaism but the Church became more and more Gentile-dominated in numbers and in its nature. By the middle of the second century the separation was clear.

A prominent fourth-century church historian, Eusebius, shows us that even back in the second century there were church leaders who emphasized their separation from the Jews by moving the date for remembering Jesus' death and resurrection away from the time of the Jewish observance of Passover. Bishop Polycrates, writing in the second century concerning keeping the memorial of Jesus' death and resurrection according to the Jewish calendar, states:

We for our part keep the day scrupulously, without addition or subtraction. For in Asia great luminaries sleep who shall rise again on the day of the Lord's advent, when he is coming with glory from heaven and shall search out all his saints ... [he lists seven martyrs] ... All of these kept the fourteenth day of the month as the beginning of the Paschal festival, in accordance with the Gospel, not deviating in the least but following the rule of the Faith.

Last of all I too, Polycrates, the least of you all, act according to the tradition of my family, some members of which I have actually followed; for seven of them were bishops and I am the eighth, and my family have always kept the day when the people put away the leaven. So I, my friends, after spending sixty-five years in the Lord's service and conversing with Christians from all parts of the world, and going carefully through all Holy Scripture, am not scared of threats. Better people than I have said: "We must obey God rather than men."[1]

Polycrates was the leader of a group known as the Quartodecimans, in Asia, who persisted in observing Jesus' death and resurrection at Passover. For many years the popes accepted this stand in Asia, until Pope Victor excommunicated the group who then organized themselves into a separate church.[2]

The Jewish Church

This means that the first Christians were Jewish Christians and Gentiles who had become "proselytes," that is, they had converted to Judaism by circumcision and submitting to the Law of Moses. These Jewish Christians had no plan for sharing their new dimension of faith with Gentiles. The thought had never crossed their minds!

Evidence of this is seen in the manner God spoke to Peter preparing him for the call to Cornelius' house (Acts 10). Peter's absolute amazement that these Gentiles should experience the same manifestation of the Spirit of the God of Israel is further evidence that the Gentiles had not been considered by the Jewish Christians. The apprehension and concern of the Church leaders in Jerusalem regarding Peter's action yet again demonstrates that, until this time, the Church was totally Jewish, with no expectation that it should embrace Gentiles other than those who had converted to Judaism.

We need to remember that God was leading his people into a new dimension of faith, revealing new truth, and that the revelation of this new truth was to devout Jews. After the blessing of Pentecost it came as utter surprise that the blessing was to be shared with Gentiles who had not previously submitted themselves to circumcision and the Law of Moses.

Now we must remember that Cornelius was not the first Gentile to put his faith in the God of Israel – there had been Rahab, Ruth and thousands of others who had all become proselytes. However, although Cornelius is described as "a righteous and God-fearing man, who is respected by all the Jewish people" (Acts 10:22) he was not a proselyte. That is why this divine revelation was so startling to the Church leaders.

As the Church expanded during a period of phenomenal growth among the Gentiles, we come to the first major problem in the Jewish Church where some taught "unless you are circumcised, according to the custom taught by Moses, you cannot be saved" (Acts 15:1). A Council in Jerusalem under the presidency of James, decided against enforcing these requirements, demanding only that they refrain from eating food used in idol worship, and from sexual immorality. They circulated a letter to all the Gentile churches informing them of the decision.

While this was satisfactory for the churches in Asia where the congregations were a mixture of Jewish and Gentile believers, the churches in Judea consisting of conservative Jewish Christians preferred to observe the Law of Moses:

> When they heard this, they praised God. Then they said to Paul: "You see, brother, how many thousands of Jews have believed, and all of them are zealous for the law. They have been informed that you teach all the Jews who live among the Gentiles to turn away from Moses, telling them not to circumcise their children or live according to our customs. What shall we do? They will certainly hear that you have come, so do what we tell you. There are four men with us who have made a vow. Take these men, join in their purification rites and pay their expenses, so that they can have their heads shaved. Then everybody will know there is no truth in

these reports about you, but that you yourself are living in obedience to the law. As for the Gentile believers, we have written to them our decision that they should abstain from food sacrificed to idols, from blood, from the meat of strangled animals and from sexual immorality."

(Acts 21:20–25)

A Greek text which is translated in verse 20 "many thousands of Jews have believed" reads "myriads of Jews have believed." The fact is clear that many more than thousands of Jews came to believe – as quoted above, there were over 50,000 Jewish Christians in Jerusalem at the time of the Council.

There was no difference of opinion so far as personal salvation was concerned between those of Jewish and those of Gentile background although their expressions of faith and life were very different. We note that they were known by different names. In Antioch the Gentile believers came to be known as "Christians" (Acts 11:26) while the Jewish believers in Jesus were called "Nazarenes" and described as a sect within Judaism:

"We have found this man to be a troublemaker, stirring up riots among the Jews all over the world. He is a ringleader of the Nazarene sect and even tried to desecrate the Temple; so we seized him."

(Acts 24:5–6)

"Meshumod!" – **"traitors"**

When the Roman armies surrounded Jerusalem the Jews who had listened to the words of Jesus remembered he had warned of this event and so heeded his instructions:

"When you see Jerusalem being surrounded by armies, you will know that its desolation is near. Then let those who are in Judea flee to the mountains, let those in the city get out, and let those in the country not enter the city. For this is the time of punishment in fulfillment of all that has been written. How dreadful it will be in those days for pregnant women and nursing mothers! There will be great distress in the land and wrath against this people. They will fall by the sword and will be taken as prisoners to all the nations. Jerusalem will be trampled on by the Gentiles until the times of the Gentiles are fulfilled."

(Luke 21:20–24)

A temporary lift in the Roman siege of Jerusalem made possible the escape of those who heeded the warning. The Jewish Christians recognized this opportunity and fled across the Jordan River seeking refuge in Pella. The siege of Jerusalem resumed during AD 68 and in the year 70 the Temple and Jerusalem were completely destroyed as Jesus had said they would be.

As a result of this action the Jewish community regarded the Jewish Christians as traitors, *meshumod*, a term which is still used to describe Jewish Christians.

Life in Pella as described by Irenaeus, a distinguished church leader of the period, shows us the Jewish Christians continued their Jewishness:

> They practice circumcision, persevere in the observance of those customs which are enjoined by the Law, and are so Judaic in their mode of life that they even adored Jerusalem as if it were the house of God.[3]

The rift widens

The destruction of the Temple and Jerusalem created a major disruption to Jewish national and religious life. The dispersed Jewish people were faced with the twofold problem of how to retain their national identity and their religious obligations which were totally dependent upon the Temple.

Yavneh was established as the administrative center of religious life near the Mediterranean coast close to modern Tel Aviv. Rabbinical Judaism developed from this center, replacing biblical Judaism. Furthermore the priest was displaced by the rabbi as the leader of religious life which now centered entirely upon the synagogue.

The new form of Judaism was not acceptable to the Jewish Christians who saw Jesus of Nazareth as the Messiah fulfilling the Mosaic Law. The authorities from Yavneh authorized the addition of an extra prayer to the daily prayers said in the synagogues, sealing their opposition to the Jewish Christians:

> Let there be no hope for the apostates and let all the sectaries perish in a moment.

Despite these attempts to force them out, the Jewish Christians continued to live among other Jews.

In AD 132 a nationalistic Jewish revolt under the leadership of Simon Bar Cochba broke out against the Roman oppressor. Against their common enemy (the Roman authorities), the Jewish Christians joined ranks with the other Jews. Amidst this battle the chief rabbi, Akiva, proclaimed Bar Cochba to be the Jewish Messiah. The Jewish Christians could not accept this declaration, and withdrew their support. They were denounced as heretics. Now they recognized that their hopes of convincing the other Jews that Jesus was the Messiah were quite vain.

The contemporary historian Justin Martyr records that many Jewish Christians were put to death. This tragic act caused the complete separation of Christian Jews from the rest of the Jewish people.

We must understand the intensely difficult situation of the Jewish Christians:

> There is no more tragic group in Christian history than these unhappy people. They, who might have been the bridge between the Jewish and the Gentile world, must have suffered intensely at the developments on both sides which they were powerless to arrest. Rejected, first by the Church, in spite of their genuine belief in Jesus as the Messiah, and then by the Jews in spite of their loyalty to the Law, they ceased to be a factor of any importance in the development of either Christianity or Judaism.[4]

CHAPTER 7

The Deluded Church

Fundamental to the mystery, too, is the truth that a Jew has to choose to be a pagan, while the Gentile has to choose not to be.[1]

Tragedy befell the Church when the truth of this statement faded into obscurity, as the Church cut herself off from her Jewish roots and Bible truth. The Church leaders failed to see that God had identified himself with the Jewish people:

> For the LORD has chosen Jacob to be his own,
> Israel to be his treasured possession.
>
> (Psalm 135:4)

They also failed to see that God had specifically said that his name would always be remembered in relationship with the Jewish people:

> God also said to Moses, "Say to the Israelites, 'The LORD, the God of your fathers – the God of Abraham, the God of Isaac and the God of Jacob – has sent me to you.' This is my name forever, the name by which I am to be remembered from generation to generation."
>
> (Exodus 3:15)

The declaration of Bar Cochba as the Jewish Messiah was the watershed for the Jewish Christians, separating them from Orthodox Judaism. In the same way the actions of Emperor Constantine of the fourth century separated the Jewish Christians from Gentile Christians and the Gentile church from Orthodox Judaism.

The Jewish Christians, as we saw in Acts 21:20, continued to see that since Messiah Jesus fulfilled the Mosaic Law as a Jew, it was both appropriate and imperative that they also retain their Jewishness.

Building on sand

The fourth century was decisive in the history of both Judaism and Christianity. Teaching and decisions made by leaders of both groups during this century had deeper and longer lasting effects upon the two groups than at any other period in their history.

The councils of Nicaea and Constantinople established the doctrines of the Church by steering their passage through various heresies and other pressures. At the same time the great Schools of Pumbeditha and Sura as well as the Patriarchate in Jerusalem were the centers of Jewish learning. Both Christianity and Judaism were active in seeking "converts" and "proselytes," which often brought them into direct confrontation.

Christianity was faced with the task of imposing moral and intellectual standards on the happy-go-lucky Roman world while Judaism was attempting to find a new basis for survival for its own community without land, central authority or Temple.

At last the Christians won the victory of official recognition – no longer were they a persecuted underground body. This brought increasing power until it influenced the whole executive government of the empire. Where earlier the Church had called for equal rights with the Jews within the empire, now that she held power, in her intolerance, she denounced them.

Superficial Christianity was widespread among the upper classes of Roman society. This brought into the Church a large membership which was probably already hostile towards the Jews.

The Jews did not passively receive these Christian attacks. There were still outbreaks of turbulence and they still had people in official places, ready to rebel at any threat to their privileges. So fierce were some of these revolts that they required military force to suppress them. This was the environment of the Church Fathers.

Christianity's privileged position under Constantine enabled the Church to impose restrictive measures against the Jewish people by banning their observances. Circumcision became illegal, thus preventing conversions to Judaism and forcing Christians to forsake their Jewish heritage – at the threat of exile or property confiscation. Jews could no longer be sent money from the Diaspora and were barred from holding public office. Even Sabbath observance was prohibited!

This dramatic change in the status of Christianity attracted many Jewish people away from the synagogue life to the Church. This movement away from the synagogue was so significant that other Jews vented their anger upon these "converts" in such harmful ways that within two years the severest of penalties were imposed upon offenders.

Jewish Christians isolated

The Jewish Christians were rejected by both the Jewish people and the Gentile Christians. They were accused both of wanting to restrict Christianity only to Jews and of wanting to impose Jewish customs on the Gentiles. This was not a new problem; it confronted the Apostle Paul.

The Church, which was now becoming a growing power in the Roman Empire, required certain confessions from Jews desiring to convert. Prospective converts were required to renounce the Jewish people, their faith and observances and to vow not to be associated in any way with them. Some "professions of faith" required the convert to confess damnation if he were to break his oath. In the words of one: "May I be an anathema in the world to come, and may my soul be set down with Satan and the devils."

The Jewish Christians held very dear the Jewishness of Jesus. They maintained that Jewish history was a total preparation for the coming of Jesus. The gospel had to be presented in its Jewishness to non-believing Jews if they were to believe in Jesus as Messiah. They also argued that Jewish believers could continue in their Jewishness and still be believers.

The Gentile Christians would not listen and concluded that the Jews were obstinately resisting Christianity. The Gentiles failed to understand what Paul had labored to explain – that the fullness and completeness of the Jewish covenants of promise could only be found in Jesus the Messiah:

As ye have therefore received Christ Jesus the Lord, so walk ye in
him: rooted and built up in him, and stablished in the faith, as ye
have been taught, abounding therein with thanksgiving. Beware
lest any man spoil you through philosophy and vain deceit, after
the tradition of men, after the rudiments of the world and not
after Christ. For in him dwelleth all the fullness of the Godhead
bodily. And ye are complete in him, which is the head of all
principality and power.

(Colossians 2:6–10, KJV)

In their blindness the Church leaders failed to heed the warnings.
The separation between the Gentile Christians and the Jewish Christians caused misinterpretation of Scripture, plunging the Church into
grievous error.

Is the Church the new Israel?

Since Judaism was looking for a Messiah still to come, the Christians
claimed that the Jews could only be expecting anti-Christ as Messiah.

Now came the great error. Since national Israel denied Jesus as
their Messiah, the Church claimed itself to be the true Israel! The
Christian writers then proceeded to read back into the prophecies
the Church in place of Israel.

Through reading the Bible this way, the writers attributed the
curses to natural Israel on the grounds of their disobedience. The
blessings of God they kept for what they considered to be the true
Israel, the Church, because she proclaimed Jesus as the Messiah.
In abandoning the basic principle of scriptural exegesis, namely,
noting who was speaking and whom he was addressing, and then
interpreting Scripture in that light, these early Church teachers lost
sight of the truth.

The influence of this teaching is evident in the Church even today.
Although the Bible contains the warning not to add to, nor subtract
from Scripture, we have Bibles published today with page headings
continuing this anti-Jewish teaching. A King James Authorized
Version with the following headings demonstrates the point:

- Isaiah 9, the prophecy of Jesus' birth and reign, is identified as
  "The church's joy in Christ's birth and kingdom."

- Isaiah 30, prophecy of God's blessing upon Israel and Jerusalem, is headed, "God's mercies towards his church."
- Isaiah 44 commences with words of comfort to Israel but is entitled, "The church comforted."
- In Isaiah 45 God declares that he will raise up Cyrus to release Israel from exile, but it bears the inscription, "God calleth Cyrus for his church's sake."
- The Lord's servant, Israel's redemption and restoration are foretold in Isaiah 49 under the title "Blessings of obedience. Christ sent to the Gentiles with gracious promises. Restoration of the church."
- Then over Isaiah 59, concerned with the sinfulness and restoration of Israel, and chapter 60, foretelling the future glory of Israel, is written the title, "The sins of the Jews. Calamity is for sin. The glorious access of the Gentiles into the church."

The seeds of anti-Semitism were sown in the Church as these writers influenced Christian writers and theologians through the centuries. This is the "replacement theology," so much inferred and sometimes explicitly taught in churches today, which baldly states that the Church has replaced Israel in God's purposes. The result is a reluctance to accept the biblical truth spoken by the prophets of God's unfailing covenant with Israel.

We find the roots of this error reaching back into the third century. Eusebius, Bishop of Caesarea, provides us with very valuable information into the teaching of this period. He wrote two volumes: of the first volume of fifteen books, all are preserved, and of the second volume of twenty books, ten have been preserved. In volume one, Eusebius claimed to have proven that Christianity is both superior to and older than all other religions.

Eusebius' subtle distinction between "Hebrews" and "Jews' pinpoints for us the heart of the problem that continues to our own time. According to him, Hebrews are the most ancient people in the world and their religion is the basis of Greek philosophy. They are neither Jew nor Gentile. From the beginning they were "Christians, and led a Christian way of life."

According to Eusebius, the Patriarchs lived lives pleasing to God and they lived as Christians not Jews. Abraham was a Christian, not a Jew. Moses was a Christian who brought a special law for the Jews which was never intended for Gentiles.

Eusebius saw the law as temporary, to be superseded by the new and superior law constantly referred to by the Hebrew prophets. He used many quotations from the prophets foretelling that the Jews will be abandoned by God as unable to receive salvation.

Eusebius presented the Jews as of no importance and contrasted them with the older "Hebrews" whom he said were the forefathers of Christianity. Hilary, Bishop of Poitiers' teaching of the Jews is summed up in his phrase that they were a "people which has always persisted in iniquity, and out of its abundance of evil has gloried in wickedness." Hilary and Eusebius presented to the pagan world a completely grotesque representation of the history of the Jews, preparing the scenario for the fourth-century tragedy.

The origin and usage of the word "Jew"

Before going further we must understand the origin and development of the word "Jew" so that we can see the abuse of the term by these early Church writers. Before the end of the New Testament period it had a pejorative use which these writers have perpetuated. We can observe nine stages of development of the term *Yehudi* which has been translated "Jew":

1. Originally *Yehudi* applied to members of the tribe of Judah, the fourth son of the patriarch, Jacob.
2. Its usage was then extended to include all those who dwelt in the area of the tribe of Judah.
3. Later, during the seven years that David reigned in Hebron, his territory was called the Kingdom of Judah (2 Samuel 5:5).
4. During the period of the two Kingdoms (Judah and Israel) "Judah" encompassed the territory of Benjamin as well (1 Kings 12:16–21). From then on, *Yehudi* applied to all residents of the southern kingdom irrespective of their tribe.
5. After the destruction of Israel (the northern kingdom), the name "Jew" was used more generally. For example, in the book of Esther 2:5 and 5:13 we discover that Mordecai is of the tribe Benjamin and also called a *Yehudi*. After Haman's

downfall, many among the people of the land converted to Judaism – *mityahadim* – Esther 8:17. At this time *Yehudi* connoted a religious, political and national entity.

6. The term "Jew" has been mainly used by Jews and non-Jews outside the land of Israel and in languages other than Hebrew. For example, Nehemiah, who was an official in the Persian court, refers to "Jews' in his personal diary. The book of Esther also was most likely written by someone close to court circles and therefore out of the land of Israel.

7. Hebrew-speaking Jews within the land were particular to call themselves *Yisrael* which means "Israel" (Israelites). It has been suggested that this was a deliberate reaction aimed at strengthening the identification with the nation's early history. For example, Ezra (in contrast to Nehemiah) uses the name *Yisrael* throughout his writings.

8. From that period on the name "Israel" is used in all Hebrew literature. The use of "Jew" and "Israel," as explained above, is evidenced in the Gospels. Nicodemus, and later the Jews who mocked Jesus, called him "King of Israel" (Matthew 27:42; Mark 15:32; John 1:49; 12:13) while Pilate and the soldiers, who were Roman, called him "king of the Jews" (Matthew 27:11, 29, 37; Mark 15:2, 9, 12, 18; Luke 23:3, 37, 38; John 19:19, 21).

9. Gentile Christians in the early Church fused together "Judaens" with Judas Iscariot who was regarded as the typical Jew. Since Judas was linked with the devil (Luke 22:3) there resulted the association of devil/Jew/Judas. From this developed the pejorative meaning of the word "Jew" that has influenced Eusebius and others and which they have perpetuated. It is worthy of note that in the nineteenth century, Jews began to call themselves "Hebrews" and "Israelites" to escape the problems associated with the name "Jew." The result, however, was that very soon these new names took on the same pejorative association as "Jew," as many nineteenth-century novels testify.[2]

It did not stop there but continues right into our usage today. The Jewish scholar Pinchas Lapide undertook a study of explanations given for the term "Jew" in modern English (British and

American), Spanish, French and Italian dictionaries. He discovered the following:

> a ruthless usurer; a person who overcharges; a person who earns money by unjust and sordid means; an avaricious individual: "Give the Jew a finger and he'll take the whole hand"; a cheater; a person of bad repute; an obstinate miscreant; a sharp trader; satanic; to over-reach, referring to the proverbial keenness of Jewish traders; to cheat by sharp business practice . . . [3]

Usury and "interest"

We now need to understand how these terms of money lending and sharp trading came to be associated with the Jewish people who were formerly farmers and peasants. Since they were prevented from owning land and barred from the Christian industrial guilds, they were reduced to work that Christians refused to do. "Let no Jew exercise any trade or calling except . . . wherein no professional associations or guilds are found," declares a Prussian law as recent as 1750.

Christians interpreted the commandment "If thou lend money to any of my people that is poor by thee, thou shalt not be to him as an usurer, neither shalt thou lay upon him usary" (Exodus 22:25, KJV), to prohibit them from lending money at interest to other Christians. The Jewish slaves who were the legal property of the Christian princes and popes were appointed as bankers, tax collectors and lenders.

Interestingly, the Jewish interpretation of Scripture came from Deuteronomy 23:19–20: "Thou shalt not lend upon usary to thy brother . . . Unto a stranger thou mayest lend upon usury; but unto thy brother thou shalt not lend upon usury" (KJV). They were licensed to make loans, rates of profit were fixed by decree, and a supply of coin was to be kept available when their owners required it. So the Jewish banker found himself excluded from ordinary walks of life, and with work nobody else would do, the distasteful task of collecting money.

An extraordinary situation arose in England when Edward I expelled all English Jewry in 1290. With the disappearance of Jewish bankers Christians had to undertake their work. Since the Christians could not lend on "usury," a new system was legalized.

The banker was entitled to compensation from the borrower for the equivalent "difference" in his wealth between the date of lending and the date of the money being returned. The amount of "difference" was decided entirely by the lender, could not be paid back before the agreed date, and the "difference" was often increased.

The "difference" system, in Latin "*quod* interest," developed into the respectable system of "interest" widely practiced by Christians. The injustices of the Christian practice led the people to protest in a popular medieval song:

> Give us back our Jews,
> For the Jews were debonair
> Greatly more, in this affair
> Than now the Christians are.[4]

This song reflects the just and accurate work of the Jewish bankers. They had come to be internationally renowned for their expertise in handling money which Christians did not want to touch. Herein lies the paradox, for it was this very issue that provoked a backlash by those who propagated the idea of a Jewish conspiracy to control the world's finance.

But we must now return to the teaching of the Church Fathers who provided the theological environment from which this behavior occurred.

Further deception

Early in the third century the most important theologian of the Church, Hippolytus, so esteemed by the Church that he was later given the title "saint," added to this error in his writings. He not only blamed the Jewish people solely for the death of Jesus but claimed that they constantly boasted of their part in his condemnation, suffering and death.

Another step in this breach with Scripture was the gradual assimilation of the heroes of the Old Testament into Christian writings until they were presented as being associated with the Church rather than being the ancestors of the Jews. The following is an example of the so-called Jewish view of ancient history as presented by the Church to her people:

Moses they cursed because he proclaimed Christ, Dathan they loved because he did not proclaim him; Aaron they rejected because he offered the image of Christ, Abiron they set up because he opposed him; David they hated, because he sang of Christ, Saul they magnified, because he did not speak of him; Samuel they cast out because he spoke of Christ; Cham they served, because he said nothing of Christ; Jeremiah they stoned while he was hymning Christ, Ananias they loved while he was opposing him; Isaiah they sawed asunder shouting his glories, Manasseh they glorified persecuting him; John they slew revealing Christ, Zechariah they slaughtered loving Christ, Judas they loved betraying him.[5]

What a travesty these distortions of Scripture present of God's elect people, the Jews. Their effect upon theology and Church teaching through the centuries has been such that God's love and purpose for the Jewish people has almost totally been unrecognized.

Poisoned thinking

Anti-Jewish venom flowed with even greater freedom during the fourth century. Since Constantine had checked the influence of Judaism, and Christianity received imperial favor, the Jewish people were no threat to the Church. Yet the venom persisted. This behavior is an obvious indication of an obsession to persecute Jewish people.

A significant preacher and writer of the time was Bishop John Chrysostom, who also was later recognized by the Church as a "saint." In a campaign to prejudice the Christians of Antioch against any contact with the Jews, he slandered the Jews in a most revolting way.

Chrysostom delivered eight sermons covering more than one hundred pages of closely printed text, expressing intense hatred and malice to Jews, making accusations that were absolute lies:

They sacrificed their sons and daughters to devils: they outraged nature and overthrew from their foundations the laws of relationship. They are become worse than the wild beasts, and for no reason at all, with their own hands they murder their own offspring, to worship the avenging devils who are the foes of our life ... they are lustful, rapacious, greedy, perfidious bandits ... inveterate murderers, destroyers, men possessed by the devil ... debauchery, drunkenness have given them the manners of the pig and the lusty goat. They know only one thing, to satisfy their gullets, get drunk, to kill and maim one another.[6]

Even worse, Bishop Ambrose of Milan organized the destruction of Jewish communities. In a letter of reply to Emperor Theodosius' demand for an enquiry into the riots, Ambrose wrote:

I declare that I have set fire to the synagogue, or at least that those who did it acted under my orders, so that there would be no place where Christ is rejected ... Moreover, the synagogue was in fact destroyed by the judgment of God.[7]

Ambrose took it upon himself to sit in God's seat of judgment on the Jewish people. Both he and Chrysostom failed to realize that God had scattered the Jewish people (Deuteronomy chapters 28–30), that they would be a blessing in the cities to which they were scattered (Jeremiah 29:7), that God would regather them to their own land in his time (Jeremiah chapters 30 and 31), that God would judge the nations according to their treatment of the Jewish people in their midst (Joel 3:1–3) and that God would restore their spiritual inheritance and purify the land (Zechariah 12:10–13:3). Even the Roman authorities were angered – the offenders were punished and the bishop required to rebuild the synagogue.

Cyril, the bishop of Alexandria, expelled all the Jews from that ancient and most important Jewish community of the whole Mediterranean region. The other major Church leaders of the time, Tertullian, Origen and Irenaeus, were not as vociferous in their anti-Jewish stance. Nevertheless they conformed to the policy of accusing the Jewish people of deicide and denying them any place in God's purposes.

To protect his new Christians against the influence of Judaism, Augustine portrayed the Jews as those who had been the sons of God and are now transformed into sons of Satan. It has been said that Augustine's influence upon Christian teaching is second only to the Apostle Paul, but they are in head-on collision regarding the Jewish people. In his commentary on Psalm 18 he wrote:

Of all nations the Jews were dispersed as witnessed of their own iniquity and of our fruit . . . thus our enemies serve us to disconcert other enemies.

Had Augustine not read Paul's explanation of why the Gentiles had been privileged with salvation?

Because of their transgression, salvation has come to the Gentiles to make Israel envious."

(Romans 11:11)

Neither did he understand God's love for the Jewish people:

As far as the gospel is concerned, they are enemies on your account; but as far as election is concerned, they are loved on account of the patriarchs, for God's gifts and his call are irrevocable."

(Romans 11:28–29)

The Jews were now being connected with the fearsome figures of Anti-Christ. Many of the Church Fathers taught that Anti-Christ would be a Jew and that the Jews would be his most devoted followers.

Severed from their roots

The deluded teaching that flowed from the lips and pens of these influential men, denying the fulfillment of God's promises to the Jewish people not only resulted in unimaginable suffering for the Jewish people in the following centuries at the hands of the Church, but also resulted in God's judgment upon the Church, precisely fulfilling the Psalmist's warning:

He who is pregnant with evil
    and conceives trouble gives birth to disillusionment.
He who digs a hole and scoops it out
    falls into the pit he has made.
The trouble he causes recoils on himself;
    his violence comes down on his own head.

(Psalm 7:14–16)

Collectively, these early Church teachers established a doctrine generally accepted in the Church and formulated into Church traditions by the early Church Councils. This led the Church along a path strewn with disaster and compromise with paganism, thereby diverging from God's Word and purpose.

At the Council of Nicea, all the remaining ties linking the Church with the Jewish people were cut. The Council changed the dates of religious festivals, moving their observance from the Jewish dates, which were in accordance with biblical instructions, to observing them on dates of pagan festivals. Christians were admonished never to attend "Jewish sacrileges."

This was a far cry from the practice of Paul who always made the synagogue his first preaching call in every town and city and only left the synagogue when all the Jewish community had heard the message of redemption in Jesus the Messiah. The Church was guilty of forsaking her first love and unless she repented as was required of the church at Ephesus (Revelation 2:4), the judgment threatening the Ephesian church would befall her.

Severance from Jewish connections meant departure from biblical observance both in doctrine, worship and behavior. The resulting void was quickly filled with religious practices adopted from the pagan temples – luxurious buildings and furniture, ceremonious and ritualistic worship. Paganisation included praying for the dead, belief in "purgatory" and the worship of saints and relics. Baptism and the Eucharist lost their biblical significance, again ignoring the stern warnings of Paul (1 Corinthians 11:27, 29–30). The struggles for influence and power among the bishops for superiority over each other and for secular power hastened Church decadence.

Jesus' rebuke to the Jewish leaders barely three centuries before now applied to the Church leaders:

> "You nullify the word of God for the sake of your tradition."
>
> (Matthew 15:6)

The Church entered into a dark age for about 1,000 years after which God in his mercy began a process of restoration with the Reformation. The seeds sown in these centuries brought forth a bitter harvest. From this experience we learn the truth of God's covenant with Abraham:

"I will bless those who bless you,
and whoever curses you I will curse."

(Genesis 12:3)

Before leaving the fourth century, let us remember that our study is concerned with the teaching and influence of the Church leaders. Generally, the relations between local Jewish and Christian communities were friendly. It was, in fact, these amicable relations that stimulated the wrath of the Church leaders, resulting in violent outbursts which sought to reproduce their own hatred for the Jewish people. Dr Lapide observes:

> Perhaps the greatest testimony to the complete falsity of the picture which the theologians painted from the second century onwards, was that it took eight hundred years to be generally believed. Not until the eleventh century did ordinary Christians come at last to believe that the Jews were children of the devil, vowed to the destruction of Christendom, and to act upon that belief.[8]

That God had not forsaken the Jewish people is apparent in many instances during these dark ages. One such instance highlights the blessing Jews were to Christians. In this angry outburst by Archbishop Agobard of ninth-century Europe, we can see the purity of Jewish worship and teaching attracting Christians:

> Things have reached a stage where ignorant Christians claim that the Jews preach better than our priests ... some Christians even celebrate the Sabbath with the Jews and violate the holy repose of Sunday ... Many of the people, peasants, allow themselves to be plunged into such a sea of errors that they regard the Jews as the only people of God, and consider that they combine the observance of a pure religion and a truer faith than ours.[9]

This is another example where Jewish people obeyed the words of their ancient prophet:

> "Seek the peace and prosperity of the city to which I have carried you into exile. Pray to the LORD for it, because if it prospers, you too will prosper."

(Jeremiah 29:7)

Tragically, the European Church during the thirteenth century literally set in stone its arrogant superiority and complete disregard for God's Word in the building of six cathedrals. This feature is particularly evident in two French cathedrals, Strasbourg and Notre Dame.

Elevated in a prominent position for all to see are the figures of two women carved out of stone. One woman stands upright, from her crowned head her long tresses blow in the wind while she clutches a cross in one hand and in the other a chalice filled with the blood of Christ. Her crowned head gazes hopefully and triumphantly into the distance. She represents the Church.

The other woman wears no crown, although dignified she is forlorn, she is downcast and blindfolded signifying her ignorance and darkness while falling from her hand is God's Law. She represents the Synagogue, the Jewish people who have been blinded to Jesus as their Redeemer Messiah. These statues in fact stand as monuments to the deluded Church.

"No Place to Rest and a Despairing Heart"

(Deuteronomy 28:65)

Conditioned by the years of the Church's perverted teaching, medieval people looked upon the Jewish population as descended from the devil, for whom they were agents to destroy Christians and ultimately to rule the world. During this period, Jews were almost wholly without legal rights. They were frequently massacred by the mob. In turn, this encouraged the Jewish tendency to exclusiveness.

These long centuries of persecution led to Jewish alienation, and to their being compulsorily restricted to the most sordid trades. This, in turn, filled the Jewish mind with bitterness towards the Gentile world. The Christian view of the Jewish people as satanic agents found its expression in the most hideous and horrific behavior. One would not expect such from any human being – far less from Christians! If this tragic situation had ceased with that Dark Age it would have still been too severe. But its influence paved the way for the Nazi Holocaust and that poisonous hatred to our very own day.

Contrasted with man's deluded behavior is God's faithfulness to his chosen people. As on a previous occasion in their history, so again he has faithfully protected and provided for them:

> He led you through the vast and dreadful desert, that thirsty and waterless land, with its venomous snakes and scorpions. He brought you water out of hard rock. He gave you manna to eat in the desert, something your fathers had never known, to humble and to test you so that in the end it might go well with you.
>
> (Deuteronomy 8:15–16)

The unholy wars

From the eleventh to the thirteenth centuries, the Crusades demonstrated the horror of this perverted Christian teaching that claimed scriptural origin. Although designed as military expeditions undertaken by Christians to recover the Holy Land from Islam, to ensure protection for Christian pilgrims, and so to establish a Christian kingdom based in Jerusalem, they were much more than this.

During the eleventh century Jews were expelled from many French and German towns. The motive was usually greed rather than a religious reason, as the seizure of Jewish property and commercial interests benefited both the Church and the state. Much of this activity had its roots in the "religious" zeal prompted by the call of Pope Urban II to the First Crusade in 1096. There began a pattern for all crusades which obliterated complete Jewish communities throughout Europe en route to the Holy Land.

Attacks upon Jewish communities reflect again the utter distortion of scriptural teaching. In 1146 a Cistercian monk challenged the crusaders in the Rhineland to avenge themselves on "those who had crucified Jesus" before setting out to fight the Muslims. A report tells of one Jew who was stabbed in five places in memory of the wounds suffered by Jesus.

After reaching and taking Jerusalem, the Crusaders were let loose in the city where all the pressure from their long privations was released in an immense and terrible blood lust. The Muslim men, women and children were murdered on the Temple Mount. The Jews were locked in their great synagogue and then burnt alive as the building was set on fire.

The massacre was such that the blood of victims was knee deep. When there was no one else to kill, the victors went in procession through the streets of the city, still littered with corpses and stinking of death, to the Church of the Holy Sepulchre to give thanks to God for his blessing.[1]

Israel's God promised to avenge his people and to destroy their unrepentant oppressors:

> "As for all my wicked neighbors who seize the inheritance I gave to my people Israel, I will uproot them from their lands and I will uproot the house of Judah from among them. But after I uproot

them, I will again have compassion and will bring each of them back to his own inheritance and his own country. And if they learn well the ways of my people and swear by my name, saying, 'As surely as the LORD lives' – even as they once taught my people to swear by Baal – then they will be established among my people. But if any nation does not listen, I will completely uproot and destroy it," declares the LORD.

(Jeremiah 12:14–17)

Still trembling from the first Crusade, the stirring of the second Crusade caused the Jewish people to cry out to the Lord, "Alas, O Lord, behold, fifty years, like the years of a jubilee, have not passed by since our blood was spilt like water, because of the sanctification of Thy great, mighty and fearful Name in the day of the great slaughter. If thou forsake us forever, what wilt Thou do for Thy great Name? Wilt Thou appoint misery a second time?"

And the Lord heard their cry and remembered his covenant and showed his lovingkindness to them. He sent Bernard, the Abbot of Clairvaux, one of the outstanding Church leaders of his century. Although Bernard was instrumental in encouraging support for the second Crusade, to release the Holy Land from oppressive Islamic domination, he spoke out with authority against the evil treatment of the Jews:

> Come, let us go up unto Zion, to the sepulcher of their Messiah; but take thou heed that thou speak to the Jews neither good nor bad; for whoever toucheth them, is like as if he had touched the apple of the eye of Jesus; for they are his flesh and bone . . . for of them is said in the Psalms, "slay them not, lest my people forget." [2]

St Bernard refused to go with the tide of anti-Semitism. In exerting his great influence on the side of truth there was a turning of the tide of wrath away from the Jews. This was most particularly evident in Germany where Bernard's influence upon King Conrad not only changed the situation for the Jewish people but resulted in the king refusing to support the Crusade.

The Church's Fourth Lateran Council in 1215 undertook the most drastic curtailment of Jewish rights under the leadership of Pope Innocent III. There is an astonishing resemblance between the

Anti-Jewish laws adopted by the Church at this Council and the Nuremburg laws of 1935 and the subsequent Nazi legislation.

This Council made a law requiring every Jewish person to wear a distinguishing mark on their clothing – known as the "law of the patch" – to further isolate them from the rest of the population. This was to become the forerunner of the infamous "Yellow Star" of the Nazi regime, pinpointing the target of ruthless attacks and death.

Medieval sculptures and paintings of biblical patriarchs and prophets wore the distinctive mark, while Jews of the day were often represented as having horns and a tail. Books of the day described a peculiar smell associated with a Jewish person, even though Jewish law required regular bathing not practiced by non-Jews in the Middle Ages.

The Crusades have become a symbol to the Jewish people of the hostility between Christianity and Judaism. No longer was the difference a theological one. Rather, Christians were seen to be the implacable enemies of the Jewish people. In this environment, the blood libel charges became widespread and, by the third Crusade, the idea of a Jewish plot against the Christian world was well established. Jewish people who lost their lives in the Crusades were venerated as martyrs for generations after, some even envied them, for they were a generation that had been tested and had proved their worth.

God's stern warning through Moses to his ancient people had become a stark reality in their lives:

> You will become a thing of horror and an object of scorn and ridicule to all the nations where the LORD will drive you.
>
> (Deuteronomy 28:37)

A Spanish inquisition

"Christian" Spain, in her zeal for maintaining purity of faith, used an Inquisitor during the fifteenth century to purge Christian heretics and Jews. Again, complete communities of Jews were wiped out; some 50,000 were forced to convert, while 300,000 fled the country. In less than twelve years, 13,000 *conversos*, Jews who had converted to Christianity, were sentenced to death because they continued to practice Judaism in secret.

The discovery of the many *conversos* who had remained true to Judaism showed that the segregation of the Jews and the limiting of their rights were not sufficient to suppress their influence. So, on 31 March 1492, an edict was signed expelling all the Jews of Spain, although it was not made known until 1 May. The exodus began.

Around 100,000 Jewish people sought temporary refuge in Portugal. On 31 July, the last Jew left Spain. Many Jews are known to have traveled with Columbus to the new world; among these were Jewish Christians of wealthy and influential families.

Lord Acton, the Catholic historian, made this pertinent statement regarding the Inquisition: "The Popes were not only murderers in the great style, but they also made murder a legal basis of the Christian Church, and a condition for salvation."[3]

This saga of Jewish anguish was another reminder of what God had declared would happen to the Jewish people when scattered among the nations:

> The alien who lives among you will rise above you higher and higher, but you will sink lower and lower. He will be the head, but you will be the tail ... Among those nations you will find no repose, no resting place for the sole of your foot. There the LORD will give you an anxious mind, eyes weary with longing, and a despairing heart.
>
> (Deuteronomy 28:43–44, 65)

But it also contained a testimony to his faithfulness to his covenant as we see in the lives of the Jews who escaped to the New World:

> "Yet in spite of this, when they are in the land of their enemies, I will not reject them or abhor them so as to destroy them completely, breaking my covenant with them. I am the LORD their God. But for their sake I will remember the covenant with their ancestors whom I brought out of Egypt in the sight of the nations to be their God. I am the LORD."
>
> (Leviticus 26:44–45)

The mass expulsion of the Jews from medieval Europe removed the greatest and the wealthiest Jews. In spite of Spain's acquisition of

Jewish wealth, historians have dated Spain's economic decline to 1492! It was evidence of God's judgment upon the Spanish nation:

> "I will bless those who bless you,
>   and whoever curses you I will curse."

(Genesis 12:3)

England expels Jews

The Jewish population of England grew extensively under William the Conqueror in 1066. Their increased fortunes, however, brought about further misfortune.

1144 saw the influence of the blood libel charges. In January, 1253, the Church became increasingly influential in repressive measures against the Jews, in ordering that Jewish worship in the synagogues be inaudible to Christians. It also ruled that Jews could not employ Christian nurses or domestic help, Jews could not eat or buy meat during Lent, and no Jew could stop another Jew from becoming a Christian.

In 1280, Jews were ordered to listen to the conversion sermons of the Dominicans, and to refrain from building new synagogues. They were to wear an oblong white badge in the form of two tables of stone, and to pay tithes to the Church. Christians were not permitted to eat at Jewish tables or to be attended by Jewish doctors.

On 18 July, 1290, the Jews were ordered to leave England before All Saints' Day. They were permitted to take with them only what they could carry, while all other possessions went to the king. Altogether sixteen thousand Jews left England, which cleared her of her Jewish population more completely than any other European country. Their exclusion from England was not ended until 1655 when Oliver Cromwell permitted their return.

A nineteenth-century English historian wrote:

> If it could be said with strict precision of language that a nation can commit a crime, it would be true that one of the greatest national crimes ever committed, was committed in England when the Jews were expelled through the combined influence of the clergy, the traders and the Barons.[4]

This tragic tearing of families from their homes, their land, their possessions, and even separation from kinsmen accords with the warnings of Moses:

> You will be pledged to be married to a woman, but another will take her and ravish her. You will build a house, but you will not live in it. You will plant a vineyard, but you will not even begin to enjoy its fruit. Your ox will be slaughtered before your eyes, but you will eat none of it ... Your sons and daughters will be given to another nation, and you will wear out your eyes watching for them day after day, powerless to lift a hand. A people that you do not know will eat what your land and labor produce, and you will have nothing but cruel oppression all your days.
>
> (Deuteronomy 28:30–33)

From a Polish haven to a Polish holocaust

The upheaval of the sixteenth-century European society forced the Jews to seek refuge elsewhere. Large numbers settled east, in the principal cities of Poland, particularly in Cracow, Lublin, and Warsaw. In peace their communities developed, they held responsible civic office, and their scholarship flourished. At a time when generally only the nobility and clergy could read or write, there was hardly one illiterate Jew.

A decadent Polish government unwittingly provided advantage for the Jewish population. An example was seen in 1643 when legislation was passed to suppress Jewish business interests. Profit margins were set; Christian merchants could make seven per cent profit while Jewish merchants were limited to three per cent. As a result, the population traded with Jewish merchants because their prices were cheaper and the Christian merchants were put out of business!

Poland had a nomadic people, the Cossacks, who worked the land. Because of ill-treatment, the Cossacks rose in 1648 against the Polish gentry who owned the land. Jews and Jesuits were the administrators of the land.

The Cossacks of the Greek Orthodox faith had long suffered persecution from the Jesuits. In the midst of the fierce battle between the Poles and the Cossacks lay the Jews who collected the taxes and acted as merchants. Protection from the Polish nobility ceased in 1648 when the Polish Army was destroyed; then followed wholesale death of the Jewish people by the Cossacks crying, "Christ killers!"

After a respite of three years, the Cossacks allied with the Czar of Russia and in 1654 massacres of the Jewish people swept Poland. Catholic Poles annihilated the Jews in Posen, Kaliz, Piotrokov and Cracow, giving their synagogues to the Dominicans. By 1660, 500,000 Jews from 700 communities had been killed.

The remainder of Polish Jewry has never been able to re-establish itself to its former strength even in pre-Second World War Poland. So the way was paved for Poland to accommodate the twentieth-century Nazi death camps.

No room in czarist Russia

The Church of Holy Russia had firmly etched in her memory the experience of the fifteenth and sixteenth centuries where nobles and even priests converted to Judaism. Russian policy was to keep the Jewish people out of Russia. Empress Elizabeth replied to a petition to allow Jews to immigrate to Russia: "From the enemies of Christ I desire neither gain nor profit."

One historian commenting on this attitude attributes it to the influence of the early Church's theology:

> Such pious royal disfavor can be traced to the very beginning of the Russian monarchy, and beyond that into the courts of Byzantium. The absolutism with which these policies were pursued derived its validation from the Greek Orthodox theology; and so deeply ingrained was this theology that every Czar to sit on the throne of Holy Russia considered it his sacred duty to protect the Russian people from Jewish economic interests, indeed even from the presence of Jews in their midst.[5]

Taxes imposed on the Jewish population were double what Christians had to pay. In 1791 a law against them confined their communities to restricted provinces – the "Pale of Settlement." By 1808 this area was further restricted to eleven provinces and laws forced Jewish people to change their occupation, language, dress

Pharaoh warns the Czar that the Jews were responsible
for the plagues of ancient Egypt.

and social habits. The country needed farmers and tillers of the land
– the Jews were to do this!

Between 1640 and 1881, six hundred laws concerning Jews were
enacted. Czar Nicholas I was aiming for one Russia, one language
and one religion. He was determined to destroy Judaism as a
distinct cultural entity.

In 1827 he instituted a system of military conscription. This
ensured that Jewish men became Russia's soldiers and imposed a
law where a soldier's son became the property of the state. Children
were taken from their homes and exiled into distant northern
provinces for periods of up to twenty-five years. The aim was to
have these children baptized. Those refusing rarely survived, and it
is said that over half never reached those camps. As many Jewish
communities could not provide their allotted number of children,
children of the Pale were constantly kidnapped.

On 13 March, 1881, Czar Alexander II was assassinated. His son,
Alexander III, began a course of autocracy. The Jewish people were
blamed for the Czar's assassination, and he enforced a plan to solve
the "Jewish problem" in conjunction with his "master planner"

Konstantin Pobedonostsev, the head of the Russian Church. One half of the Jews would be baptized and one half would be starved to death.

Six weeks later dreadful pogroms began to sweep the land. In 160 towns and villages Jews were killed and their property destroyed. Priests and Russian peasants came to the defense of the terror-stricken Jews, demonstrating it was the power of the Czar and not the people who were responsible for these measures against the Jewish people. In response to world protests at this carnage, the Russian government, to clear itself, said the pogroms were a result of the "harmful consequences of the economic activity of the Jews on the Christian population."

On 3 May, 1882, new laws known as the "May Rules" provided some protection for the Jewish people but also prohibited them from settling or buying new land in the Pale. They forced Jewish merchants to close on Sundays and Greek Orthodox holidays. These were followed by restrictions in education; later graduates were prevented from practicing their profession. Large numbers of Jews sought refuge elsewhere. Many fled to America.

Beginnings of the second exodus

A Jewish doctor, Leon Pinsker, called for a second exodus. He wrote:

> Let us obtain dry bread by the sweat of our brow on the sacred soil of our ancestors.[6]

Societies emerged all over Europe and in America stimulated by the vision. In 1882, three settlements were established in Palestine, populated by Rumanian and Russian exiles. Assisted by finance from Baron Edmond de Rothschild, others were able to follow. They were known as the BILU settlers. The name arose from the initial letters of the Hebrew phrase "House of Jacob, come and let us go!"

God had promised not only discipline but also restoration:

> "I will block her path with thornbushes;
>   I will wall her in so that she cannot find her way.

She will chase after her lovers but not catch them;
   she will look for them but not find them.
Then she will say,
   'I will go back to my husband as at first,
   for then I was better off than now.' . . .

In that day I will respond,"
   declares the LORD . . .
"I will plant her for myself in the land;
   I will show my love to the one I called 'Not my loved one.' "

(Hosea 2:6–7, 21, 23)

Czar Nicholas II's accession to the throne in 1894 put him in control of the largest Jewish population in the world – 6,000,000. He commenced to slaughter the Jewish population through an organization of agents known as the "Black Hundreds" with the cry "Give them more blood." The Czar's repressive policies were forced on the whole Russian population, not only the Jews, and resulted in his murder in the revolution of 1917.

Blood libel

The cruelest allegation against the Jewish people perpetrated by Christians (with which, ironically, the early Church was charged) was the "blood libel." It was alleged that Jews murdered non-Jews, especially Christians, to obtain the blood for Passover or other rituals.

While blood sacrifice was practiced by pagan religions it was prohibited by the Law of Moses. The origin of this accusation reaches back before the time of Jesus to the Greek ruler, Antiochus Epiphanes, and it has been suggested that the story was spread as propaganda to justify his desecration of the Temple.

The early Church also suffered such allegations. The second-century Church Father Tertullian complained:

> We are said to be the most criminal of men, on the score of our sacramental baby-killing and the baby-eating that goes with it.[7]

Tertullian also describes the torture Christians suffered as a result of these evil accusations.

As Christianity spread through Western Europe, influencing popular thinking and imagination, stories developed around the alleged inhumanity and sadism of the Jews. In Norwich in 1144 it was alleged that the Jews had "bought a Christian child before Easter and tortured him with all the tortures wherewith our Lord was tortured, and on Long Friday hanged him on a rood in hatred of our Lord."[8]

This accusation of torturing and murdering Christian children in the form of Jesus' Passion continued in various forms throughout the twelfth and thirteenth centuries.

We see the persistence of the perpetrators of these allegations which were continued even after thorough investigations had proved them false. Emperor Frederick II of Hohenstaufen decided to clear up the matter concerning a particular allegation once and for all. He said he would have all the Jews of the empire killed if the accusation proved true, and he would publicly exonerate them if it proved false. To be sure that he would get the truth he commissioned "decent and learned converts" from among the Jews of the West to undertake the investigation.

The thorough investigation found absolutely no evidence to support the charges. Frederick exonerated the Jews and Pope Innocent IV did likewise but little notice was taken of either the state leader or the Church leader.

In the nineteenth century, leaders of Jewish hatred used the blood libel as a weapon to arouse the uneducated masses in order to achieve their political goals. This was especially true in Eastern Europe. The Nazis used the blood libel in full force for anti-Jewish propaganda. Russia had been the main perpetrator of the blood libel in modern times, particularly until the 1917 Revolution.

The British statesman, David Lloyd George, concisely summarized the illogical dilemma that besets the Jewish people scattered among the nations:

> Of all the bigotries that savage the human temper there is none so stupid as the anti-Semitic. It has no basis in reason; it is not rooted in faith; it aspires to no ideal; it is just one of those dank and unwholesome weeds that grow in the morass of racial hatred.
>
> How utterly devoid of reason it is may be gathered from the fact that it is almost entirely confined to nations who worship Jewish

prophets and apostles, revered the national literature of the Hebrews as the only inspired message delivered by the Deity to mankind and whose only hope of salvation rests on the precepts and promises of the great teachers of Judah.

Yet in the sight of these fanatics, the Jews of today can do nothing right. If they are rich, they are birds of prey. If they are poor, they are vermin. If they are in favor of a war, it is because they want to exploit the blood feuds of the Gentiles to their own profit. If they are anxious for peace, they are either instinctive cowards or traitors. If they give generously – and there are no more liberal givers than the Jews – they are doing it for some selfish purpose of their own. If they do not give – then what could one expect of a Jew but avarice? If labour is oppressed by great capital, the greed of the Jew is held responsible. If labour revolts against capital – as it did in Russia – the Jew is blamed for that also. If he lives in a strange land he must be persecuted and pogrommed out of it.

If he wants to go back to his own, he must be prevented. Through the centuries in every land, whatever he does, or intends, or fails to do, he has been pursued by the echo of the brutal cry of the rabble of Jerusalem against the greatest of all Jews – "Crucify him!"[8]

Hear, O Israel

But the God of Israel who had the first word also has the last word. He will not be defied and he will triumph:

> The LORD called you a thriving olive tree
>   with fruit beautiful in form.
> But with the roar of a mighty storm
>   he will set it on fire,
>   and its branches will be broken.
>
> (Jeremiah 11:16)

Paul explains simply how those broken olive branches are to be grafted in again so that the olive will thrive as never before:

> If some of the branches have been broken off, and you [Gentiles], though a wild olive shoot, have been grafted in among the others

and now share in the nourishing sap from the olive root, do not boast over those branches. If you do, consider this: You do not support the root, but the root supports you. You will say then, "Branches were broken off so that I could be grafted in." Granted. But they were broken off because of unbelief, and you stand by faith. Do not be arrogant, but be afraid. For if God did not spare the natural branches, he will not spare you either.

Consider therefore the kindness and sternness of God: sternness to those who fell, but kindness to you, provided that you continue in his kindness. Otherwise, you also will be cut off. And if they do not persist in unbelief, they will be grafted in, for God is able to graft them in again. After all, if you were cut out of an olive tree that is wild by nature, and contrary to nature were grafted into a cultivated olive tree, how much more readily will these, the natural branches, be grafted into their own olive tree!

(Romans 11:17–24)

We Gentile Christians must understand two important lessons from this:

Firstly, God is disciplining Israel among the nations. The nations are not given the right to discipline Israel. God made this very clear in his statement through Zechariah:

Thus says the Lord of hosts: I am jealous for Jerusalem and for Zion with a great jealousy. And I am very angry with the nations that are at ease; for while I was but a little displeased they helped forward the affliction and disaster.

(Zechariah 1:14–15, AMP)

Paul warns us that we too will be disciplined by God if we are disobedient.

Secondly, the Psalmist reminds Israel of God's faithfulness to his people:

He will not let your foot slip –
    he who watches over you will not slumber;
indeed, he who watches over Israel
    will neither slumber nor sleep.

The LORD watches over you –
  the LORD is your shade at your right hand;
the sun will not harm you by day,
  nor the moon by night.

The LORD will keep you from all harm –
  he will watch over your life.

(Psalm 121:3–7)

Then God encourages Israel with the assurance:

"For a brief moment I abandoned you,
  but with deep compassion I will bring you back.
In a surge of anger
  I hid my face from you for a moment,
but with everlasting kindness
  I will have compassion on you,"
  says the LORD your Redeemer . . .
  " . . . no weapon forged against you will prevail,
  and you will refute every tongue that accuses you.
This is the heritage of the servants of the LORD,
  and this is their vindication from me,"
declares the LORD.

(Isaiah 54:7–8, 17)

Preparing the Way for the Holocaust

The Holocaust was the work of Christians . . . and the fulfillment of Christianity.

Such is the damning judgment of Yoram Shaftel, Israel defense attorney in the trial of John Demjanjuk (March 1987), who was accused of being "Ivan the Terrible" of the infamous Treblinka death camp.[1]

A mixture of truth and deception

Martin Luther, who received and declared the new truth of justification by faith not by works, also perpetuated an old lie. As a young man he was friendly to Jews and even fought against those who hated them. In 1523 in a pamphlet, *Jesus Was Born a Jew*, he wrote:

Our fools, the popes, bishops, sophists and monks, these coarse blockheads, dealt with the Jews in such a manner that any Christian would have preferred to be a Jew. Indeed, had I been a Jew and had seen such idiots and dunderheads expound Christianity, I should rather have become a hog than a Christian . . .

They were called names and had their belongings stolen. Yet they are blood-brothers and cousins of the Savior. No other people have been singled out by God as they have; they have been entrusted with his Holy Word . . .

I would advise and beg everybody to deal kindly with the Jews and to instruct them in the Scriptures; in such a case we could expect them to come over to us.[2]

Luther's attitude was clearly in hope that pure Christianity would succeed in attracting the Jewish people. In later years, however, a bitter Luther completely reversed his opinion. Lashing out vehemently at the Jewish people, he wrote:

> The Jews deserve the most severe penalties. Their synagogues should be leveled, their homes destroyed, they should be exiled into tents like the gypsies. Their religious writings should be taken from them. The rabbis should be forbidden to continue teaching the Law. All professions should be closed to them. Only the hardest, coarsest work should be permitted them. Rich Jews should have their fortunes confiscated, and the money used to support Jews who are willing to be converted. If all these measures are unsuccessful, the Christian princes have the duty of driving the Jews from their lands as they would rabid dogs.[3]

On 14 February, 1546, four days before his death, Luther preached his last sermon. His subject was the Jews, demanding that they be driven from all German lands. Ironically, Luther's understanding of Paul's teaching of justification by faith was influenced by a commentary on Romans written by a fourteenth-century Jewish Christian, Nicholas of Lyra.[4]

Four centuries later a German historian wrote:

> It is difficult to understand the behavior of most German Protestants in the first Nazi years unless one is aware of two things; their history and the influence of Martin Luther. The great founder of Protestantism was both a passionate anti-Semite and a ferocious believer in absolute obedience to political authority. He wanted Germany rid of the Jews ... advice that was literally followed four centuries later by Hitler, Goering and Himmler ...
>
> Luther employed a coarseness of language unequalled in German history until the Nazi time ... In no country, with the exception of Czarist Russia, did the clergy become by tradition so completely servile to the political authority of the State.[5]

In the early days of his career, Hitler cunningly used Scripture and a spurious profession of the Christian faith to win respectable support from the "Christian" Germans. In a speech as early as 12 April, 1922, he had the audacity to say:

> In boundless love, as a Christian and a human being, I read the passage which tells us how the Lord at last rose in his might and seized the scourge to drive out of the Temple the brood of vipers and adders. How terrific was his fight against the Jewish poison; I realize more profoundly than ever before the fact that it was for this that he had to shed his blood upon the Cross.[6]

Hitler's hatred for Jews permeates all his writing:

> I hated the mixture of races displayed in the capital, I hated the motley collection of Czechs, Poles, Hungarians, Ruthenians, Croats, etc., and above all, that ever-present fungoid growth – Jews, and again Jews.[7]

Moses had declared to his people the horror of walking contrary to God's commands:

> All these curses will come upon you. They will pursue you and overtake you until you are destroyed, because you did not obey the LORD your God and observe the commands and decrees he gave you. They will be a sign and a wonder to you and your descendants forever. Because you did not serve the LORD your God joyfully and gladly in the time of prosperity . . .
>
> The LORD will bring a nation against you from far away, from the ends of the earth, like an eagle swooping down, a nation whose language you will not understand, a fierce-looking nation without respect for the old or pity for the young.
>
> (Deuteronomy 28:45–47, 49–50)

And God constantly reminded his people of his faithfulness to them:

> "I gave you my solemn oath and entered into a covenant with you, declares the Sovereign LORD, and you became mine."
>
> (Ezekiel 16:8)

> This is what the LORD says –
>   he who created you, O Jacob,
>   he who formed you, O Israel:

"Fear not, for I have redeemed you;
 I have summoned you by name; you are mine."

(Isaiah 43:1)

"Listen to me, O house of Jacob,
 all you who remain of the house of Israel,
you whom I have upheld since you were conceived,
 and have carried since your birth.
Even to your old age and grey hairs
 I am he, I am he who will sustain you.
I have made you and I will carry you;
 I will sustain you and I will rescue you." ...

"I say: My purpose will stand,
 and I will do all that I please ...
I will grant salvation to Zion,
 my splendor to Israel."

(Isaiah 46:3–4, 10, 13)

The Protocols of the Learned Elders of Zion

Germany

During World War II, the Nazi determination to destroy the Jewish people was "justified" by some writings of an earlier time known as *The Protocols of the Learned Elders of Zion*. These were widely distributed by the Third Reich and often quoted in their literature. It is important that we understand something of the background of these writings as they are still used and influential in creating anti-Jewish activity.

Before the rise to power of the Nazis, the *Protocols* were most popular in Germany. These writings claimed the Jewish people exercised an occult power, and that they were determined enemies of German-Christian culture. This well suited those in Germany who were looking for scapegoats for Germany's defeat; the Nazi Party used this theme right from its start.

Switzerland

A fact that is not well known is that the Jewish community of Switzerland, in Berne, 1934, took the distributors of the *Protocols* to trial. The court clearly established that the *Protocols* were forged and therefore were not what they purported to be. This meant that the contents of the *Protocols* were false, they were malicious lies. But this did nothing to stop their misuse.[8]

Let us now look at the history of the *Protocols*. During the Middle Ages, many bizarre stories of Jewish behavior were told by Christians. Often these arose from legends that the Jewish people were responsible for poisoning of wells and the spreading of plagues. (It should be noted that the Jewish people were often protected from some of these plagues because they lived by the Law of Moses, which incorporates sound standards of hygiene.) The next stage of these anti-Jewish plots was to say that there was a worldwide Jewish conspiracy determined to reduce the Gentiles to slavery and even to exterminate them!

Spain

Later in Spain, this thinking turned from a religious to a political emphasis. It spread to France where Catholic writers broadened the threat by linking Freemasons and Jews in an anti-Christian plot. In the late nineteenth century, the legend of the "Elders of Zion" was written in Paris by an unknown author to encourage Czar Nicholas II to set up the secret police against the Jews.

The unknown forger used an old French political pamphlet by Maurice Joly which had been originally written to expose the ambitions of Napoleon III. It mentioned nothing about Jews or Judaism. In rewriting them, the unknown author introduced a mythical conference of the leaders of world Jewry who, he claimed, already had control of the policies of numerous European states and were not far from world domination.

Russia

Even Nicolas II, who was so dedicated to wiping out the Jewish population, recognized the *Protocols* were untrue. He noted in the margin of the manuscript given to him, "One does not defend a worthy cause by vile means."[9]

People were looking for a basic reason for the wholesale slaughter during World War I which so dramatically changed the face of Europe, followed by the Russian Revolution in 1917 and the uprisings in Germany. The ground was fertile for the propagandists

Frontispiece to a Polish edition of the *Protocols*, Poznan, 1937.
The caption reads: "After Russia and Spain – it is Poland's turn!
She must have a blood bath! Only ruins and cinders should remain!
Already the Jew leads Death to her harvest in Poland!
Let us watch this marching column and let us be awake,
for woe to us! Woe!!!"

to suggest a "Jewish Revolution" which was responsible for the pogroms in southern Russia between 1918 and 1920.

The *Protocols* were then spread in the West. Many reputable newspapers raised questions on their authenticity and in 1921 a journalist, Philip Graves, pointed to the close similarity between the text of the *Protocols* and the pamphlet originally written by Joly. While this resulted in responsible people refusing to take them seriously, they were nonetheless, translated into all the main world languages and widely circulated.

Egypt

President Nasser of Egypt ensured they were distributed to all his troops. It has been reported that the *Protocols* were, after the Koran, the most frequently cited book at the International Conference of Muslim Scholars gathered in Cairo in 1968. An article in the Egyptian state-owned newspaper *al-Akhbar* on 3 February, 2002 stated:

All the evils that currently affect the world are the doings of Zionism. This is not surprising, because the *Protocols of the Elders of Zion*, which were established by their wise men more than a century ago, are proceeding according to a meticulous and precise plan and time schedule, and they are proof that even though they are a minority, their goal is to rule the world and the entire human race.

In October 2002, a private Egyptian television company Dream TV produced a forty-one-part "historical drama" entitled *A Horseman Without a Horse (Fares Bela Gewad)*, largely based on the *Protocols*. This ran for a month on seventeen Arabic-language satellite television channels, including government-owned Egypt Television (ETV), causing concerns in the West. Egypt's Information Minister Safwat El-Sherif announced that the series "contains no anti-Semitic material."[10]

Iran

The first Iranian edition of the *Protocols* was issued during the summer of 1978 before the Iranian Revolution. In 1985 a new edition of the *Protocols* was printed and widely distributed by the Islamic Propagation Organization, International Relations Department in Tehran. The Astaneh-ye Qods Razavi (Shrine of Imam Reza) Foundation in Mashhad, Iran, one of the wealthiest institutions in Iran, financed publication of the *Protocols* in 1994.

Parts of the *Protocols* were published by the daily Jomhouri-ye Eslami in 1994, under the heading *The Smell of Blood, Zionist Schemes*. *Sobh*, a radical Islamic monthly, published excerpts from the *Protocols* under the heading *The text of the Protocols of the Elders of Zion for establishing the Jewish global rule* in its December 1998– January 1999 issue, illustrated with a caricature of the Jewish snake swallowing the globe.

In April 2004, the Iranian television station Al-Alam broadcast *Al-Sameri wa Al-Saher*, a series that reported as fact several conspiracy theories about the Holocaust, Jewish control of Hollywood, and the *Protocols*. The Iran Pavilion of the 2005 Frankfurt Book Fair had the *Protocols*, as well as *The International Jew* (reprints from Henry Ford's *The Dearborn Independent*) available.[11]

Saudi Arabia

Saudi Arabian schoolbooks contain explicit summaries of the Protocols as factual:

> *The Protocols of the Elders of Zion:* These are secret resolutions, most probably of the aforementioned Basel congress. They were discovered in the nineteenth century. The Jews tried to deny them, but there was ample evidence proving their authenticity and that they were issued by the elders of Zion . . .
>
> The cogent proof of the authenticity of these resolutions, as well as of the hellish Jewish schemes included therein, is the [actual] carrying out of many of those schemes, intrigues and conspiracies that are found in them. Anyone who reads them – and they were published in the nineteenth century – grasps today to what extent much of what is found there has been realized.

According to Freedom House 2006 report, a "Saudi textbook for boys for Tenth Grade on Hadith and Islamic Culture contains a lesson on the 'Zionist Movement.' It is a curious blend of wild conspiracy theories about Masonic Lodges, Rotary Clubs, and Lions Clubs with anti-Semitic invective. It asserts that the *Protocols of the Elders of Zion* is an authentic document and teaches students that it reveals what Jews really believe. It blames many of the world's wars and discord on the Jews."[12]

Malaysia

Dr Mahatir Mohammed, former president of Malaysia, a persistent opponent of Israel speaks of "Zionist plots" and "international Jewish media." He has said that "the expulsion of the Jews from the Holy Land 2,000 years ago and the Nazi oppression of the Jews have taught them nothing. If at all, it has transformed the Jews into the very monsters that they condemn in their propaganda. They have been apt pupils of Dr Goebbels."[13]

Malaysia has become a racist nation, patterning its actions literally after Nazi Germany.

Japan

Although Japan has a very small Jewish population, the influence of the *Protocols* is becoming increasingly evident. There has been a spate of anti-Semitic books published in Hiroshima.

The best-selling author, Masami Uno, argues that an "international Jewish conspiracy" has created Japan's present economic troubles. He says that Jews control major US corporations and have engineered "a targeted bashing of Japan." He further asserts that the reports of mass killings of Jews by the Nazis during World War II are exaggerated.

It has been reported that two books by Uno, one entitled *If you Understand the Jews, You Can Understand the World* have sold at least 800,000 copies, thereby qualifying them as best-sellers. He claims that the bribery indictment of former Prime Minister Kakuei Tanaka in 1976 and the rise of South Korea as a competitor were part of the plot. Uno tells us that Jewish bankers have created the strengthened yen to subvert and subjugate the Japanese economy.

Other books that have also appeared on the Japanese market include *Miracles of the Torah which Control the World, Understanding the Protocols of the Elders of Zion* and *Make Money with Stocks Targeted by the Jews.*[14]

The Jerusalem Post for 23 April 2006 was headlined "*Protocols* still being used to stir up hatred of Jews." The article claims:

> A century-old forgery used to justify ill-treatment of Jews in Czarist Russia and widely circulated by the Nazis is distributed even today in many languages to stoke hatred of Israel, an exhibit at the US Holocaust Museum says.
>
> Colorfully bound editions of *The Protocols of the Elders of Zion* have appeared recently in Mexico and in Japan, where there are few Jews, says exhibit historian Daniel Greene. High school texts in Syria, Lebanon and schools run by the Palestinian authority use the book as history, he says ... "The Internet has about 500,000 sites where the book is discussed – about half and half for and against," Greene estimated ...
>
> When Egyptian government-sponsored TV showed a series based on *The Protocols* in 2002, the State Department condemned it. In 2005, a new edition of the book was published in Syria. This Syrian edition of *The Protocols* claims that the terrorist attacks in the US on September 11, 2001, were orchestrated by a Zionist conspiracy.

We must recognize this subtle conspiracy for what it is. This is not a conspiracy of Jewish origin against the world but the very reverse –

a world conspiracy against the Jewish people! Now that the Jewish people have the opportunity of living in their promised homeland, the life of the ghetto is past, but the conspiracy is now centered upon their homeland, Israel.

"Zionism is racism"

The United Nations Assembly passed Resolution 3379 on 10 November, 1975, declaring "that Zionism is a form of racism and racial discrimination." The significance and motive of this action is further highlighted by three points.

10 November, 1975 was the thirty-seventh anniversary of the horrific Nazi *Kristallnacht* – "the night of broken glass" – when Hitler's program of genocide was launched against the Jews of Europe. During that night in all the cities, towns, villages and hamlets throughout greater Germany, hundreds of synagogues were set on fire, Jewish shops were looted, and Jews were beaten up in the streets.

The Secretary-General of the United Nations in November 1975 was the controversial Kurt Waldheim, who later became the premier of Austria.

Seventy-two nations voted in favor of the resolution while thirty-five nations voted against the resolution with thirty-two abstentions. Of those favoring the resolution only fourteen were true democracies, nineteen were communist and twenty-two were Muslim nations. It is encouraging to know that New Zealand, Australia, the United States of America and Britain voted against the resolution. This was revoked 16 December, 1991, by Resolution 4686 as Israel's precondition to be involved in the Madrid Peace Conference.

The New York Times rightly put into perspective the situation which questions the faithfulness of the United Nations to its own charter:

> The unholy alliance of Communist and Arab Governments that pushed through the General Assembly in the odious resolution equating Zionism with "racism" was, in effect, challenging the very right to existence of Israel, a member state created by act of the United Nations itself. The original objective of the Arab bloc was to expel Israel forthwith.

On the Zionism Issue...
IT WAS DEMOCRACIES vs DICTATORSHIPS
An analysis of the political systems of the nations voting on the U.N. resolution to identify Zionism as a form of racism shows—

VOTING FOR THE RESOLUTION: 72 MEMBERS

Afghanistan	One-man rule	Madagascar	Military dictatorship
Albania	Communist dictatorship	Malaysia	Parliamentary democracy
Algeria	One-party	Maldive	
Bahrain	Sheikdom	Islands	Parliamentary democracy
Bangladesh	Martial-law dictatorship	Mali	Military dictatorship
Brazil	Military dictatorship	Malta	Parliamentary democracy
Bulgaria	Communist dictatorship	Mauritania	One-party rule
Burundi	Military dictatorship	Mexico	Parliamentary democracy
Byelorussia	Soviet republic	Mongolia	Communist dictatorship
Cambodia	Communist dictatorship	Morocco	Kingdom
Cameroon	Parliamentary democracy	Mozambique	One-party rule
Cape Verde	Parliamentary democracy	Niger	Military dictatorship
Chad	Military dictatorship	Nigeria	Military dictatorship
China	Oman		Absolute monarchy
Congo	Military dictatorship	Pakistan	Nominal democracy
Cuba	Communist dictatorship	Poland	Communist dictatorship
Cyprus	Mixed rule	Portugal	Military rule
Czechoslovakia	Communist dictatorship	Qatar	Sheikdom
Dahomey	Military dictatorship	Rwanda	Military dictatorship
Egypt	One-party rule	Sao Tome	
Equatorial		e Principe	Parliamentary democracy
Guinea	One-party rule	Saudi Arabia	Absolute monarchy
Gambia	Parliamentary democracy	Senegal	Parliamentary democracy
East Germany	Communist dictatorship	Somalia	Military dictatorship
Grenada	Parliamentary democracy	South Yemen	Leftist dictatorship
Guinea	One-party rule	Soviet Union	Communist dictatorship
Guinea-Bissau	One-party rule	Sri Lanka	Parliamentary democracy
Guyana	Nominal democracy	Sudan	Military dictatorship
Hungary	Communist dictatorship	Syria	One-party rule
India	Emergency one-woman rule	Tanzania	One-party rule
Indonesia	Military dictatorship	Tunisia	Parliamentary democracy
Iran	Absolute monarchy	Turkey	Parliamentary democracy
Iraq	One-party rule	Uganda	Military dictatorship
Jordan	Kingdom	Ukraine	Soviet republic
Kuwait	Family dynasty	United Arab	
Laos	Communist dictatorship	Emirates	Sheikdoms
Lebanon	Parliamentary democracy	Yemen	Military dictatorship
Libya	Military dictatorship	Yugoslavia	Communist dictatorship

Of the 72 members voting for the resolution, only 14 were true democracies. The other 58 were run by dictators, strong men or elite groups.

VOTING AGAINST THE RESOLUTION: 35 NATIONS

Among these nations, which included the U.S. and most nations of West Europe, were 27 democracies and only 8 countries run by dictators or strong men.

Democracies: Australia, Austria, Bahamas, Barbados, Belgium, Britain, Canada, Germany, Honduras, Iceland, Ireland, Israel, Italy, Liberia, Luxembourg, the Netherlands, New Zealand, Norway, Sweden, U.S.

Others: Central African Republic, Haiti, Ivory Coast, Malawi, Nicaragua, Panama, Swaziland, Uruguay.

Note: 32 countries abstained and 3 were "not present".

Zionism is Racism UN voting chart
(*US News & World* Report, Nov 24, 1975)

A cartoonist's impression of the United Nations "Zionism is Racism"
resolution links the activity of the UN in the conflict
with the Palestinians, with that of Hitler
(Par **Aldor** de "El Tiempo" de Bogotá)

This same fervor for the destruction of Israel is keenly reflected in
the fiery speech of PLO leader Yasser Arafat as he addressed the
Palestinian National Council in Algiers on 20 April, 1987:

> We will continue the armed struggle . . . the Palestinian gun shall not
> be put aside until we reach Palestine . . . Our nation has determined
> that it will write its history in words of blood and fire, because the
> [Palestinian] soil is indivisible, and so is our will . . . I call upon our
> brethren in Iran to reach agreement [with Iraq] and to put an end to
> this war, so that all the guns may be directed to the liberation of

Palestine from the clutches of Zionism and colonialism ... We will continue to maintain fighting contact with the Israeli foe, until our revolution is victorious. We will fight, not just for the sake of fighting, but for the imposition of a just and comprehensive solution in our region, based on the legitimate rights of the Palestinian people – its right of return, of self-determination and the establishment of the Palestinian state with Jerusalem as its capital.[15]

Thirty years after the UN Resolution, the author received from Church leaders in Jerusalem a collective statement embodying the "Zionism is racism" resolution and reflecting the antagonism of Yasser Arafat's statement. This document, entitled *The Jerusalem Declaration on Christian Zionism*, was published 22 August, 2006. The signatories to the declaration are: the Latin Patriarch of Jerusalem, Michel Sabbah; the Syrian Orthodox Patriarch of Jerusalem, Swerios Malki Mourad; the Episcopal Bishop of Jerusalem and the Middle East, Riah Abu El-Assal; and the Evangelical Lutheran Bishop in Jordan and the Holy Land, Munib Younan.

It is a statement directed at Christians who accept that God made covenants with Israel which he is fulfilling in these days – they are described as "Christian Zionists":

> Christian Zionism is a modern theological and political movement that embraces the most extreme ideological positions of Zionism, thereby becoming detrimental to a just peace within Palestine and Israel. The Christian Zionist programme provides a worldview where the gospel is identified with the ideology of empire, colonialism and militarism. In its extreme form, it places an emphasis on apocalyptic events leading to the end of history rather than living Christ's love and justice today.
>
> We categorically reject Christian Zionist doctrines as false teaching that corrupts the biblical message of love, justice and reconciliation.
>
> We further reject the contemporary alliance of Christian Zionist leaders and organizations with elements in the governments of Israel and the United States that are presently imposing their unilateral pre-emptive borders and domination over Palestine. This inevitably leads to unending cycles of violence that undermine the security of all peoples of the Middle East and the rest of the world.

We reject the teachings of Christian Zionism that facilitate and support these policies as they advance racial exclusivity and perpetual war rather than the gospel of universal love, redemption and reconciliation taught by Jesus Christ. Rather than condemn the world to the doom of Armageddon we call upon everyone to liberate themselves from the ideologies of militarism and occupation. Instead, let them pursue the healing of the nations! . . .

We call upon all people to reject the narrow worldview of Christian Zionism and other ideologies that privilege one people at the expense of others . . .

With urgency we warn that Christian Zionism and its alliances are justifying colonization, apartheid and empire-building . . .

A bizarre twist

On the one hand we hear Yasser Arafat and the Muslim world denouncing Zionism as racism, while they deny the right of the Jewish people to return to their ancient homeland, to their own sovereign state, with its own democratic government, its unique culture and ancient religion as expressed in the Old Testament (the Jewish Tenach). On the other hand Arafat is guilty of trying to strip Jesus of his Jewish identity and branding him a Palestinian. On 24 December, 1995, at the annual celebration of Jesus' birth in his birthplace, Bethlehem, Yasser Arafat, a Muslim, publicly declared that Jesus is a Palestinian, not a Jew. *The Jerusalem Post* (25 December, 1995) reported this event in an editorial entitled "Arafat and the Church":

> It is difficult not to feel a grudging admiration for Yasser Arafat. When he first started describing Jesus as a Palestinian around 15 years ago, he was mocked even by some of his supporters. This egregious insult to history and elementary knowledge was dismissed as a silly propagandistic canard, an unfortunate manifestation of Arafat's contempt for the world's intelligence . . .
>
> The Big Lie, as it has often done in the past, has easily won the day. Arafat arrived in Bethlehem on Saturday and said "This is the birthplace of our Lord the Messiah, the Palestinian, the Palestinian," and the media reported it as if it is simply a statement of fact. Even before he arrived, NBC-TV announced that he would greet the

Yasser Arafat, a Muslim, is changing the sign over Jesus' cross
from "Jesus of Nazareth King of the Jews" to
"Jesus of Nazareth King of the Palestinians."
This is symbolic of the increasing Islamisation of Christianity.
(*The Jerusalem Post*, 16 January, 1996)

multitudes not far from where another Palestinian was born almost
2,000 years ago. This mindless deference to nonsense recalled the
time Hanan Ashrawi [a Palestinian Arab leader] said at the opening
of the Madrid conference that she was a descendent of the first
Christians. The 200 correspondents in her audience not only refused
to be offended by this mockery of truth. They got up and cheered.

Nor has the Church protested. There have been some noises
from Rome about turning Christmas festivities into a celebration of
Arafat, especially after Italian journalists reported that "Arafat has
stolen the show from Jesus." And when officials of the Palestinian
Authority suggested that as part of the Christmas celebration a
laser beam display would show Arafat and Jesus walking together
in the Bethlehem sky, church officials balked . . .

But in general the local clergymen seem to have made toadying
to the PLO an article of faith. Following the PLO line, the Latin
Patriarch Michel Sabbah (who yesterday led the procession from
Jerusalem to Bethlehem) told the Catholic Church in Lebanon
recently that the Church of Jerusalem was concerned about the
"new reality" that has inserted itself in the Holy Land – the Jewish
factor. (As a letter writer pointed out in *The Jerusalem Post*, "surely
he knows that had 'the Jewish factor' been a new reality here . . .

there would have been no Christianity.") And neither he nor any other voice has been raised in Jerusalem or Rome to protest Arafat's rape of Christian history and belief.

It should not be too painfully difficult for the Church to remind its Arab flocks that Jesus was a Jew who lived in Judea, as the New Testament testifies. Nor should its officials be diffident about mentioning that the name Palestine, which is never mentioned in the New Testament, is a distortion of "Philistine," a derisive appellation coined by the Romans to offend the Jews (including those who followed Jesus).

Having subscribed to some murderous Big Lies in the past, the Church may want to throw a few words of truth in the direction of the Holy Land. In this day of much-trumpeted conciliation, such words should prove a most salutary contribution indeed.

The Palestinian propaganda is a total denial of Christianity's roots in biblical Judaism. It is an interpretation of the Bible as being only a Christian revelation. It portrays Christianity as a new religion totally divorced from the Jewish Scriptures, the *Tenach*, the Old Testament, in the divine history of salvation. It presents the Church as the New Israel with no connection whatsoever with the Jewish people. Bat Ye'or in her masterly work *Eurabia*, states in the chapter "The Islamization of Christianity":

> For the Palestinians – both Muslim and Christian – Israel is thus just a symbolic name devoid of concrete reference to history and cultural reality. Futhermore, Palestinian Christians have been convinced that they had always lived happily with the Muslims until the restoration of the State of Israel . . . replacement theology, fed by the Palestinian Arab Churches, spreads today among Catholics as well as Protestants – and incorporates the theological and political components of modern European anti-Zionism.
>
> (p. 214)

"The nation or kingdom that will not serve you will perish" (Isaiah 60:12)

While this book focuses on how the Church's extremely distorted interpretation of Scripture prejudices the position of the Jewish people, it must inevitably recognize the effect upon the nations. We have seen God's judgment upon the Church for her rejection of the Jewish people. We must also realize that God has been judging nations and national leaders according to their treatment of the Jewish people.

Many people accept the interpretation of history by secular historians who often see events as a confusion of incidents which do not relate together nor have any purpose. For the Christian who regards the Bible as the authoritative Word of God, there is meaning. This is not simply acknowledging that God is in control and all will work out well in the end, but recognizing definite direction according to the declared purpose and will of God.

Unless we have a clear understanding of God's purpose for Israel and the Jewish people, we need a new perspective of history, which is more clearly stated as *His Story*. We will note eight important biblical facts concerning Israel and the nations:

1. The Apostle Paul tells us that the hand of God is controlling the nations of the earth and their boundaries in order that human beings may come to know him:

   > From one man he [God] made every nation of men, that they should inhabit the whole earth; and he determined the times set for them and the exact places where they should live. God did this so that men would seek him and perhaps reach out for him and find him, though he is not far from each one of us.
   >
   > (Acts 17:26–27)

2. Daniel tells us that God controls the appointment of rulers over the nations:

   > "The Most High God is sovereign over the kingdoms of men and sets over them anyone he wishes."
   >
   > (Daniel 5:21)

3. Jeremiah reveals to us that God disciplines the nations using Israel as his instrument:

   > "You are my war club,
   >   my weapon for battle –
   > with you I shatter nations,
   >   with you I destroy kingdoms,

with you I shatter horse and rider,
    with you I shatter chariot and driver,
with you I shatter man and woman,
    with you I shatter old man and youth . . .
    with you I shatter governors and officials."

(Jeremiah 51:20–23)

Isaiah elaborates further upon God's use of Israel as an instrument of discipline, making four points:

(a) God is sovereign: "do not be dismayed, for I am your God. I will strengthen you" (Isaiah 41:10).
(b) Israel will not be destroyed: "those who oppose you will be as nothing and perish" (Isaiah 41:11).
(c) Israel is nothing in her own strength: "Do not be afraid, O worm Jacob, O little Israel, for I myself will help you" (Isaiah 41:14).
(d) Israel is to be used by God to discipline the nations:

"See, I will make you into a threshing sledge,
    new and sharp, with many teeth.
You will thresh the mountains and crush them,
    and reduce the hills to chaff.
You will winnow them, the wind will pick them up,
    and a gale will blow them away.
But you will rejoice in the LORD
    and glory in the Holy One of Israel."

(Isaiah 41:15–16)

The threshing sledge was a deadly instrument. The very sharp metal teeth under this heavy sledge slashed through and crushed the stalks and heads of wheat so that all was dust and only then could the wind separate the precious kernel of wheat from the chaff.

4. Micah reaffirms this function of Israel. The nations are pictured gathered together against Israel but they do not realize their own dangerous position because they do not know God's purpose:

But they [the nations] do not know
    the thoughts of the LORD;

they do not understand his plan,
   he who gathers them like sheaves to the threshing floor.

"Rise and thresh, O Daughter of Zion,
   for I will give you horns of iron;
I will give you hoofs of bronze
   and you will break to pieces many nations."

You will devote their ill-gotten gains to the LORD,
   their wealth to the LORD of all the earth.

(Micah 4:12–13)

5. Not only does judgment face those who harm the Jewish
   people but God even says that he judges nations according to
   their treatment of the Jewish nation:

"In those days and at that time,
   when I restore the fortunes of Judah and Jerusalem,
I will gather all nations
   and bring them down to the valley of Jehoshaphat.
There I will enter into judgment against them
   concerning my inheritance, my people Israel,
for they scattered my people among the nations
   and divided up my land."

(Joel 3:1–2)

6. God also declares that nations will come against Jerusalem
   and that they will suffer as a result of their actions:

"I am going to make Jerusalem a cup that sends all the
surrounding peoples reeling. Judah will be besieged as well as
Jerusalem. On that day, when all the nations of the earth are
gathered against her, I will make Jerusalem an immovable rock
for all the nations. All who try to move it will injure
themselves."

(Zechariah 12:2–3)

7. Zephaniah provides us with an example of God's dreadfully
   severe judgment upon Moab and Ammon because they have
   discredited the Jewish people and expanded their borders into
   the land allocated by God to the Jewish people – they are to
   be completely destroyed:

"I have heard the insults of Moab
 and the taunts of the Ammonites,
who insulted my people
 and made threats against their land.
Therefore, as surely as I live,"
 declares the LORD Almighty, the God of Israel,
"surely Moab will become like Sodom,
 the Ammonites like Gomorrah –
a place of weeds and salt pits,
 a wasteland forever.
The remnant of my people will plunder them;
 the survivors of my nation will inherit their land."

This is what they will get in return for their pride,
 for insulting and mocking the people of the LORD Almighty.
           (Zephaniah 2:8–10)

8. It was known among the nations that Israel was chosen by God and that judgment would fall on those who stood against the Jewish people. This fact is made clear in the severity of the warning given to the Gentile Haman, the Prime Minister of Persia, when he sought to destroy Mordecai, the Jew:

> "Since Mordecai, before whom your downfall has started, is of Jewish origin, you cannot stand against him – you will surely come to ruin!"
>
>   (Esther 6:13)

Obviously it is God's ultimate purpose on earth that all people should come to know him. His judgment is always balanced by his mercy. Persistent wrong has always drawn God's judgment in the hope that the wicked man will turn away from his wickedness and live righteously (Ezekiel 18:21). This is the reason why Paul wrote:

> I urge, then, first of all, that requests, prayers, intercession and thanksgiving be made for everyone – for kings and all those in authority, that we may live peaceful and quiet lives in all godliness and holiness. This is good, and pleases God our Savior, who wants all men to be saved and to come to a knowledge of the truth.
>
>   (1 Timothy 2:1–4)

God expressed his purpose for the Jewish people:

> "For as a belt is bound round a man's waist, so I bound the whole
> house of Israel and the whole house of Judah to me," declares the
> LORD, "to be my people for my renown and praise and honor."
>
> (Jeremiah 13:11)

"I will enter into judgment against them" (Joel 3:2)

History has clearly demonstrated the truth of God's declaration to
Israel:

> The nation or kingdom that will not serve you will perish;
> it will be utterly ruined.
>
> (Isaiah 60:12)

God is sovereign ruling the nations, using the nations to discipline
Israel and using Israel to discipline the nations. He is a righteous and
a just God:

> "I will have mercy on whom I have mercy,
> and I will have compassion on whom I have compassion."
>
> (Romans 9:15)

An example of his blessing and cursing, judgment and mercy, is seen
in the message Samuel conveyed to the newly anointed King Saul of
Israel:

> This is what the LORD Almighty says: "I will punish the Amalekites
> for what they did to Israel when they waylaid them as they came
> up from Egypt. Now go, attack the Amalekites and totally destroy
> everything that belongs to them . . ."
>
> Then he said to the Kenites, "Go away, leave the Amalekites so
> that I do not destroy you along with them; for you showed
> kindness to all the Israelites when they came up out of Egypt."
>
> (1 Samuel 15:2–3, 6)

On another occasion God promised judgment upon the Babylonians
for their destruction of Jerusalem:

"Before your eyes I will repay Babylon and all who live in Babylonia for all the wrong they have done in Zion," declares the Lord.

(Jeremiah 51:24)

The archaeologists testify that this superpower was completely destroyed as the Lord had declared. There are many other scriptural examples of leaders removed from power and nations toppled as a result of their treatment of the Jewish nation.

Spain

Today's wide usage of the Spanish language, reaching from Spain to the Southern and Central Americas, accompanied by the many Spanish place names dotting the world, serve to remind us of the once-great Spanish Empire. She was an empire of great sea power, enormous wealth and renowned discoverers. This empire, like Babylon, disappeared because of her treatment of the Jews.

Britain

Unlike Spain, Britain reversed her decision to expel the Jews but only after three and a half centuries of banishment were they permitted to re-settle in Britain. Not only was Britain given a second chance but she was given the privilege of administering the Jewish homeland prior to statehood.

In 1917 the British government (in the Balfour Declaration) viewed "with favor the establishment in Palestine of a national home for the Jewish people" and promised to "use their best endeavours to facilitate the achievement of this object . . . "

Golda Meir states that the Chamberlain government's White Paper on Palestine (1939) "gave way to Arab blackmail in much the same fashion that it was giving way to the Nazis. The White Paper, in effect, ended the British mandate, although the death throes were to go on for another nine years ... Today the answer seems incredible, even to me. The truth is that all that the *yishuv* (Jewish community) wanted from 1939 to 1945 was to take as many Jews as could be saved from the Nazis."[16]

Britain broke her covenant with the Jewish nation and the Britannia who once ruled the waves, today possesses nothing of her empire.

Foreign Office,

November 2nd, 1917.

Dear Lord Rothschild,

I have much pleasure in conveying to you, on behalf of His Majesty's Government, the following declaration of sympathy with Jewish Zionist aspirations which has been submitted to, and approved by, the Cabinet.

"His Majesty's Government view with favour the establishment in Palestine of a national home for the Jewish people, and will use their best endeavours to facilitate the achievement of this object, it being clearly understood that nothing shall be done which may prejudice the civil and religious rights of existing non-Jewish communities in Palestine, or the rights and political status enjoyed by Jews in any other country".

I should be grateful if you would bring this declaration to the knowledge of the Zionist Federation.

Arthur James Balfour

Letter from Lord Balfour, Foreign Secretary, to Baron Edmond de Rothschild, favouring the homeland for the Jewish people in Palestine. This letter came to be known as "The Balfour Declaration." It was raised to the status of a treaty when it was embodied in the Mandate for Palestine conferred upon Britain by the League of Nations at the San Remo Conference on 25 April, 1920.

Poland

Poland boasted of the largest European Jewish community and enjoyed the benefits which this former refugee people (the Jews) contributed to their magnificent country. But Poland's repeated massacring of the Jews has brought its own pall of oppression and destruction, leaving her a derelict nation.

Poland's notorious ghettos of Warsaw and Lodz saw 3,000,000

Jews die in Auschwitz and other death camps. It was because of Poland's anti-Semitic reputation that Hitler was able to build most of his death camps there.

In recent times it was not Warsaw or Lodz that was a concentration camp but the whole of Poland. While the Russian army controlled Poland, chief Soviet Communist Party officials enjoyed the finest homes, food and service at the expense of the Poles who stood in long food lines for limited and overpriced food and waited for fifteen years to get an apartment.

Germany

The "superior" German race who arrogantly sought to rule the world, was divided by the same concrete walls, barbed wire and guard dogs they used to separate themselves from the Jewish people at Auschwitz, Dachau, Madjanak, Sobibor, Treblinka, Buchenwald, Ravensbruck, Bergen-Belsen. The Berlin Wall was a replica of the concentration camp fences the Germans built around the Jews. The wall divided Germany until it was opened on 9 November, 1989, but Germany was not reunited until 3 October, 1990.

Built in 1949, the 165-kilometer wall was to keep East Germans from fleeing communism. There were two 12-foot-high parallel walls electrified to electrocute anyone touching them and 12,000 border guards. Between the fences were machine-gun posts ready to shoot any trespasser, and vicious dogs running loose trained to kill. A visit to Dachau, the museum concentration camp, shows that the Russians had built the same wall around the Germans as the Germans built around the Jews!

After 2.5 million East Germans had escaped to freedom in the West (nearly one out of every six people), during the night of Saturday 12 August, 1961, a 40,000-man special security and police force cut across streets, rail lines and tram tracks around the 1,395-kilometer East–West border with barbed wire, trenches and concrete blocks. This was the night of the Wall.

Berliners woke on Sunday morning to discover the two Germanys were separated – many family members were separated with no possibility of reunification. West Berlin, which lay 180 kilometers inside East Germany, was surrounded by the wall and was totally dependent on a few special air and surface access routes. It has been estimated that the Wall cost $35 million.[17] There is a remarkable similarity between these events and the German treatment of the Jewish people from 1933 till 1945.

The Soviet Union

The Soviet Union's notorious anti-Semitic behavior was witnessed in the 1980s by the 300,000 Russian Jews who had been refused their right to emigrate to Israel. Not only did Russia prevent her 2.7 million Jews the freedom to travel, but the nation became a ghetto of fear where all Russians, except for a privileged few, were denied their rights to travel outside her borders. Russia sponsored the PLO who trained terrorists responsible for bombing civilians in Israel.

Syria became a Soviet surrogate state enabling the Russians to stockpile offensive military equipment in Syria aimed at the destruction of Israel. Israel's entry into Lebanon in 1982 uncovered hundreds of tons of Russian-made weapons and ammunition hidden in miles of tunnels. All this revealed plans for a massive attack upon northern Israel which would have been a premature Armageddon. God has declared his judgment upon Russia in Ezekiel chapters 38 and 39. When Russia eventually strikes Israel upon her mountains, God will destroy the Russian military power.

In his covenant with Abraham, God had stated,

> "I will bless those who bless you,
>   and whoever curses you I will curse."

> (Genesis 12:3)

History shows us that God means exactly what he says

> "Whatever you did not do for one of the least of these, you did not do for me."

> (Matthew 25:45)

The awesome precision of the fulfillment of God's warnings to the Jewish people is further witnessed as the nations met to discuss the solution to the Jewish problem. God had warned through Moses:

> The LORD will scatter you among all nations, from one end of the earth to the other . . . Among those nations you will find no repose,

no resting place for the sole of your foot. There the LORD will give you an anxious mind, eyes weary with longing, and a despairing heart. You will live in constant suspense, filled with dread both night and day, never sure of your life.

(Deuteronomy 28:64–66)

At the same time the nations stand warned about their responsibility in meeting the needs of the Jewish people. Jesus presents us with a scene of the judgment of the nations (Matthew 25:31–46). The nature of each (whether a "sheep" or a "goat" nation) is decided according to how that nation has treated the people whom Jesus describes as "brothers of mine." Jesus' brothers are the Jewish people (see chapter 2) and judgment of the nations is according to their treatment of the Jewish people. This is in agreement with God's covenant with Abraham (Genesis 12:3); it is reaffirmed in Joel's prophecy of the judgment of the nations (Joel 3:2) and again in Zechariah 2:8.

An easy escape from our own guilt is to find someone else to be the scapegoat. While we so readily blame the Nazis for the Holocaust for which they were responsible, there was an opportunity for the nations to save the Jewish people from the Holocaust.

President Roosevelt organized a conference which met in July 1938 at Evian-les-bains, France.[18] Only fifteen weeks after Hitler annexed Austria, the delegates from thirty-two nations met to decide on a method for rescuing the Jews of the "Greater German Reich." Also attending were officials of thirty-nine refugee organizations including twenty Jewish organizations who had come prepared with photographs, reports and eyewitness accounts which provided an obvious picture of the doom facing the Jews of Europe.

At that time, the Jews could get out of Europe – that was not the problem. Where could the Jews go? Who would accommodate the Jews? That was the problem.

Two days before the conference began, Anne McCormick, a columnist for *The New York Times*, stressed its utter importance:

It is heartbreaking to think of the queues of desperate human beings around our consulates in Vienna and other cities waiting in suspense for what happens at Evian. But the question they underline is not simply humanitarian. It is not a question of how many unemployed this country can safely add to its unemployed millions. It is a test of civilization . . . Can America live with itself if it lets Germany get away with this policy of extermination, allows the fanaticism of one man to triumph over reason, refuses to take up this pledge of battle against barbarism?[19]

The leading US delegate, Myron Taylor, at the request of the American Jewish leaders, met with Sir Michael Palairet (the deputy head of the British delegation) to ask that the head of the Jewish Agency for Palestine, Dr Chaim Weizmann, be permitted to present the case for immigration to Palestine. Palestine had received more Jewish refugees than any other country. Sir Michael replied that his government "would naturally prefer that this meeting should not take place."[20] Taylor agreed not to speak with Weizmann before the conference.

The thirty-nine representatives of the refugee organizations were allocated ten minutes each to put their case, including the World Jewish Congress representing 7,000,000 Jews. The Jewish population of Germany at that time was only 350,000 and of Austria 222,000. If each of the thirty-two nations had accepted 17,875 Jews, there would have been no Jews left for the Reich.

One by one the national representatives gave reasons why their nation could not accommodate the Jewish refugees. Australia stated, "As we have no real racial problem, we are not desirous of importing one."[21] They accepted 15,000 over three years. New Zealand was unwilling to lift its restrictions. Sir John Shuckburg reported that the British colonial empire contained no territory suitable to the large-scale settlement of the Jewish refugees – they received 9,000 Jewish children. Canada wanted only agricultural immigrants. The Dominican Republic accommodated 500. Only Holland and Denmark opened their doors to the Jewish people.

At the conference, the delegation of Jews from Germany were refused the opportunity to speak but were restricted to written submissions. Golda Meir described the conference:

> I was there in the ludicrous capacity of the "Jewish observer from Palestine," not even seated with the delegates but with the audience, although the refugees under discussion were my own people, members of my own family, not just inconvenient numbers to be squeezed into official quotas, if at all possible.

Sitting there in that magnificent hall, listening to the delegates of thirty-two countries rise, each in turn, to explain how much they would have liked to take in substantial numbers of refugees and how unfortunate it was that they were not able to do so, was a terrible experience. I don't think that anyone who didn't live through   it can understand what I felt at Evian – mixture of sorrow, rage, frustration and horror. I wanted to get up and scream at them all, "Don't you know that these 'numbers' are human beings, people who may spend the rest of their lives in concentration camps, or wandering around the world like lepers, if you don't let them in?" Of course, I didn't know then that not concentration camps but death camps awaited the refugees whom no one wanted.[22]

The bitter report of the *Danziger Vorposten* sums up the effect of the Conference:

We see that one likes to pity the Jews as long as one can use this pity for wicked agitation against Germany, but that no state is prepared to fight the cultural disgrace of central Europe by accepting a few thousand Jews. Thus the conference serves to justify Germany's policy against Jewry.[23]

Hitler interpreted the refusal of the nations to do anything about the Jewish people as approval for him to implement his "Final Solution."

Standing against the tide

There were Christian leaders who did stand against the tide of popular opinion. Sadly, Archbishop of Canterbury Cosmo Lang, who served from 1928 to 1941, declared that "the Jews themselves were to blame for the excesses of the Nazis." On the other hand William Temple, his successor, saw the situation in a totally different light. He was an outspoken advocate for the Jewish victims of Hitler. His forceful advocacy appeared in public speeches, articles and letters to the British press during 1942 and 1943.

Temple expressed both his "burning indignation" at the Nazi mass murders and his strong disappointment at the response of the Allies. The Jews were "caught between the hammer of the enemy's brutality and the anvil of democracy's indifference," he said. "In comparison with the monstrous evil confronting us the reasons for hesitation usually advanced by officials have an air of irrelevance."

Archbishop Temple was not intimidated by strong opposition to his urging England and its allies to grant asylum "to any Jews who are able to escape the clutches of the Nazis." In an especially stirring speech before the House of Lords in March 1943, he urged the Allies to take "immediate measures on the largest and most generous scale" to aid the Jews. He argued against the British public opposing Britain taking in refugees claiming that "by skilful use of the wireless," the government could easily win public support for helping those who were "being delivered to almost certain death." It was time for action: "We at this moment have upon us a tremendous responsibility. We stand at the bar of history, of humanity, and of God."

The archbishop's stand drew the attention of both British and American officials concerned at this influential Christian leader heading a growing wave of public criticism over the Allies' indifference to Hitler's Jewish victims. The public interest by early 1943 caused British officials to begin planning an Allied conference on refugees. An internal Foreign Office memorandum concerning this singled out the Archbishop of Canterbury as one of those who had been "agitating the public conscience."

When the British government suggested the conference be held in Washington, the State Department blocked the idea. Beckinridge Long, an American official, wrote in his diary, "to talk here would put us in a bad position with Canterbury giving publicity in the press and all the pressure which would be coming from the locally organized groups in this country."

The conference was held, but in isolated Bermuda. More negative criticism arose as a result of the conference's decisions especially from the Emergency Committee to Save the Jewish People of Europe (more popularly known as the Bergson group). Using the headline "We all stand before the bar of history, humanity, and God," they published a series of full-page advertisements in American newspapers and magazines.

Archbishop Temple's stand influenced millions of Americans, even to the point of motivating the Roosevelt administration to take action. They did aid Jewish refugees near the end of the war, though it was both belated and limited.

Rafael Medoff who wrote the *Jerusalem Post* article "Remembering William Temple," concluded:

> Today, we may look back and wonder how different history might have been if other church leaders, in America and England, had followed Archbishop Temple's lead. Or if his predecessor, Cosmo Lang, had spoken out for the rescue of Jewish refugees in the 1930s, before the Nazi persecutions turned to mass murder. Similarly, one wonders how history, humanity, and God – to borrow Rev. Temple's memorable phrase – will judge those church leaders who today are siding with the enemies of Israel.[24]

Rotten roots (Isaiah 5:24)

We have seen how early Christian misinterpretation of the Bible quickly gave grounds to a world's hatred for the Jewish people. The same Christian misuse of Scripture has established a teaching that has continued to influence Christian thinking and behavior towards these ancient chosen people of God. This also influences the attitudes of the Church, the nations and the world towards the State of Israel today.

Although today many people may not have heard of the *Protocols of the Elders of Zion*, this perverted teaching has influenced multitudes in their attitudes and behavior towards the Jewish people. A combination of the teachings of Martin Luther, resurgent German nationalism and the influence of the occult as well as the anonymous writings of the *Protocols* prepared the mind of a complete nation to conceive and execute the most hideous plan ever devised by man – the Nazi effort to annihilate the Jews. The greater tragedy is that most of the Church remained silent!

Professor Rupp concluded a lecture on Luther by observing:

> As we follow Luther through the years, we find a signal instance of how we become like what we hate. We see a growing obstinacy, a hardening of heart, a withering of compassion, a proneness to contemptuous abuse – the very things he thought were the marks of judgment on the Jews.[25]

We have witnessed that this observation equally applies to many others through history.

"I Will Bless Those Who Bless You"

(Genesis 12:3)

> The crucifixion and the resurrection of the Jewish people is a sign that God is not mocked, that pride brings the biggest battalions low in the end, that the Author and Judge of history blesses the Suffering Servant and brings the human hero low. Do the baptized believe these truths, or must they be numbered among the blind and deaf when the Messiah comes? [1]

Peter Abelard was one of "the baptized" who not only believed these truths but stood up early in the twelfth century with the Jewish people against a background of severe Jewish persecution. At first he was denounced by the notable monks of Clairvaux, then by other church authorities and finally by Pope Innocent II.

Abelard's courageous stand, like that of Bernard of Clairvaux, reminds us that all through these dark centuries of anti-Jewish activity there were strong men of God – Church dignitaries and ordinary Christians – who stood out against the tide of wicked teaching and its subsequent infamous action against the Jewish people.

Jacob shall return ... the Puritans' teaching

A turning of the tide was evidenced during the seventeenth century, particularly in England. The Puritans, who upheld Bible truth and authority, widely influenced public thinking and attitude in England and Holland. A vital concern for the Jewish people was born, and although not all Puritan aspirations were accomplished during their period, the Jews were readmitted to England. We can trace from the Puritan influence some action that later blossomed into the restored Jewish homeland.

In January, 1649, Ebenezer and Joanna Cartwright, English Puritans living in Amsterdam, petitioned the English government:

> That this Nation of England, with the inhabitants of the Netherlands, shall be the first and the readiest to transport Israel's sons and daughters to their ships to the Land promised to their forefathers, Abraham, Isaac and Jacob for an everlasting Inheritance.[2]

The petitioners were not only moved to see the Jewish homeland restored but also expressed concern for the return of Jewish people to England. The petition continued, that the Jews "may again be received and permitted to trade and dwell amongst you in this Land." After 350 years' banishment from English shores, this petition – "Petition of the Jews for Repealing the Act of Parliament for their Banishment out of England" – was part of the process that reversed this decision. The petition also reflects the power of the Bible upon people's attitudes and action in a nation.

In returning to the Bible, the Puritans gave much attention to the Old Testament, emphasizing Hebraism in the family and community life. The names of the heroes and patriarchs were conferred upon their children at baptism. Sunday observance was colored by the ancient Sabbath. Their conduct was based upon the lifestyle and principles of the faithful as recorded in the books of the Judges and Kings.

Accordingly, priority was given to the Hebrew language even above Greek, the New Testament language. The three "biblical languages," Hebrew, Greek and Latin, were taught to children and were prerequisite to theological study – the main attraction at the universities. Biblical scholarship and exegesis dominated the intellectual activity of the age. Interest in the Jewish people was not confined to the scholars but was widespread, touching the people through books, treatises, lectures and sermons.

In December 1655 Cromwell, the Protector of England, convened a special committee of judges, clergy and merchants to consider re-opening the doors for Jewish people to return to England. The statement of the clergy acknowledges the unique responsibility they believed England had towards the Jewish people: "The good people of England did generally more believe the promises of the calling of the Jews and more correctly pray for it than any other nation."

The clergy were convinced that in admitting the Jews to England, they might bring about this "calling." They believed this instance provided England with an opportunity to repent of her sins towards the Jewish people: "We are children of the same Father Abraham, they naturally after the flesh, we believers after the Spirit."[3]

England did permit the re-entry of Jews. But we need to notice what really motivated Puritan interest in the Jewish people being restored to England and why they should have been restored to the Promised Land. Puritans believed that Jesus was to reign for the millennium in Jerusalem and that prior to his return to earth, the Jewish people would have to be restored to their land. Permitting their re-admission to England could have facilitated their "conversion," fulfilling a biblical requirement for Jesus' return.

Some historians argue that England's readmission of the Jews was dictated by the aid the Jewish community could have contributed in the war with Spain. That may have been a factor at the time, but it is obvious that it was the teaching of the Puritans and the power of biblical conviction that changed the English heart convincing her to make right her wrongs to the Jewish people.

Jerusalem shall be inhabited

The Puritan fire was quenched as the age of reason undermined the authority of Scripture during the eighteenth century. No longer could the Bible be interpreted – certainly by the Christians of that day – to convey the hope of the Lord's return, since prophecy was "irrational," and so any thought of a Jewish homeland was dropped.

Although Puritans were ejected from the Established Church, excluded from membership in institutions of learning and deprived of civil rights until 1689, they persisted in keeping alive their tradition until a better season. The season was the nineteenth century and the harvest was the Evangelical Revival.

Emphasis upon the Old Testament was renewed as the authority of the Bible was restored. Stimulated by the prophecies of Jerusalem's restoration and the return of the Jewish people to their ancient land, Christians felt bound to assist this restoration process.

A characteristic of the Evangelical Revival was the birth of many gospel societies including the Baptist Missionary Society, the British and Foreign Bible Society, the Religious Tract Society, the Church Missionary Society and the London Society for Promoting Christianity among the Jews. For a long time the last of these, known as the Jews' Society, was the most popular of all the missionary societies.

At the Jews' Society meetings, sermons presented Jesus as the Jewish Messiah. The Jews' Chapel was established with free education for Jewish children. Christian support for the work was phenomenal: after five years the society had the support of 2,000 contributors.

Records show that by 1841 both the Archbishops of Canterbury and York along with twenty-three bishops, many priests and noble gentry, were among the patrons. By 1850 the society, later known as the Church's Ministry among the Jewish People (CMJ), had seventy-eight missionaries serving in thirty-two branch offices scattered from London to Jerusalem.

Britain's early influence on Jewish restoration

A driving force in this movement was Anthony Ashley Cooper, the seventh Earl of Shaftsbury. As an evangelical Christian, Ashley's deep concerns were for improving the morals, working conditions, and general standard of life in Britain. He was highly motivated by his belief in the nearness of the return of Jesus which "has always been a moving principle in my life for I see everything going on in the world subordinate to this great event."[4]

Ashley knew that the return of the Jewish people to their own land was a requirement before Jesus could return. From the inscription on the ring worn on his right hand, his heart-concern was obvious: "Oh, pray for the peace of Jerusalem!" One can almost hear the echo of the Psalmist voice:

> "If I forget you, O Jerusalem,
>   let my right hand wither!
> Let my tongue cleave to the roof of my mouth,
>   if I do not remember you,
> if I do not set Jerusalem
>   above my highest joy!"

(Psalm 137:5–6, RSV).

Ashley, a leader of the Jews' Society, envisaged an Anglican bishopric in Jerusalem, believing that a transplant of the work in England on to the soil of Eretz Israel (the land of Israel promised to Abraham) would lead to the restoration of the Jewish homeland. The extent of his enthusiasm to this end is seen in his writing when Britain appointed the first vice-consul of any nation to Jerusalem:

> Took leave this morning of Young, who has just been appointed Her Majesty's Vice-Consul at Jerusalem! The ancient city of the people of God is about to resume a place among the nations, and England is the first of Gentile kingdoms that ceases "to tread her down."[5]

Ashley liberally shared his views with politician friends and used opportunities whenever they arose to win support for the Jewish cause. Following the publication of the first of many books on travel in the Holy Land, he reviewed the book to publicize his dream of a restored Jewish homeland under the care of the Anglican Church. He used as evidence for the urgent fulfillment of his dream, a letter received from Poland describing increasing persecution which was creating a resurgence of desire among the Jews of Russia and Poland to return to their ancient homeland.

Enthusiastically, Ashley described the Jews' Society's plan to build an Anglican Church in Jerusalem, preferably on Mount Zion. He explained that already missionaries were holding the first-ever Protestant services in Hebrew for the small congregation of proselytes "on the Mount of the Holy City itself in the language of the prophets and in the spirit of the Apostles." His words mirror his satisfaction from the occasion as "one of the most striking that have occurred in modern days, perhaps in any days since the corruptions began in the Church of Christ."[6]

While Ashley's motivation for this Jewish homeland was scriptural, he had also surveyed practical requirements. He noted that Eretz Israel was suited to agriculture and foresaw that it would be ideal for producing cotton, silk and olive oil, thereby creating employment as well as trade appropriate to England's needs. He also saw that the "recall of the Jews to their ancient homeland" could become a stabilizing influence in the shaking

Muslim-controlled Ottoman Empire. It is important to note that Ashley made no suggestion of developing an independent Jewish state, and that all this activity was taking place twenty years *before* the birth of Theodore Herzl.

First bishop to Jerusalem

Although a change of government prevented any further action towards a Jewish homeland, the Church of England did create a bishopric in Jerusalem. A former Jewish rabbi was consecrated as its first bishop, Michael Solomon Alexander, who had been professor of Hebrew at King's College. This event was the greatest achievement of the Jews' Society and was seen by that Society as a sign for the restoration of the ancient kingdom of Israel as a Church of England diocese.

On Sunday 7 November, 1841, in Lambeth Palace, Alexander was consecrated Bishop of Jerusalem by the Archbishop of Canterbury and the bishops of London, Rochester and New Zealand in the presence of a distinguished company. Working among the Jewish people proved laborious, reaping a small harvest, and taking its heavy toll upon his strength. Within four years he was dead. The weight of the task was summed up in the words of one Jewish observer, "the hill of Zion is not a likely place for a Jew to forsake the faith of his fathers."

The Puritans had motivated the British to re-admit the Jewish people to England and sown the seed of a Jewish homeland. The Evangelicals, and especially the London Jews Society (later known as The Church's Ministry Among Jewish People) and the seventh Earl of Shaftsbury, pursued the vision of a Jewish homeland until definite steps were made in establishing that homeland.

Although the Evangelical enthusiasm for the Jewish people and their homeland waned, and the Jewish people refused to be inspired by a move from their comfortable homes to endure the hardships of settling and developing their ancient homeland, the interest was taken up from a very different direction. At first this was for imperial reasons, but then by Christians looking backwards into history to understand the Jewish roots of their faith, rather than to see themselves fulfilling prophecy or looking for the return of Jesus.

Britain's part in spying out the land

Benjamin Disraeli's rise to prominence in politics, and onward to serve as Britain's prime minister at the zenith of her imperial power, certainly demonstrated the English heart change towards Jewish people. This Jewish man, who identified with the Christian faith, precisely defined the Christian debt and responsibility to the Jewish people in his speech on Jewish Emancipation in the House of Commons:

> Where is your Christianity if you do not believe in their Judaism? On every altar ... we find the table of the Jewish law ... All the early Christians were Jews ... every man in the early ages of the Church by whose power or zeal or genius the Christian faith was propagated, was a Jew ... If you had not forgotten what you owe to this people ... you as Christians would be only too ready to seize the first opportunity of meeting the claims of those who profess this religion.[7]

Disraeli's distinction was that of an empire builder who had no association with Ashley, nor was he a Jewish nationalist. His part in securing the Jewish homeland under British control was primarily concerned with Britain's interests abroad. As Britain's empire expanded eastward in the later nineteenth century, he acquired for Britain the Suez Canal, a vital link with India and the developing extremities of her empire. Simply, Suez had to be guarded and Eretz Israel's close proximity provided an excellent guard-post for the British.

Rationalism replaced Evangelicalism in the unfolding drama of the Jewish return to their homeland. Rationalist Christians were determined to prove the Bible as history in contrast to the Evangelicals who needed no proof of the Bible's accuracy or historicity but looked forward to prophetic fulfillment.

This was an age of scientific discovery and the questioning of a myriad of previously held facts. Human history was born in the Holy Land. Jewish roots were therefore the roots of mankind and certainly the roots of Christianity – they had to be investigated. One man wrote about the Jewish prophets, "they taught men the true nature of God, that he was a God of love as well as of justice, the

Father as well as the judge of mankind."[8] The task they set themselves was to recover the authentic past and discover the real people of the Bible, which was accomplished through the fields of archaeology, topography, meteorology, botany and zoology.

Even the War Office was caught up in this interest in the Holy Land. The War Office supported the Palestine Exploration Fund of which Shaftsbury was a founding member. Engineers were sent out on a task never before undertaken – surveying and mapping the Holy Land! They set out to discover the sites of ancient cities, they identified tribal boundaries, discovered important markers and boundary stones, and uncovered ancient highways. The dead, unknown past came alive! Former skepticism that this was once fertile land "flowing with milk and honey" was not only totally disproved by their discoveries, but it was realized that this once highly productive land required only cultivation to restore its fertility.

If the Puritans and the Evangelicals had widely disseminated the idea of a Jewish homeland and stimulated action towards this end, the Rationalists measured the land, observed its nature, and investigated its potential. Their verdict was that the ancient Jewish homeland had the potential to support a large population. The British now knew Eretz Israel thoroughly and were equipped and prepared to defend it.

A Jewish homeland at last!

Even if she desired to, Britain was not in a position to give the land to the Jewish people as a homeland, since Palestine was not among her possessions. Long ago she had realized the danger of a world ruler dominating Europe and controlling the Middle East. Protection from Cairo to Constantinople was vital to maintain, plus free access to the Far East. Therefore, Britain diligently patrolled the Mediterranean.

In order to maintain that balance she had consistently supported the crumbling Turkish Empire against pressures from Russia, France, Prussia and Germany, believing that the disappearance of the old Turkish Empire would drastically change the face of the Middle East.

We can now see why the British War Office was so actively

involved in measuring the ancient Jewish homeland. Britain had prepared herself thoroughly for that day when the Turkish Empire fell. Disraeli's securing of the Suez Canal and Cyprus had been strategic then, but proved even more so when the storm clouds burst forth in World War I. The Islamic Turkish Empire, which had dominated the Middle East for 400 years, at last crumbled.

The scene was set for a man of conviction to lead favorably disposed leaders to proclaim this as the Jewish homeland. Arthur Balfour was that man. Formerly Britain's Prime Minister, now Foreign Secretary, Lord Balfour wrote to Baron Edward de Rothschild as the representative of the Jewish people, on 2 November, 1917:

> His Majesty's Government view with favour the establishment in Palestine of a national home for the Jewish people, and will use their best endeavours to facilitate the achievement of this object, it being clearly understood that nothing shall be done which may prejudice the civil and religious rights of existing and non-Jewish communities in Palestine, or the rights and political status enjoyed by Jews in any other country.[9]

Balfour had been schooled in the Bible since childhood, the characters and places of the Bible being very real to him. Unlike the Puritans and Evangelicals he was not a religious enthusiast, nevertheless he was very interested in the "people of the Book."

Unlike other Christian Englishmen who assisted the restoration of the Jewish people to their land, Balfour's concern was for the Jews as people to whom Christians owed an "immeasurable debt" – which could in part be paid by returning them to their homeland. He was in no way motivated by any biblical interpretation of a millennium, nor by imperialist gains. He wrote that "the position of the Jew is unique. For them race, religion and country are inter-related as they are inter-related in the case of no other religion and no other country on earth."[10]

We cannot move on before we recognize the remarkable contribution made by a Jewish scientist to the war effort in Britain. Although the Allies were marching to victory, Britain was desperately short of gunpowder to arm her navy. Winston Churchill, First Lord of the Admiralty, approached a brilliant Jewish chemist,

Chaim Weizmann who in turn produced 30,000 tons of synthetic acetone that was used in the manufacture of cordite gunpowder.

Dr Weizmann was asked how the British Government might reward his services. He replied, "There is only one thing I want . . . a national homeland for my people." The Balfour Declaration was Britain's response. Again we are reminded of God's covenant with Abraham:

> "Abraham will surely become a great and powerful nation, and all nations on earth will be blessed through him."
>
> (Genesis 18:18)

General Edmund Allenby, also conversant with the Bible, was the commander of the allied forces in Palestine who officially received the handover of Jerusalem on 11 December, 1917. During 1918 he completed the conquest of the old Empire, succeeding where the Crusaders had failed, to bring the whole of this territory under "Christian" rule for the first time in history. From that time Britain assumed responsibility for the area until 1922 when the League of Nations officially conferred upon her the Palestine Mandate.

Although several significant Christian contributions towards the rebirth of Israel could be mentioned, we will only refer to one – the very practical contribution of a biblically literate army captain whose influence is even today evident in Israel: Orde Wingate. It is impossible for us to understand his motivation unless we know something of his belief.

Soon after Wingate's arrival he explained to a Jewish military commander that his sympathies were with Zionism and that "there is only one important book on the subject, the Bible, and I have read it thoroughly." He continued:

> This is the cause of your survival. I count it as my privilege to help you fight your battle. To that purpose I want to devote my life. I believe that the very existence of mankind is justified when it is based on the moral foundation of the Bible. Whoever dares lift a hand against you and your enterprise here should be fought against. Whether it is jealousy, ignorance or perverted doctrine such as have made your neighbors rise against you, or "politics" which make some of my countrymen support them, I shall fight

with you against any of these influences. But remember that it is your battle. My part, which I say I feel to be a privilege, is only to help you.[11]

Captain Wingate was posted as an intelligence officer to a most unsettled Jerusalem in 1936. Since the Arab riots of 1929 the peaceful atmosphere was never regained, but both the British and Jewish policy remained one of defense. Coinciding with Wingate's arrival, a new wave of Arab terror broke out where guerrillas destroyed homes, towns, and agricultural settlements in the most savage outbursts. It was clear to this young officer that there were three factions in this land – the Arabs, the Jews, and the British Administration who failed to keep their agreement.

Wingate trained special units of men (known as the Special Night Squads) in unusual techniques that proved extremely successful in defense from the marauding Arab attacks. In contrast to the official defense policy employed, where many Jews and British were being killed, his objective was to attack and claim the land surrounding settlements – thereby affording protection.

Techniques introduced by this courageous soldier continue to be in Israeli military use. Men trained by him included subsequent commanders, a minister of Defence and Chiefs of Military Staff. Because of the value of Wingate's unique contribution to the security and morale of the Jewish people of Israel, he is still held in highest regard seventy years later in Israel today.

We have seen the role played by Bible-believing Christians in the restoration of Israel: Let us now turn to investigate the influence of the changed Christian attitude towards the Jewish people.

The Time to Favor Zion Has Come

I am not ashamed of the gospel, because it is the power of God for the salvation for everyone who believes; first for the Jew, then for the Gentile.

(Romans 1:16)

The purity and holiness of these men attracted me; their earnestness and the firmness of their convictions drove me to investigate their faith, which made them much better than myself or any people I ever knew.[1]

This conviction of a Viennese Jew in 1843 is typical of many Jewish encounters with Christians recorded during the later nineteenth century. It marked a distinctive change in the Jewish–Christian relationship and resulted in many Jewish people embracing Jesus of Nazareth as the Messiah of Israel.

The power of righteousness

Contrasted with the harsh Christian treatment of previous centuries of forced conversions and baptisms at the cost of banishment or death, a new Christian era emerged. We can trace this new attitude to the seventeenth-century Puritan zeal to see Jewish people receive equal rights and be restored to their homeland. But more than this, these Christians were concerned for the Jewish people, which of course meant seeing them come into the fullness of faith in the Messiah.

Jewish people came to desire baptism, but not forced baptism.

Both the quality of personal faith and the availability of the New Testament played an essential part in presenting the truth of the gospel in its proper setting. This enabled the Jewish mind to understand the Jewishness of Christianity and to recognize a depth of meaning unknown to the Gentile experience.

That the nineteenth century marks a turning point in Jewish people being "grafted in" again is confirmed by the record of the Reverend J. F. de le Roi (a missionary of the London Society for Promoting Christianity among the Jews) in his book *Jewish Baptisms in the 19th Century* published in 1899. According to his records, in that century 224,000 Jewish people were baptized. It also needs to be pointed out that baptism was, at this period, generally a choice of social convenience rather than personal conviction.

Upholding these facts but disputing the figures *The Universal Jewish Encyclopaedia* (1941) states: "These figures are manifestly too low ... Actually the number of converts during this period must have been considerably higher."[2] The encyclopedia lists some two hundred eminent Jews of the nineteenth century, recognized for their notable contribution to human endeavor, who professed faith in Christ.

Arthur Morse in his book *While Six Million Died* records that in late 1938 "it was necessary to find new homes for 660,000 persons still living in Germany and Austria. Of this total, 300,000 were Jews; 285,000 were Christians of sufficient Jewish ancestry to fail the Nuremberg racial tests ..."[3]

Statistical precision is not important for our purposes. The point established is that the Jewish people were embracing faith in their Messiah to an extent not known since the early Church and that there were more Christians favorably disposed towards the Jewish people than there had been since the early Church period. The British *Church Times* of 17 August, 1883, published the following observation of the situation:

> There is reason to believe that there is no family of the human race which, on the whole and in proportion to its size, yielded more converts to Christianity.[4]

One Jewish Christian, the Reverend Elias Newman, estimated that prior to World War II, of the 16,000,000 Jews in the world, at least half a million professed faith in Christ. Newman further claimed that there were more than three times the number of Jewish Christian ministers than those finding their origins in any other non-Christian religion. There are also figures ranging from 250,000 to one and a quarter million Jewish Christians among the 6,000,000 Jewish people destroyed in the Holocaust.[5]

Surpassing the impact of any statistics is the richness of the Jewish contribution to the Church. We should so expect it to be so for they are "the natural olive branches." The shame is that Gentile members of the Church have tended to overlook this fact, which is rarely found recorded in the history books. It is also significant that the Jewish Christians (who understood both Judaism and the Jewish mind) were able to present Christ acceptably to the Jewish people. Indeed, as they explain, many felt a compulsion so to do. We need to take careful notice of these men and their contribution.

Defenders of the faith

Gentile members of the Church are indebted to Alfred Edersheim, a scholar and theologian, for his depth of research into the Jewish nature of our faith. Edersheim's writings give us a portrait of Jesus as a Jew, describing Jewish life in the Gospel period and earlier, and illuminating the teaching of the rabbis. They also introduce the world of Jewish thinking and explain the sacrificial system and ministries associated with the Temple.

Where Edersheim illuminated the gospel for the world to receive deeper insight into Christ, August Neander presented the ongoing work of Christ in his Church in a dynamic thrust toward a pre-destined end. In an age conditioned by rationalism, Neander inspired faith by his clear presentation of Christ's working in the world in a continuum of predetermined purpose. True to his word, Neander defended the Christian faith against a tide of rationalist destruction threatening not only Germany but the whole of Christendom.

Another defender of the Christian faith, extraordinarily des-cended from a family who escaped the terror and torture of the Spanish Inquisition, was Isaac da Costa. A deepening awareness of the uniqueness of his people led to further study of Jewish history.

Da Costa's strong convictions expressed in his courageous writings and speeches won him many friends among the nobility of his native Holland as well as in England, France, Germany and Switzerland. They also attracted many enemies. Da Costa emphasized to the Church its duty and debt to Israel, while he proclaimed to the Jews Jesus as their Messiah.

Carl Caspari's interest was captured by Saul of Tarsus' persecution of the Jewish Christians. Intrigued by the book of the Acts of the Apostles, he then went on to carefully study the New Testament. When convinced that this Jewish book revealed truth, he put his faith in Christ and set about telling his Jewish brethren and Gentiles of his discovery. Caspari's activity was considerably governed by his conviction of Israel's ultimate place in God's purposes.

Another man of the time, Abraham Capadose, was a cousin to Caspari. Although a physician, he also labored in sharing his faith with Jewish people, particularly through his writing.

David Baron was born into a Polish orthodox Jewish family, destined to become a rabbi. Burdened by original sin, he struggled to find peace within his studies. Finally he found peace in Christ but rejection from his family. Baron's missionary zeal led him to the Jewish communities along the Russian border, in Germany, Austria, Hungary, Galicia and Bohemia.

The spreading of their faith consumed the energy of many of these gifted men. Already we have referred to the work of Michael Alexander, the former rabbi who, as bishop of Jerusalem, established Christ Church. Selig Cassel served as a member of the Prussian Parliament, which position he relinquished to serve as preacher and teacher in a Berlin church. Solomon Ginsburg, the son of an honored Polish rabbi, triumphed over intense opposition to establish many churches in Brazil. Haymin Herschell left his training for the rabbinate to teach the gospel to Jewish communities in London and Europe.

Leon Levison, born in Tiberias, was knighted for his political and economic contribution to Britain during World War I, distinguished for his work for the Russian Jewish Relief Fund. He was actively concerned for mission work among the Jews and the continuation of fellowship for Christian Jews, which resulted in his forming the International Hebrew Christian Alliance.

Shabbetai Rohold was born in Jerusalem where he became a proficient Talmudic scholar, later moving to Scotland then Canada where he established a Christian synagogue, finally returning to the mission station in Eretz Israel. Henry Stern traveled widely with the gospel to Eretz Israel, Baghdad, Persia, Abyssinia and England. Joseph Wolff also traveled taking the gospel to Egypt, Eretz Israel, Syria, Baghdad, Persia, Greece, Turkey, India and England.

The power of the Word

Many of the Jewish men who came to put their faith in Christ were sons of rabbis. Some had trained to be rabbis, while others had served as rabbis. Consequently these men had acquired an extensive knowledge of Hebrew, detailed learning in the Torah and the Talmud, as well as a deep knowledge of the prophets and writings. Such men knew the Old Testament at a depth not known by Gentiles, and when they came to recognize Jesus as the Messiah, they received revelation of God's purposes that equipped them for unique service.

Raphael Biesenthal was born in Prussia of pious parents who intended him to be a Jewish scholar and rabbi. He achieved these to an exceptional standard, although not quite as his parents had hoped.

Biesenthal's prolific writing made him a household name in Germany. He wrote commentaries on the Gospels, the Epistles to the Romans and Hebrews, and the Psalms; he compiled a Hebrew lexicon, translations into Hebrew of the book of Acts and Romans. His *History of the Christian Church* was written especially for Jews to show the Jewishness of the early Church.

Isodor Lowenthal was sent as a missionary to Afghanistan. Not only did he translate the New Testament into Pushtu – the chief language of Afghanistan and parts of India, but he also compiled a dictionary in Pushtu. This was left in manuscript form when he was shot by his servant after only seven years in the country, at thirty-eight years of age.

Isaac Salkinson from Lithuania expressed a deep concern for his own people. He translated into Hebrew Milton's *Paradise Lost*. Salkinson's greatest achievement and satisfaction was translating the Greek New Testament into idiomatic Hebrew.

Joseph Schereschewsky's outstanding ability in linguistics well equipped him for the remarkable saga of revising and completing the Bible in Mandarin Chinese and the Wenli dialect. After the Mandarin Bible was completed in 1875, Joseph was stricken by a serious illness, which left him totally paralyzed.

Schereschewsky's translation of the Bible into these dialects made the Scriptures available to a potential 250,000,000 people. In addition to preparing a concordance in Chinese for the entire Bible, he wrote grammars and dictionaries to assist in the study of Chinese. It was said of him: "Schereschewsky is one of the six most learned Orientalists in the world."[6]

David Ginsburg, of Polish descent, completed an extensive study and published the amended Hebrew text. He was elected to the Board of Old Testament Revisers and he searched to recover all the notes available from these Jewish scholars – the *Massorah*. Ginsburg handled a large volume of the textual criticism which he finally published in one volume. This work has enabled Bible scholars and translators to consider how far the old manuscripts agree in their variations, additions and deficiencies.

The long list of Jewish Christians actively sharing the new light of their faith encompasses many varied places in society – Britain's empire-building prime minister, Benjamin Disraeli; Germany's illustrious musician and composer, Felix Mendelssohn; England's astronomer William Herschel. The list includes teachers, writers, church builders and leaders – Isaac Helmuth of Poland; Ludwig Jacoby, Freidrich Philippi, Freidrich Stahl and Max Wertheimer of Germany; Christian Kalkar of Sweden; Julius Kobner of Denmark; Aaron Saphir, Iechiel Lichtenstein and Charles Schonberger of Hungary; Joseph Rabinowitz of Russia.

Joseph Rabinowitz was described by Hugh Schonfield as "the Herzl of Jewish Christianity." Rabinowitz was brought up strictly within Judaism and was concerned by the influence of anti-Semitism. Exploring the possibility of mass migration to Eretz Israel, he visited the Holy Land using as a guidebook a Hebrew New Testament given him years before. On the Mount of Olives he came to the conclusion: "The key to the Holy Land is in the hands of our brother Jesus."

Rabinowitz returned to Kishniev to establish "Israelites of the New Covenant." Determined not to become another denomination of the Church he labored to present the Jewish Messiah in all his Jewishness to Jews and deliberately refrained from being baptized in a church. That created a stir not only within Judaism but also in the Church. He became the darling of Jewish missions who distributed his testimony, which stimulated inflated expectation of their work.

Accounts of Rabinowitz' work range from belittlement to exaggeration depending upon the source. It was in complete contrast to Jewish missions of his time, which were essentially denominations of the Church as reflected in their identity, "Hebrew Christians." Rabinowitz' ministry undoubtedly was the beginning of the restoration of Messianic Judaism. The emphasis was on remaining Jewish in expressions of faith and identity when embracing the Jewish Messiah Jesus.

Rebirth in Zion

The appointment of Michael Solomon Alexander, a former rabbi and oriental scholar, as "Bishop in Jerusalem" in 1841 set the spiritual clock ticking again in the Promised Land. Alexander was the first Jewish believer in Jesus to attempt to establish a congregational base in Jerusalem with the sole purpose of restoring the truth of the new covenant, that Jesus is Israel's Messiah. He was the first Jewish bishop since the first century to follow the New Testament tradition of Jewish bishops of Jerusalem.

There had been churches represented in Jerusalem through the centuries. They were Gentile churches preoccupied with their self-preservation and ecclesiastical activities, oblivious to the salvation needs of the small surrounding population. But now there appeared believers in Jesus of Jewish descent, concerned for the spiritual well-being of the Jewish population. They were picking up where the Messianic Jews of the first century had left off. It was an event that did not go unnoticed and definitely did not go uncontested. Into this scene stepped Bishop Michael Solomon Alexander.

On the one hand there were those who were euphoric at the event. They sensed that the magnitude of what they were caught up in was far beyond their imagination or dreams. That integral milestone of divine purpose was captured by *The Church of England Quarterly Review* of April 1843:

> A Bishop of the Hebrew race and a Bishop of Jerusalem, cannot but excite attention among the Jews, and if it leads to nothing farther

than provoking to jealousy, in the first instance, even this is preparation for another step, whether that be their gathering into the Christian Church, or reinstating them in the land which was so often promised to their fathers.[7]

On the other hand there came a prediction of doom. An English Jew responded to Alexander's appointment: "The Hill of Zion is not a likely place for a Jew to forsake the faith of his fathers."[8] If not prophetic this was certainly a realistic appraisal of the situation in the sense that Alexander was seen by Jews as a Jew who had forsaken the faith of his fathers, thus drawing intense opposition from Zion's devoutly religious Jews. That intensity can be measured in his shortened life.

Of Bishop Alexander's ministry, the London Jews' Society, the parent body, in the 1843 issue of their *Jewish Intelligence*, nearly two years before his death wrote prophetically of their expectation:

> ...The most efficient means, indeed, the only means, for the national conversion of any people, is the rise of a visible Church of natives. All people are suspicious of a foreign religion and foreign teachers – the Jews peculiarly so ... By the visibility of a national church alone can this be removed; and where can the national Church of Israel command more attention, or find a more genial soil, than on the holy hill which *"is beautiful for situation, and the joy of the whole earth?"*
>
> And be it remembered that this is no longer a mere vision or theory. An infant Jewish Church already exists in that sacred locality ... It is now a year since a Hebrew bishop again, after a lapse of many centuries, took up his seat in the Holy City ... Why have the efforts of Christians not been concentrated upon that one spot, which prophecy, Providence, memory, hope and every sacred association, point out as the most important upon the earth's surface?

Less than four years after Bishop Alexander's appointment, "one of the largest blood-vessels near his heart ruptured." Alexander died on 22 November, 1845. This tragedy for his family and for the restorationist movement is described by Muriel Corey using the words of Jesus, "Except a corn of wheat fall into the ground and die, it abideth alone, but if it die, it bringest forth much fruit."[9] History has borne out her assessment. Christ Church was built and consecrated on 21 January, 1849.

About a decade after Bishop Alexander's death a Jewish visitor to Jerusalem, Ludwig Frankel recorded:

> When all the Jewish converts residing in Jerusalem are assembled in this church, they form an imposing and numerous congregation. What other Jewish congregation in the world, even when all its members are assembled, can boast like that of Jerusalem of having a hundred and thirty baptized Jews in one church?[10]

Jewish historian Barbara Tuchman elevated the significance of the London Jews' Society to international level, to the birthing of a nation, in her book *The Bible and the Sword*: "If the Jews' Society had concerned itself only with conversion we could ignore it. It was that vital linked factor, the restoration of Israel, that gives the Society's work historical importance."

The battle for Zion

Alfred Sawyer, a former rector of Christ Church, helps us to see the miracle of how Christ Church pioneered the way for Protestant churches into the Middle East:

> Building an Anglican Church in Jerusalem in the middle of the last century was not as simple as it sounds. To begin with it was against the law to build a church – or a synagogue for that matter.
>
> There hadn't been a church built in Jerusalem since the Crusades. The reason was simple. Whilst Islamic law – which had prevailed in Jerusalem since the defeat of the Crusaders in 1187 – tolerated the presence of Christians and Jews, it would not permit any new non-Islamic places of worship to be built. Old churches and synagogues could be refurbished. But there is no provision in Turkish law for the expansion of the Christian community other than by an increased birth rate.
>
> Evangelism by Christians was strictly prohibited. The Turks enforced this dictum with the enactment of the Status Quo, an agreement whereby the property, rights and privileges of the

various communities were frozen in time. The rule was: what was, is, and shall be forever.

One of the consequences of the Status Quo was to force the ancient Christian communities of the Holy Land to focus on maintenance instead of mission. The critical issue for most Christian communities living under the rule of Islam in the Holy Land and elsewhere in the Middle East was simply survival.

It must have struck the Turks as a bit odd that an Anglican missionary society from England and a Lutheran Prince from Prussia wanted to establish a joint "Protestant" bishopric in Jerusalem. The Prince was Kaiser Frederick Wilhelm IV. The missionary society was called the London Society for the Promotion of Christianity Amongst the Jews, or, as it was popularly known, the London Jews' Society [L.J.S.].

As early as 1838 the L.J.S. had urged the establishment of a bishopric in Jerusalem and the building of a church, to be called Christ Church, which would serve as a base for the society's evangelistic work amongst the city's Jews. Not surprisingly, the Turks firmly rebuffed the proposal. Neither were the ancient Christian churches keen on the idea. The Jewish community naturally opposed the plan.

Even some Anglicans recoiled at the thought of a joint venture with the Prussians. One of the leading English Tractarians, John Henry Newman, wrote in his memoirs concerning the establishment of the Jerusalem bishopric, "The Anglican Church might have apostolic succession, as had the monophysites; but such acts as were in progress led me to the gravest suspicion, not that it would soon cease to be a Church, but that, since the 16th century, it had never been a Church all along."

Newman strongly opposed the agreement which would link the Anglicans to a Church that did not hold to the doctrine of apostolic succession. The agreement called for bishops to be appointed alternately by the English and the Prussians.

Permission to build Christ Church was given grudgingly by the Turks. Had it not been for Britain's status as a superpower and the help she gave the Ottoman Empire in putting down a war, it is doubtful that Christ Church would have ever been built.

In the end the Ottomans agreed to allow construction of Christ Church to proceed under one condition: It would not be called a "church." Instead, it would be officially referred to as the private "chapel" of the British Consul. The result was what some contemporary observers thought was an architectural nightmare, a neo-Gothic church with a house stuck literally on the side of it.

Despite being aesthetically unexceptional, Christ Church broke new ground. The Islamic taboo against new churches was shattered. In the ensuing years new church buildings and guest houses for pilgrims cropped up all over Jerusalem. Other European powers quickly moved in as well, giving what had been a relatively unimportant provincial hill town a cosmopolitan status in the decaying Ottoman Empire.

Most importantly an evangelical witness had been established in the Mother City of the Christian faith. Those early years saw numbers of Jewish people, including several rabbis, come to faith in Jesus as their Messiah.[11]

An identity crisis

A name is all about identity. As Jewish people came to faith in the Promised Land, they struggled with their identity. Jewish believers in Jesus outside the land were generally known as Hebrew Christians. They belonged to the Church into which they integrated. Among missions to Jewish people the liturgy was simply translated into Hebrew and their hymns sung in Hebrew.

Gershon Nerel who serves on the Executive Board of the Messianic Jewish Alliance of Israel observes:

> The emergence of the Messianic Jewish [Hebrew Christian] self-identity between the years 1917 and 1967 is a unique phenomenon in the history of the *"Yishuv"* [the Jewish Community] in Eretz-Israel, the land of Israel. By "Messianic Jews" it is meant Jews who voluntarily decided to embrace faith in *Yeshua* [Jesus] of Nazareth as Son of God and Redeemer, or as in one single case . . . merely as Messiah and Prophet. The originality of this segment in Israeli society – which in Mandatory Palestine numbered circa 120 persons and roughly 150 around 1967 – was that they insisted on not being regarded as "converts to Christianity," but rather stressed their being called "Completed Jews" or "Messianic Jews."[12]

During the latter nineteenth century the term "Hebrew Christian" was used by both the London Jews' Society (later known as the Church's Ministry among Jewish People – CMJ) and the American Christian and Missionary Alliance (C & MA). But for the Hebrew-speaking Jewish believers in Jesus settling in the land of their patriarchs, this was a new day of restoration.

To them "Hebrew Christian" or "Jewish Christian" was both alien and an association with a past painful experience of Jewish identification with the Gentile Church. "Messianic Jew" is an identity that is Jewish. Their purpose was to return to the Acts of the Apostles, to the faith and practice of the first-century believers who were initially all Jewish.

The Messianic Jews weaned themselves from their attachment to the missionary organizations located in Jerusalem, Jaffa, Haifa, Safed and Tiberias in the early twentieth century as they assimilated into the developing distinctive Hebrew-speaking Jewish society. They saw the need to observe the holy days of Leviticus especially circumcision, the Sabbath and Passover. Misunderstanding of their motives brought opposition from the Christian community, which charged them with "self-exalting behavior."

The use of the term Hebrew Christian was used when connecting with the international Messianic Jewish body but in Hebrew they were known as *Yehudim Meshihiim*, Messianic Jews. In 1931 "The Hebrew Christian Fellowship of Palestine" was formed as an interdenominational body with the intention of being independent of church organizations and hoping to unite Messianic Jews in Palestine.

The organization changed its name in 1933 to Hebrew Christian Alliance of Palestine and the Near East. The following were the requirements for admission: "Expression in public of faith in Messiah Jesus as personal Savior and Lord; belief in the divinity of Messiah Jesus; belief in his sacrificial death and resurrection; acceptance of the Old and New Testaments as the word of God and as the rule for their faith and lives." It is noteworthy that neither belief in the Trinity nor the practice of water baptism, somewhat controversial subjects, were listed as requirements for membership, thereby minimizing obstacles to wider membership.[13]

"Nicodemus Jews"

Opposition from the orthodox Jewish community did not prevent Jewish people from coming to faith in Jesus but it successfully drove them underground. "Nicodemus Jews" were the secret believers as in the days of Jesus "for fear of the Jews" (John 7:13). Of course by nature of their secrecy we have no idea of their number.

Roger Allison, a minister whom CMJ posted to Palestine in 1941, provides a significant report demonstrating the seriousness with which some orthodox Jews considered the New Testament, remembering that it was a "forbidden" book to Jewish people:

> Early in the 1940s I learned that there existed in the all-Jewish city of Tel Aviv a group of up to one hundred orthodox Jews, who were meeting secretly to study and discuss the New Testament. This became known to me because, although no Gentile was admitted to that closed circle, our Jewish co-worker Weinstock, recognized as a Christian believer and trusted by the group, was once and once only invited to visit them, in order to help them over some particularly knotty problem.
>
> That incident alone provided evidence that, quite apart from the slightest "missionary" activity, the Holy Spirit was quietly working in the Jewish conscience – perhaps even more so among the orthodox than the secular. There can be no doubt that something new is taking place in the Jewish soul, the corporate soul of the nation and even of worldwide Jewry.
>
> An orthodox rabbi has gone on record as saying that there is "a Jesus wave" going through Israel today. The Messianic Jews, whose number is constantly growing, are those who, while remaining Jews (as they insist) and loyal Israelis (as they prove), have taken the big, open leap of faith into the kingdom which Jesus announced, inaugurated and embodied.[14]

At the conclusion of the British Mandate in 1948 when the British departed, concern was raised about the safety of the Jewish believers in Jesus. Many were linked to the British, both missionaries and government. The British were seen as the enemy since the enforcement of their 1939 White Paper which prevented Jewish refugees from entering Palestine. Most of these refugees were survivors of the Nazi death camps and were now being deported to camps in Cyprus.

"Operation Mercy" evacuated from Palestine all Hebrew Christians who chose not to remain in the Jewish State. It is estimated that about a dozen Jewish believers in Jesus remained. Operation Mercy resulted in disunity and those believers assimilated into the non-Jewish churches. This meant that the community of Jewish believers in Jesus in Eretz Israel ceased to exist.

Independence: political and spiritual

Roger Allison recognized an important change in 1948:

> The establishment of the new State had, I believe, quite a lot to do in fostering this gradual change of attitude towards the One whose very name had for so long been a name to be shunned, afraid of and suspected. What was happening seemed to be that, together with political independence, there was coming to birth an independence of thought, unfettered by the closed mind of a kind of ghetto mentality. They now had a new and, hopefully, honoured place in the comity of nations.[15]

Gershon Nerel explains the effect of that independent thought:

> Following the establishment of the State of Israel in 1948, a new era began in the history of the Jewish believers in Jesus in the Land. Those very few who remained, reinforced by the new Jewish believers in Jesus who moved into the Land through the massive *aliya* [immigration] waves of the 1950s and 1960s, together formed a new foundation for local believers. They worked strongly to eliminate their minority status within the expatriate minorities of churches and missions in Israel. In fact, gradually they did become a self-determined ideological minority of their own.[16]

Menahem Ben Hayim is a Messianic pioneer whose family came from Eastern Europe and settled in America. He emigrated with his wife to Israel in 1963 as a Jewish believer in Jesus. Menahem highlights the diversity of the body with its inherent problems. He recalls:

The Messianic movement was developing rapidly. More young people were coming to faith, and the influence of the American "Jews for Jesus" became noticeable in Israel. We received wide coverage from the media.

The Messianic Jewish Alliance seeks to link Jewish believers from all congregations with each other. Many Messianic believers still don't feel accepted in Israel. We flutter around like a bird which hasn't yet learned to fly. We haven't developed strong wings with which we can rise like an eagle.

The problem is that we're still such a mixture. Don't forget every Jew has a different background ... Israel is a huge melting pot. At the same time our congregations still maintain many of the characteristics of the churches with which they have been in contact in the *diaspora*, or through which they came to faith, including the way in which they conduct worship. We have charismatic and non-charismatic, evangelical free church, liturgical and others.

Often it's a strong personality which keeps a congregation together. Sometimes the problems are not on a theological level, but concern the personality of the leader. This has occasionally hindered the growth of the Messianic Jewish part of the body of Messiah in Israel.[17]

A new heart

Reuven Berger, pastor of The Congregation of the Lamb on Mount Zion, which meets in Christ Church, Jerusalem, describes his experience of arrival in Israel. Reuven observed a turning point when the Jewish believers in Jesus were not confined to new immigrants but Israeli-born young people began to come to faith:

When did the Messianic movement begin? It began when Jesus was on this earth. What we are experiencing today is only the continuation and restoration of what was begun two thousand years ago and what went into ruins not many years after that. As we look at the State of Israel today it is really impossible to separate the Messianic movement from the restoration of Israel as a nation.

We have lived in this land since 1970. In those years this whole Messianic movement developed. When we came to Israel there were very few Jews who believed in Jesus. There were very few

Messianic congregations. There were one or two in Jerusalem made up of some older Jewish believers. There was one in Haifa. Basically, there was very little to be seen in the land.

At the end of the 1970s it was like the beginning of a revival, a small revival. Through that the Lord began to establish the foundation of the body through which eventually he was going to work into the whole nation of Israel. It was quite an amazing thing to see, just within a period of years a number of young Israelis met the Lord. It was something completely new.

At the time of the book of Acts, the great question in the early Church was not "How do Jews believe in Jesus?" but, "What do we do with the Gentiles? Where have they come from?" Today the Church has so departed from its understanding of the word of God that it is surprised and finds difficulty understanding, "What do we do with the Jews who believe in Jesus?"

Many think that a Jew who believes in Jesus is no longer a Jew. As we look at Church history we see that Jews were asked to deny their Jewishness in their conversion to Jesus. This was more a conversion to Christianity than it was a conversion to the Messiah and a conversion of the heart.

When we speak of conversion in this land we mean a conversion of the heart from the old to the new, from the flesh to the Holy Spirit, and of course that's what it is for all people, whether they are Jews or Gentiles. We know that throughout the ages people have tried to convert the Jews in all kinds of missions to the Jews.

The interesting thing that's happening in our time is that it is a sovereign, prophetic move of the Lord ... throughout the generations there were always Jews who came to faith in Jesus; most often they entered into the Gentile Christian denominations. We can see many Jews became Catholics in the Catholic countries. We can see that today many Jews who have come from what was the Soviet Union became believers and were in the Orthodox Church of Russia. Some of them were in an evangelical church.

Barry Segal, a Messianic leader, speaking in 1992 described events after his arrival in 1981:

In the mid-1980s all of a sudden there was a rumbling here in the land. There was a pouring out suddenly upon some of the local people and in the last five to eight years there has been a whole new wave of indigenous congregations throughout the land.

If you came to Jerusalem in 1984 there were two or three indigenous fellowships; today, there are more than a dozen. Maybe there will be twenty-four, something like that. And I think what Jerusalem has become or is becoming is the magnetic force for every angelic and demonic force in the heavenlies.

Ethiopian immigrants

The two large operations known as "Operation Moses" in 1984–85 and "Operation Solomon" in 1991 airlifted Ethiopian Jews to Israel. Amharic-speaking, generally from primitive rural living conditions, these Ethiopian Jews were transported through a time warp into twentieth-century Israel. Among them are believers in Jesus who came to faith during a revival in Ethiopia associated with evangelical and Pentecostal fellowships which was of an indigenous nature and not involved with foreign missions. There are a number of Amharic-speaking congregations scattered around Israel who keep a low profile, cautious to protect their identity.

In March 1999 a newspaper article reported on a meeting in Ashdod held by the anti-missionary organization Lev L'Achim. This was attended by several highly respected Ethiopian religious leaders, the deputy mayor and the city's chief rabbi, who gathered to discuss the missionary activities of the Ethiopian community in Israel. According to the press the meeting decided "to act against the pestilence of the activities of the mission . . . and to maintain a strong connection between Lev L'Achim, the Ethiopian community and the members of the Shas party who are doing much on the subject of the mission."[18]

Russian immigrants

The collapse of the Soviet Union following the *glasnost* and *perestroika* policies in 1989 flung open the gates for Jewish people to leave. During the next decade the flood of a million "Russian" Jews arrived in Israel in large waves of immigration. These had a wide impact on Israeli society, including the Messianic body.

Those conducting a survey in 1998–99 conclude:

> The arrival of Russian immigrants has meant not only an increase
> in members in already existing congregations but also an increased
> number of congregations. Of the 81 groups included in this survey
> some 57 were founded in the 1990s. The fact that "only" some 20
> of these congregations or groups were started by Russians and have
> Russian as their only or first language does not adequately reflect
> the situation. In other congregations established in the 1990s, over
> 90 percent of the members are Russians and the work began mainly
> as an outreach to Russians.[19]

Coincidence or act of God?

Is it a coincidence that this Jewish revival of interest in Jesus of
Nazareth blossomed at the time Jewish people began to leave
Eastern Europe to settle in their promised homeland? Is it by chance
that Herzl and the Zionists emerged onto the stage of history at this
time in the wake of this movement, clamoring for their homeland?
Is it incidental that by mid-twentieth century the Jewish homeland
was internationally recognized as a State? Is it an accident of history
that the nineteenth-century Christian outreach to the Jewish people
was followed by revivals of increasing magnitude during the
twentieth century?

No! These events are not by coincidence, chance, incidence or
accident – they are the unfolding plan and purpose of God triggered
off by obedience to his principles. Paul revealed the truth when
he said, "... salvation has come to the Gentiles to make Israel
envious" (Romans 11:11).

God had declared:

> When all these blessings and curses I have set before you come
> upon you and you take them to heart wherever the LORD your God
> disperses you among the nations, and when you and your children
> return to the LORD your God and obey him with all your heart and
> with all your soul according to everything I command you today,
> then the LORD your God will restore your fortunes and have
> compassion on you and gather you again from all the nations

where he scattered you. Even if you have been banished to the most distant land under the heavens, from there the LORD your God will gather you and bring you back. He will bring you to the land that belonged to your fathers, and you will take possession of it. He will make you more prosperous and numerous than your fathers. The LORD your God will circumcise your hearts and the hearts of your descendants, so that you may love him with all your heart and with all your soul, and live. The LORD your God will put all these curses on your enemies who hate and persecute you.

(Deuteronomy 30:1–7)

Israel Regathered by God (Jeremiah 31:10)

On 7 June, 1981, Israel dispatched a flight of F-15 and F-16 fighter aircraft at 4:40 pm local time, with orders to knock out Iraq's $260 million nuclear-research reactor. Israel reasoned that her implacable enemy would soon be making nuclear bombs. At 5:10 pm the lead fighter penetrated Iraqi airspace and at 5:30 pm they attacked their target.

TIME magazine provided a thorough covering of the event. The "Publisher's Letter" raised the question of Israel's constant appearance before the world:

> In its first cover story on Israel, dated August 16, 1948, TIME hailed the newborn nation and its Prime Minister, David Ben-Gurion, with some prophetic words: "Although, in years to come fighting might break out again and again ... it was time to stop pondering the settled question of whether there would be a Jewish State, time to start asking what kind of a nation Israel was" ... As a result, Israel and its role in the Middle East have been subjects of 35 TIME cover stories, more than any other country or geographic area except the Soviet Union.
>
> ...says Bureau Chief David Aikman: "There is something almost cosmic about Israel's conflict with its neighbors. Where else in the world would the chief of the Air Force quote the Bible in answer to a reporter's question?" [1]

Mr Aikman points to the unique character of Israel and to the only source for hope and understanding of what is taking place in Israel and the Middle East – the Bible!

GENERAL ASSEMBLY
SESSION 49
ROLL-CALL FORM

PLENARY MEETING 128 DATE Nov 29

COMMITTEE _____ TIME _____

Question at Issue: Palestine Partition

	YES	NO	ABSTAIN		YES	NO	ABSTAIN
AFGHANISTAN		X		LEBANON		X	
ARGENTINA			X	LIBERIA	X		
AUSTRALIA	X			LUXEMBOURG	X		
BELGIUM	X			MEXICO			X
BOLIVIA	X			NETHERLANDS	X		
BRAZIL	X			NEW ZEALAND	X		
BYELORUSSIAN S.S.R	X			NICARAGUA	X		
CANADA	X			NORWAY	X		
CHILE			X	PAKISTAN		X	
CHINA			X	PANAMA	X		
COLOMBIA			X	PARAGUAY	X		
COSTA RICA	X			PERU	X		
CUBA		X		PHILIPPINES	X		
CZECHOSLOVAKIA	X			POLAND	X		
DENMARK	X			SAUDI ARABIA		X	
DOMINICAN REPUBLIC	X			SIAM			—
ECUADOR	X			SWEDEN	X		
EGYPT		X		SYRIA		X	
EL SALVADOR			X	TURKEY		X	
ETHIOPIA			X	UKRAINIAN S.S.R.	X		
FRANCE	X			UNION OF SOUTH AFRICA	X		
GREECE		X		UNION OF SOVIET SOCIALIST REPUBLICS	X		
GUATEMALA	X			UNITED KINGDOM			X
HAITI	X			U.S.A.	X		
HONDURAS			X	URUGUAY	X		
ICELAND	X			VENEZUELA	X		
INDIA		X		YEMEN		X	
IRAN		X		YUGOSLAVIA			X
IRAQ		X					
TOTAL for Column				TOTAL:	33	13	10

The voting chart of the United Nations General Assembly
on the partition of Palestine – 29 November, 1947

The "Publisher's Letter" underlines the fact that Israel is
constantly in the news and frequently the center of it. God said this
would be so. In fact he declared it about 2,800 years ago:

In that day the Lord will reach out his hand a second time to reclaim
the remnant that is left of his people from Assyria, from Lower
Egypt, from Upper Egypt, from Cush, from Elam, from Babylonia,
from Hamath and from the islands of the sea.

He will raise a banner for the nations
> and gather the exiles of Israel;
he will assemble the scattered people of Judah
> from the four quarters of the earth."

(Isaiah 11:11–12)

God makes two unique statements of what he will do uniquely with his people Israel. He says he will regather them a second time from the places he has scattered them and he will raise a banner for the nations by the regathering of Israel.

We know that following their seventy-year exile in Babylon there was a regathering of the Jewish remnant under Nehemiah in the sixth century BC In the scripture quoted from Isaiah 11 the Lord is referring to a second regathering.

Since the return from Babylon there has never been an occasion in history until the twentieth century when a large body of Jewish people has returned to Israel.

Wave the flag for all to see

What is a banner? It is a flag bearing symbols immediately identifying whom, or what, it represents. When, for example, the blue flag with Union Jack and Southern Cross was unfurled at the Olympics, every New Zealander present shouted excitedly.

God said, "I'm going to raise a flag and everybody is going to see it! Everybody is going to know Israel is here!" But, only those who know the meaning of the symbol will know who put the flag there and why it is there.

To ensure that we know what he is saying without any doubt in our minds, God specifies from where he will regather this remnant – "the four quarters of the earth." He wants us to be very sure that this regathering is not confused with his first regathering from Babylon which would have been from one corner of the earth.

It is important to note who is bringing the Jewish people to Israel. Isaiah said, "the Lord will reach out his hand a second time..." Then in Jeremiah 31:10 we are informed:

> "Hear the word of the LORD, O nations;
> > proclaim it in distant coastlands:

'He who scattered Israel will gather them
and will watch over his flock like a shepherd.' "

The God of Israel, who scattered her, is now regathering his people to Israel and his purpose is to be a shepherd, caring intensely for his people. God, the Lord of history is drawing his people home. This is no human design or historic accident, but an unfolding of God's pre-ordained plan.

The *TIME* publisher draws attention to the constant focusing upon Israel which is apparent to us in our media daily, whether the subject be conflict with her neighbors, terrorism of her people at home or abroad, criticism through the UN, comments on her economy, or dramatic rescues of her people from oppressed countries.

It is not only as though Israel were constantly in the news but rather that she invariably hits the headlines dramatically as the center stage of events – with her rebirth on 14 May 14, 1948; by the startling victory and recapture of Old Jerusalem in the Six Day War, June, 1967; by surviving the Yom Kippur War, 1973; by the finesse of the Entebbe rescue, 1976; by the dramatic rescue of over half of the Ethiopian Jewish community, January 1985. God has raised her as a banner to the nations.

Clearly, the God of Israel is not content with just the regathering of the Jewish people to their homeland, but he wants all mankind to know about it.

Don't you believe it?

The rebirth of Israel has had a marked impact upon the other two monotheistic religions associated with Israel: Christianity and Islam.

Many Christians have believed that Israel was finished. "God has replaced Israel with the Church." So they said, "Israel's done!" Islam goes even further. Islam teaches that God has finished with both Israel and the Church. "God has given his new truth to us!" they shout.

God was fully prepared for this one. He declared what would happen about 2,500 years before the event:

"Who has ever heard of such a thing?
Who has ever seen such things?

> Can a country be born in a day
>   or a nation be brought forth in a moment?
> Yet no sooner is Zion in labor
>   than she gives birth to her children."
>
> (Isaiah 66:8)

What an embarrassment to those who said Israel will be no more. Then for the pessimists who said it wouldn't last long, Israel has reached her fifty-ninth year. And to make absolutely sure he had silenced the critics he planted Israel in the Islamic heartland where she belongs!

> "This is what the Sovereign LORD says: This is Jerusalem, which I have set in the center of the nations, with countries all around her."
>
> (Ezekiel 5:5)

With the blessing of God

At 4:30 pm Iyyar 5, 5708 (Jewish date), or 14 May, 1948, the National Council met in the Tel Aviv Museum Hall. Ben-Gurion, who presided, announced: "I shall read you the Foundation Scroll of the State of Israel, which has been approved in the first reading by the National Council." As he continued with the appeal, "Let us accept the Foundation Scroll of the Jewish State by rising," the entire audience rose. Rabbi Fishman thereupon pronounced the traditional blessing:

> Blessed art Thou, O Lord, our God, King of the Universe, who has kept us alive and preserved us and enabled us to reach this season.

Ben-Gurion announced: "The State of Israel has arisen. This session is closed."[2]

> *"Come, they say, "Let us destroy them as a nation,*
> *   that the name of Israel be remembered no more."*
>
> (Psalm 83:4, emphasis added)

The next day 650,000 Jews were surrounded by forty million Arabs with one and a half million of them armed. Eighty thousand Jews in

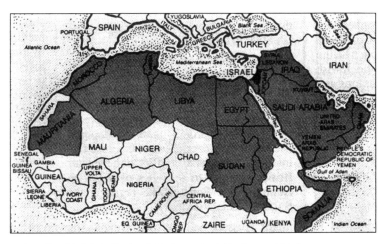

Israel's rebirth is in the Land God promised Abraham which is now among Islamic nations. The dark areas indicate Islamic Arab nations.

Jerusalem were cut off from the rest of Israel. The miracle is that Israel was born and she was not and could not be destroyed. The Lord had said:

> "No weapon forged against you will prevail,
>   and you will refute every tongue that accuses you."
>
> (Isaiah 54:17)

It was at this time that, with their intended destruction of the new Jewish state, most Arab leaders called their people (the Arabs) to stay especially in cities like Haifa. Many Arab peasant farmers feared the war and fled with their families to Lebanon and Egypt. In some places like Ramleh and Lod they were expelled. Naturally the fleeing Arabs did not choose to return in a state of war, thereby creating the "refugee" problem for which Israel has been blamed ever since. Considerable propaganda has been written on this subject.

TIME reported on 16 August, 1948,

> Out of the concentration camps, ghettos, courtrooms, theatres and factories of Europe the Chosen People had assembled and had won their first great military victory since 166–160 BC Israel's victory came after the worst of a thousand persecutions.

كيـف نستعمــل نجمة اسرائيل ٠٠

How to use the star of David . . . (Iraqi daily *Al Manar*, 8 June, 1967)

Again prophetic words were fulfilled:

> "Arise, shine, for your light has come,
>   and the glory of the LORD rises upon you.
> See, darkness covers the earth
>   and thick darkness is over the peoples,
> but the LORD rises upon you
>   and his glory appears over you."

(Isaiah 60:1–2)

Relevant today

We have settled the question that God raised Israel for world attention. Why did God do this? We find the answer in the teaching of Jesus.

You will remember the events of Jesus' journey to Emmaus with Cleopas. Jesus explained his life and ministry from the Law, Prophets and Psalms:

> "This is what I told you while I was still with you: Everything must be fulfilled that is written about me in the law of Moses, the Prophets and the Psalms."

Then he opened their minds so that they could understand the Scriptures. He told them, "This is what is written: The Christ will suffer and rise from the dead on the third day, and repentance and forgiveness of sins will be preached in his name to all nations, beginning at Jerusalem. You are witnesses of these things."

(Luke 24:44–48)

In doing this Jesus demonstrated the importance and accuracy of the Old Testament even after his death and resurrection. He is saying, "All that has happened in my life to date, and that you have witnessed has been declared by my Father in the Law, the Prophets and the Psalms."

The covenants are related?

Much misunderstanding has been created through the use of the terms Old Testament and New Testament. It is essential that we understand the importance of one of the most frequently used words in Hebrew Scripture – covenant.

In chapter 3 we studied the covenant God made with Abraham and the succeeding four covenants which developed from that covenant. We saw that the permanent new covenant replaced the temporary Mosaic covenant. Dr David Bivin sheds important light upon this subject:

> The best known commemoration of God's covenant with his people is called in Hebrew *be-RIT mi-LA*, the covenant of circumcision. In rabbinic literature this is also called "the covenant of Abraham our father."
>
> Hebrews 12:24 speaks of Jesus as the mediator of "a new covenant." This is a reference to the well-known prophecy uttered by Jeremiah:
>
> "The time is coming" declares the LORD,
>   "when I will make a new covenant
> with the house of Israel
>   and with the house of Judah."
>
> (Jeremiah 31:31)

However, nowhere in the New Testament is the term "new covenant" used as a name for the collection of books which

Christians refer to as the New Testament. "Scripture" for the early followers of Jesus meant the Hebrew Scriptures. The term "New Testament" was coined much later in history.

Nevertheless, *habe-RIT hahada-SHA* (the new covenant), is the term used in Hebrew today to refer to the "New Testament." What Christians call the "Old Testament" is referred to in Hebrew as *ta-NAK*. This is an abbreviation of the Hebrew words for the three sections of the Jewish Bible (*to-RA*, Torah; *nevi-IM*, Prophets; *ketu-VIM*, Writings).

Calling the Jewish Scriptures the "Old Testament" denigrates the Hebrew Bible. "Old Testament" seems to imply that the Jewish Scriptures have been replaced by the Christian New Testament, and that God somehow has abrogated the covenant he made with the Jewish people. Consequently, some Christians have concluded that the "Old Testament" is out of date and does not warrant such serious study as the New Testament.

Actually, the Hebrew adjective "new" used with "covenant" does not necessarily imply the replacement of an earlier covenant, but may only imply its renewal. Furthermore, the translation "testament" in this context is unfortunate because it misses the connection with Jeremiah 31:31, and also may be misconstrued by the English reader to mean testament in the sense of last will and testament, rather than covenant.[4]

Concerning the Law and the Prophets Jesus did not say they are null and void, but forcefully stressed their continuance until completely fulfilled:

> "Do not think that I have come to abolish the Law or the Prophets;
> I have not come to abolish them but to fulfill them. I tell you the
> truth, until heaven and earth disappear, not the smallest letter, not
> the least stroke of a pen, will by any means disappear from the Law
> until everything is accomplished."
>
> (Matthew 5:17–18)

The writer to the Hebrews refers to these covenants, saying:

> By calling this covenant "new," he has made the first one obsolete;
> and what is obsolete and ageing will soon disappear.
>
> (Hebrews 8:13)

The emphasis here is introducing and seeing the fulfillment of the new covenant which is related to the old. The new covenant is not something totally different from the old, but rather it follows on from the former or Mosaic covenant.

Today we sometimes see old cars driven on the road. A car from the 1920s, no matter how carefully restored, simply cannot match a car of 2006 in performance, speed, comfort, and ease of driving. In 1920 they did not have the technological understanding of successive years, therefore, we expect improvement which makes the old version "obsolete."

However, the old car has an engine that propels it forward on four wheels, directed by a steering wheel, gears that assist the engine load, an accelerator providing speed control, and a braking system. The "new" version is a continuation of the principles of the old with substantial improvements through new revelation. In similar manner there is a continuing relationship between the former covenant and the "new." The "new" covenant is superior in revelation and it is eternal in nature.

Some people speak as though God finally gave up on the Law and the Prophets as though he had made a great blunder in his estimation of the people with whom he made the covenant. Then he decided to produce another covenant of a totally different nature with some other people. Thus God discarded the first covenant.

Firstly, such thinking does not agree with these words of Jesus who goes out of his way to forcefully explain that all God has declared in the Law, through the Prophets and in the Psalms, will be totally fulfilled.

Secondly, this thinking does not take into account the reliability of God's Word:

> "The grass withers and the flowers fall,
> but the word of our God stands forever."

(Isaiah 40:8)

Or as God says on another occasion:

> Even to your old age and grey hairs
> I am he, I am he who will sustain you.

I have made you and I will carry you;
   I will sustain you and I will rescue you . . .
Remember the former things, those of long ago;
   I am God, and there is no other;
   I am God, and there is none like me.
I make known the end from the beginning,
   from ancient times, what is still to come.
I say: My purpose will stand,
   and I will do all that I please.

(Isaiah 46:4, 9–10)

Benjamin Disraeli expressed it this way:

> In all church discussions we are apt to forget the second Testament
> is avowedly only a supplement. Jesus came to complete "the Law
> and the Prophets." Christianity is completed biblical Judaism, or it
> is nothing. Christianity is incomprehensible without Judaism, as
> Judaism is incomplete without Christianity.[5]

Unlocking the prophetic word

Before his death Jesus told the disciples he had much more to
explain to them, but that they had learned all they could understand
at that time. He promised that the Holy Spirit would teach them in
the future (John 16:12). After Jesus spoke with Cleopas he remained
with the disciples for forty days before ascending to heaven. During
that time he taught them much that they could not have understood previously.

Following this time of teaching and empowered by the Holy
Spirit, Peter explained to an eager crowd the significance for them
of Jesus' death and resurrection and events that would precede his
return:

> "Repent, then, and turn to God, so that your sins may be wiped
> out, that times of refreshing may come from the Lord, and that he
> may send the Christ, who has been appointed for you – even Jesus.
> He must remain in heaven until the time comes for God to restore
> everything, as he promised long ago through his holy prophets."

(Acts 3:19–21)

Jesus will remain in heaven until the time comes for God to restore everything to its rightful order. The details of God's restoration program are contained in the prophets. Since Jesus has not yet returned to earth, the key to our understanding of what God is doing today lies with the prophets. When we turn to the prophets we find God telling us the accuracy of his Word:

> "I am the LORD,
> who has made all things . . .
> who carries out the words of his servants
>> and fulfils the predictions of his messengers."
>
> (Isaiah 44:24, 26)

> . . . so is my word that goes out from my mouth:
>> It will not return to me empty,
> but will accomplish what I desire
>> and achieve the purpose for which I sent it.
>
> (Isaiah 55:11)

> Then the LORD said to me, "You have seen well, for I am watching over my word to perform it."
>
> (Jeremiah 1:12, NASB)

> Surely the Sovereign LORD does nothing
>> without revealing his plan
>> to his servants the prophets.
>
> (Amos 3:7)

Why did Jesus weep over Jerusalem?

Overlooking Jerusalem, part way up the Mount of Olives, stands a modern church, prominent for its unusual design. The roof is shaped like a teardrop.

> As he [Jesus] approached Jerusalem and saw the city, he wept over it and said, "If you, even you, had only known on this day what would bring you peace – but now it is hidden from your eyes. The days will come upon you when your enemies will build an embankment against you and encircle you and hem you in on

every side. They will dash you to the ground, you and the children within your walls. They will not leave one stone on another, because you did not recognize the time of God's coming to you."

(Luke 19:41–44)

"Then let those who are in Judea flee to the mountains, let those in the city get out, and let those in the country not enter the city. For this is the time of punishment in fulfillment of all that has been written. How dreadful it will be in those days for pregnant women and nursing mothers! There will be great distress in the land and wrath against this people. They will fall by the sword and will be taken as prisoners to all the nations. Jerusalem will be trampled on by the Gentiles until the times of the Gentiles are fulfilled."

(Luke 21:21–24)

Jesus wept over Jerusalem because he knew how the people's rejection of him would affect them and the generations to come. As we have discovered, Jesus spoke of the fulfillment of the Law, the Prophets and the Psalms. He knew what they contained and he knew what their rejection of him would mean for the nation of Israel.

Within a generation these words of Jesus completely described the dreadful events that occurred in Jerusalem. Under the orders of the Emperor Vespasian, Titus commanded an army of many legions that surrounded Jerusalem. Titus wanted the Jewish people who were trapped within the walls of Jerusalem to surrender and come under the authority of the Roman Empire, but they resisted, hoping for victory over the Roman army.

The Jewish people's determination to win and heroism was evident to the Romans. Flavius Josephus, a Jew who turned himself over to the Romans, wrote accounts of the Jewish rebellion against Rome. His detailed reports show the accuracy of Jesus' words.

God's hand upon Titus may well be seen from an opening scene in the siege of Jerusalem where Titus found himself ambushed by Jews. Lacking his armor, Titus battled with his sword, scattering his enemy while arrows rained over him although not touching him!

Jerusalem was cut off. The food supply rapidly dwindled. Jews turned against Jews in their efforts to survive. Jews lay dead around the city, unburied. All decency and restraint disappeared as hunger reigned. Wives robbed their husbands, children their fathers, and mothers their babes! Food was snatched from the mouths of dear ones dying. Locked doors were broken open to steal food. People were mercilessly tortured or even battered to death for their morsels of food.

Josephus says:

> To give a detailed account of their outrageous conduct is impossible, but we may sum it up by saying that no other city has ever endured such horrors, and no generation in history has fathered such wickedness. In the end they brought the whole Hebrew race into contempt in order to make their own impiety seem less outrageous in foreign eyes, and confessed the painful truth that they were slaves, the dregs of humanity, bastards, and outcasts of their nation.
>
> . . . It is certain that when from the Upper City they watched the Temple burning they did not turn a hair, though many Romans were moved to tears.[6]

Titus authorized the execution of Jewish prisoners by crucifixion in full sight of the Jews, hoping this would lead to surrender. The opposite happened. The Jewish leaders forced Jews desiring to give themselves over to the Romans to see their fate. The countryside was stripped of trees used for fortifications and crosses:

> The Romans, though it was a terrible struggle to collect the timber, raised their platforms in twenty-one days, having as described before stripped the whole area in a circle round the town to a distance of ten miles. The countryside like the City was a pitiful sight; for where once there had been a lovely vista of woods and parks there was nothing but desert and stumps of trees.
>
> No one – not even a foreigner – who had seen the old Judea and the glorious suburbs of the City, and now set eyes on her present desolation, could have helped sighing and groaning at so terrible a change; for every trace of beauty had been blotted out by the war, and nobody who had known it in the past and came upon it suddenly would have recognized the place: when he was already there he would still have been looking for the City.[7]

It was reported that through one gate of the city alone, 115,880 Jewish corpses were taken between the dates of 14 April (the day the

Romans encamped) and 1 July. Six hundred thousand pauper bodies were known to have been removed from the city and it was known there were many others not accounted for.

On 10 August, AD 70, the very day when – centuries before on 9th Av in 586 BC – the king of Babylon had burned the Temple, the temple was burned again:

> As the flames shot into the air the Jews sent up a cry that matched the calamity and dashed to the rescue, with no thought now of saving their lives or husbanding their strength; for that which hitherto they had guarded so devotedly was disappearing before their eyes.[8]

Jerusalem was totally destroyed, not one stone of the Temple was left upon another. The Jewish people were defeated, crushed under the foot of the Roman army and those who survived were taken as slaves and scattered throughout the Empire.

As Jesus stood on the Mount of Olives overlooking Jerusalem, towards the end of his earthly ministry, he knew that it was now too late for a change of attitude – "but now it is hidden from your eyes." Jesus knew the dreadful suffering and destruction that would befall Jerusalem and its people in the future. That is why he wept. No doubt the words of the Law were ringing in his ears:

> If you fully obey the LORD your God and carefully follow all his commands that I give you today, the LORD your God will set you high above all the nations on earth. All these blessings will come upon you and accompany you if you obey the LORD your God . . .
>
> However, if you do not obey the LORD your God and do not carefully follow all his commands and decrees I am giving you today, all these curses will come upon you and overtake you.
>
> (Deuteronomy 28:1–2, 15)

Jesus wept because these "brothers" of his had not responded to his teaching, they had missed their opportunity – "but now it is hidden from your eyes . . . because you did not recognize the time of God's coming to you." As we have seen, this passage by Moses from Deuteronomy is an historical summary of what has actually befallen most Jewish people from the time of Jesus weeping on the Mount of Olives until today!

The justice and mercy of God

God is both just and merciful. God's justice would be meted out for disobedience to his will and purpose.

Jeremiah describes God's justice to Israel:

> "I will repay them double for their wickedness and their sin, because they have defiled my land with the lifeless forms of their vile images and have filled my inheritance with their detestable idols."
>
> (Jeremiah 16:18)

God's mercy is also available to the penitent. Isaiah tells us that when Israel is "holy,"

> Instead of their shame
>   my people will receive a double portion,
> and instead of disgrace
>   they will rejoice in their inheritance;
> and so they will inherit a double portion in their land,
>   and everlasting joy will be theirs.
>
> (Isaiah 61:7)

Moses also declares God's mercy to the Jewish people when they return to him and promises rich blessing:

> Then the LORD your God will make you most prosperous in all the work of your hands and in the fruit of your womb, the young of your livestock and the crops of your land.
>
> (Deuteronomy 30:9)

Some teach that God has finished with the Jewish people because of their disobedience. It is clear from this portion of the Law that there is a way back to accomplishing God's purposes "to set them high above all the nations on earth." There is the promise of the restoration of their fortunes.

The Restoration of Israel

What did the prophets say? We have seen that Isaiah prophesied the return of the Jewish people from "the four corners of the earth." Isaiah 43:5–7 gives us more detail about the promised return:

> "Do not be afraid, for I am with you;
>   I will bring your children from the east
>   and gather you from the west.
> I will say to the north, 'Give them up!'
>   and to the south, 'Do not hold them back.'
> Bring my sons from afar
>   and my daughters from the ends of the earth –
> everyone who is called by my name,
>   whom I created for my glory,
>   whom I formed and made."

God has made it extremely clear that he will regather the Jewish people from all over the world at a time in history which cannot be confused with his regathering them from Babylon in the sixth century BC. Then they returned to Israel from a north-easterly direction but this second regathering will be from everywhere.

Michael Elkins, a BBC correspondent in Jerusalem, described the early years of the "ingathering":

> They came from all of Europe, they came from Russia, from the United States, South Africa, Canada, Argentina, Australia, Iraq, Turkey, Iran, Tunisia, from the Atlas Mountains in Morocco. They came from places where most people hardly imagined that there could be Jews – from India, China, from the Hadramaut of Aden,

from the mountains and jungles of Ethiopia. They came from 42 countries; from Western cultures, Eastern cultures, from tribal cultures as primitive as those of the Stone Age. They were monogamous, polygamous. They were doctors, lawyers, merchants, goldsmiths, witchdoctors, goat-herders. They hunted with blowpipes, with clubs, bows and arrows. They were Jews, all of them Jews.

They come from the North

God commands the North:

> "I will say to the north, 'Give them up!' "
>
> (Isaiah 43:6)

A command, "Give them up!" would only come if the people were being forcefully held back. A parent seeing his children bullied would shout with all the authority at his command, "Give them up! Let them go!" In this way the Father of an oppressed Jewish people is commanding their oppressor, "Give them up!"

When we look at a world map we see that Germany is north of Israel. Between 1935 and 1945 Hitler's systematic extermination program killed 6,000,000 Jewish people, of which 1,000,000 were children. When the death camps were opened in 1945 the Jewish survivors set their course for Israel. The one thing in the heart of European Jews who survived World War II was to go to their homeland, Palestine, as it was known then.

It is of further significance that when one traces the longitudinal line north through Jerusalem it passes through the former Soviet Union and particularly through the Russian capital, Moscow. By the late 1980s it was estimated that there were approximately 3,000,000 Jews in the Soviet Union. Of these, 300,000 had applied for exit visas to emigrate, but had been refused. They were known as *refuseniks*.

Many Jews who applied to emigrate to Israel were severely penalized, either by losing their jobs, or by imprisonment on trumped-up charges. Some were sent to grim labor camps in the Siberian wilderness for teaching Hebrew or for teaching the history and culture of Judaism. The release of Anatoly Shcharansky in February 1986 after twelve years of exile and imprisonment and much public protest from the West, and also that of Ida Nudal in October 1987 following a similar struggle for sixteen years, were seen not only as a victory but also as bringing hope to many Jews in the Soviet Union.

> "I will say to the north, 'Give them up!' "

Further emphasis and detail on this matter is given by Jeremiah:

> "So then, the days are coming," declares the LORD, "when people will no longer say, 'As surely as the LORD lives, who brought the Israelites up out of Egypt,' but they will say, 'As surely as the LORD lives, who brought the descendants of Israel up out of the land of the north and out of all the countries where he had banished them.' Then they will live in their own land."
>
> (Jeremiah 23:7–8)

Every year for 5,766 years, the Jewish people have remembered their deliverance from Egypt under Moses by celebrating the Passover. This event marked not only their deliverance from bondage but also their establishment as a nation.

It is almost too difficult to imagine the Jewish people annually commemorating another event which will eclipse the Passover. Yet the prophet declares that such a time will come when the Lord has brought the Jewish people home to "their own land" from "the north and out of all the countries where he has banished them."

As the result of inner turmoil and erosion within the Communist system a policy of *glasnost*, "open doors," led to the collapse of the entire Soviet system and the opportunity for Jewish people to emigrate in the late 1980s. During the 1990s some 1,000,000 Jewish people emigrated from the Soviet Union to Israel.

Reports from Christians scattered through the countries of Europe describe how both individuals and groups had prepared in various ways for migration of God's people through Europe. These people had acted upon what they believe to be the direction of God, quite independently of each other, in fact ignorant of other preparations.

Food has been stockpiled, clothes gathered, accommodation prepared for large groups of people, ships and buses purchased for their transport, and Russian Bibles distributed – all awaiting a mass movement of people!

Will these be provision for the Jewish people of this region who have not emigrated to Israel and who may find themselves trapped by anti-Semitism? The organizers believe so.

God had vividly foretold this:

"With weeping they will come,
And by supplication I will lead them;
I will make them walk by streams of waters,
On a straight path in which they will not stumble;
For I am a father to Israel,
And Ephraim is My firstborn."

(Jeremiah 31:9, NASB)

An important aspect of their preparations in Finland, Norway, Sweden, Denmark, West Germany, the Netherlands, and Belgium, is that the program has not been organized by a leader but rather, by individuals who have undertaken their projects only to hear later about others making similar preparations. Then they have realized they are a part of a large network. It is believed that this preparation is to receive an exodus of Jews from the Soviet Union – "I will say to the north, 'Give them up!' "

However passages in Ezekiel 39 indicate that the bulk of the Russian Jews will not return to Israel until after the defeat of the Russian armies on the mountains of Israel:

"On the mountains of Israel you will fall, you and all your troops and the nations with you."

(Ezekiel 39:4)

"Then they will know that I am the LORD their God, for though I sent them into exile among the nations, I will gather them to their own land, not leaving any behind."

(Ezekiel 39:28)

They come from the south

On 4 January, 1985, world headlines reported that the Israeli government had undertaken an evacuation from Ethiopia of over half of the Jewish community. About 15,000 people were snatched from a Marxist government and settled in Israel. This was called "Operation Moses." Over several years Ethiopian Jews, known sometimes as *Falashas*, had been flown out through Sudan, via Europe, to Israel.

Extraordinarily in 1991, another well-planned and executed top-secret rescue operation, "Operation Solomon," rescued another 15,000 Ethiopian Jews within a twenty-four-hour period from Addis Ababa, the Ethiopian capital. This exodus and release from Marxist oppression in a drought-stricken country where they have been held in bondage, relates closely to the words of the prophet,

> "I will say ... to the south, 'Do not hold them back!'"

I received a report from a contact in Israel who has worked among these new immigrants. This woman reported that time and time again these Ethiopian people explained that they have not left Ethiopia because of the drought – they have known drought and hardship throughout their lives – but that they believe now is time for them to come home to Israel!

One Ethiopian priest – they have priests, not rabbis, because rabbis are not mentioned in the Books of Moses (the Law of Moses) which they read, know and live by – wrote to the Chief Priest of the Jews in Jerusalem:

> Has the time arrived that we should return to you, our city, the Holy City of Jerusalem? For we are poor people and have neither prince nor prophet, and, if the time has arrived, send us a letter which will reach us to say that the time has arrived. The men of our country say, "Separate yourselves from the Christians and go to your country, Jerusalem, and reunite yourselves with your brothers."

This letter was written in 1862 and it was answered, but not for 122 years! It shows us the heart-love of these people for God and for the Land he has promised his people.

The report describes the situation:

> When the communists took over Ethiopia, at first it looked like it was going to be a very passive situation for the Ethiopian Jews. For the first time in centuries they were given land, because under the

communists everyone is equal. That was short-lived, for soon after that the communists outlawed Judaism and their condition became even worse than initially. As famine and drought increased, their neighbors blamed it upon them. We have many stories of men and women who were dragged out of their homes and were brutally beaten, torn apart and murdered, because they were blamed for the famine and drought – it was the Jews' fault, so they claimed!

Finally, they were being conscripted into the army and posted to extremely hazardous positions. So they wanted to leave Ethiopia to avoid the draft. Really and truly, the major reason for emigration is because they came to the realization that they no longer had any chance to survive as a community. They knew if they continued in Ethiopia that their Judaism and their race would be finished.

To reach Sudan they had to trek through the mountains. In Ezekiel 34:25–31 God said that he would keep them from fear of wild animals because many times lions and beasts would attack them on their journey. Most of the time they had only a little water with them. Most food or medications were stolen from them by robbers along the way. They had heard reports, from the young men, and young women, who had left several years earlier – the brave ones that made it through the mountains and wrote home – who said, "Come, there is a road that leads through the mountains into Jerusalem."

So, come they did. Again the younger ones would leave. Some of them didn't make it. Some of them were captured by soldiers. Some were sent back if they were not killed, beaten or imprisoned. Those who went back left again with larger groups: families, sometimes whole villages would pack up and leave.

When they reached Sudan they found out that they were not yet in Israel, in fact they were in a worse situation than ever. In Sudan they suffered more persecution and hatred from the Christians and the non-Jewish Ethiopians in the camps because food was so competitive, space was so competitive. Many of them tried to hide their identities as Jewish Ethiopians. Mostly they huddled together in their small huts, and every day was filled with fear. However, they did have one advantage over the other Ethiopians, they knew in their hearts they were going home. There was always the hope of Israel. So by an act of God, a real miracle, they were brought by aeroplanes to Israel.

The hope of these people is promised by God,

> "They will no longer be plundered by the nations, nor will wild animals devour them. They will live in safety, and no one will make them afraid. I will provide for them a land renowned for its crops, and they will no longer be victims of famine in the land or bear the scorn of the nations. Then they will know that I, the LORD their God, am with them and that they, the house of Israel, are my people, declares the Sovereign LORD."
>
> (Ezekiel 34:28–30)

The Jews can't be stopped from coming

Let us see how precisely the prophetic word has been fulfilled in God's regathering the Jewish people to Israel.

> "They will return from the land of the enemy.
> So there is hope for your future."
>
> (Jeremiah 31:16–17)

In October, 1981, I heard Dr M. Jaffe, then Chairman of the Union of Synagogues in Israel, describe his feelings when he visited the death camps of Europe in 1945. He said:

> If I were asked how long it would be before the Jewish people had their own homeland, I would have replied, "Over one hundred years!" A third of our people had been carefully exterminated: scientists, physicians, teachers and lawyers were hunted and killed. If you were to operate on a human body and remove one third of his organs he would die. But that is what happened to my people! Today we are a nation! We have a university in Jerusalem, in Tel Aviv, in Beer Sheva and in Haifa. It's a miracle!

A miracle it is, as the prophetic word of the Lord has been established in history.

Further verses describe the regathering after the Holocaust:

> "Return, faithless people," declares the LORD, "for I am your husband. I will choose – one from a town and two from a clan – and bring you to Zion."
>
> (Jeremiah 3:14)

"In those days the house of Judah will join the house of Israel, and together they will come from a northern land to the land I gave your forefathers as an inheritance."

(Jeremiah 3:18)

Dr Derek Prince, who lived in Jerusalem following World War II, noted that this "northern land" was the area from which many of the Jewish refugees came from, to Israel. Many times he heard survivors describe how they were the only surviving member of their Berlin family but since arriving in Israel had discovered a relative from another city, say Hanover. Many times he has heard a similar story with reference to other cities: in fact "one from a town and two from a clan" now in Israel.

Another distinct reference to a specific group of Jewish people whom God decreed would return to Israel as a part of the ingathering are from China:

"See, they will come from afar –
    some from the north, some from the west,
    some from the region of Sinim."

(Isaiah 49:12)

Lance Lambert points out that *Sinim* in Modern Hebrew means "the land of the Chinese." Jews have been reported in China as far back as the ninth century when 1,000 men, women and children migrated from either Persia or India. In the thirteenth century Marco Polo's reports indicated a sizeable Jewish community.

The rise of Nazism led 18,000 to 20,000 Jewish victims to China between 1938 and 1941, raising the population to about 30,000. Many of these Jews immigrated to Israel at the time of her rebirth.

Gentiles will prepare the way

God gives further insight into his strategy for their return after the Holocaust:

"I will beckon to the Gentiles,
    I will lift up my banner to the peoples;
they will bring your sons in their arms
    and carry your daughters on their shoulders.

Kings will be your foster fathers,
and their queens your nursing mothers."

(Isaiah 49:22–23)

During the horrors of the Holocaust many Gentiles, at great personal risk to themselves and their families, hid Jewish people from the Nazis and their informers, ensuring the preservation of Jews, and subsequently enabling them to return to Israel.

Today in Jerusalem at *Yad Vashem* (the memorial to the Holocaust) an avenue of carob trees provides access to the memorial hall. This avenue is "The Avenue of the Righteous Gentiles" – a tribute to individual people and families of Gentiles who are known to have protected Jewish lives from this demonic attempt to wipe them all from the face of the earth. A special medal has been struck by the Israeli government in recognition of the Righteous Gentile.

Each of these carob trees bears a plaque at its base naming the righteous Gentile. We find there are many names, mainly from European countries, among them Corrie ten Boom whose story is related in *The Hiding Place* and Raoul Wallenberg who mysteriously disappeared when the Russians entered Hungary after Raoul had saved at least 100,000 Hungarian Jews!

When the Nazis moved into Denmark, making the usual announcement that Jews were to wear a yellow Star of David as a means of ready identification in preparation for their extermination, King Christian declared that all the citizens of Denmark are Danes and all shall wear the yellow star. The Danish Jews, thus concealed, were remarkably protected during the whole war. God said the Gentiles would bring the Jewish people home and kings would be their *"foster fathers,"* and that is exactly how it has been.

A magic carpet

A most unusual regathering from Yemen and Iraq is foretold in these words:

In a desert land he found him,
in a barren and howling waste.
He shielded him and cared for him;
he guarded him as the apple of his eye,

like an eagle that stirs up its nest
    and hovers over its young,
that spreads its wings to catch them
    and carries them on its pinions.

(Deuteronomy 32:10–11)

In 1948 some 48,000 Yemeni Jews, from a community dating back to the times of King Solomon, began to move across the desert sands towards the British Colony of Aden. Persecuted by the Moslems they lived in a feudal-type community, cut off from the modern world of cars and airplanes and the technology we take for granted. One law demonstrating their persecution decreed that fatherless Jewish children under thirteen should be taken from their mothers and raised as Moslems in Moslem homes.

The total community moved across the large desert to Aden. A prophet from their midst centuries before predicted that they would be taken back to the Promised Land on the wings of a great silver bird before the Messiah comes. That is precisely what has happened.

In "Operation Magic Carpet" between June 1949 and June 1950, the RAF airlifted the Yemeni Jewish community to Israel in DC4 Skymaster aircraft. To the pilots' consternation some of the passengers lit fires on the aircraft to cook their food! The miracle is that they escaped from the hostile Yemeni regime.

From 1949 to the present day, about 130,000 Jews have fled to Israel from Iraq in three major movements. In the early 1940s they made the journey on foot; during the 1950s, there were a number of airlifts and, in more recent times, during the 1970s, they have traveled by donkey through Kurdistan. Some had left considerable fortunes behind, and all arrived in Israel penniless after having their goods confiscated by the Iraqi government. Mordechai Ben Porat, a former Minister without Portfolio, left Iraq as a young man in 1945. He described his adventure:

> I came overland by foot from Baghdad to Israel. I came with five of my friends from our underground Zionist movement, and it took us one month to get there. By 1949, I was a major in a combat unit in the army, and when I was released, went back to Iraq to smuggle Jews from Iraq to Persia, and from Persia to Israel. In order to get into Iraq in 1949, I entered as a Bedouin in traditional dress. In two-

and-a-half years I smuggled 15,000 Jews. I was caught four times. Others were caught and sent to the gallows. I was tortured each time, finally escaped, and came back to Israel.

In 1979, after Khomeini returned to Teheran, I was sent to Iran to help the Persian Jews. We succeeded in getting about 2,000 Jews out. Just as the revolution was taking place, the 33 of us working there were rescued. I was in the Israeli Embassy seven minutes before Khomeini's mobs stormed it; for a week afterward, we fled from house to house until we were rescued by an American jet.[1]

"Operation Babylon" took place between May 1950 and January 1952, when the American-owned Near East Transport company flew some 104,000 Jews – about 95% of Iraqi Jewry – from Iraq to Israel via Cyprus. This was twice as many as had returned from Babylon in the sixth century BC. *The New York Times* described it as "the biggest air migration in history."

Former Knesset Speaker, Shlomo Hillel, under an alias, arranged this movement. Two years earlier he had managed to smuggle 13,000 Iraqi Jews from Iraq into Iran, and from there had flown them to Israel.

Israel offers these people a home and the hope of a new life as God has declared:

> "This is what the Sovereign LORD says: I will take the Israelites out of the nations where they have gone. I will gather them from all around and bring them back into their own land. I will make them one nation in the land, on the mountains of Israel. There will be one king over all of them and they will never again be two nations or be divided into two kingdoms."
>
> (Ezekiel 37:21–22)

Considering the collapse of Iraq in the last decade, this rescue operation of Iraq's Jewish population again demonstrates the faithfulness of Israel's God in regathering his ancient people to their land.

A wilderness cultivated

God not only declared how he would regather the people to "their own land," but he foretold their activities on arrival:

They will rebuild the ancient ruins
    and restore the places long devastated;
they will renew the ruined cities
    that have been devastated for generations.

(Isaiah 61:4)

It is true that the Jews rebuilt the ancient ruins and repaired the ancient cities on their return from Babylon in the sixth century BC after the exile which lasted seventy years. This rebuilding, however, was not of cities which were "devastated for generations." The latter prophecy surely describes the second exile of the Jewish people since the destruction of Jerusalem in AD 70 and many even before then. The devastation of about forty-seven generations has been restored by those who have returned.

All over Israel the fulfillment of this prophecy is to be found, in the cities, towns and settlements. There are many examples: Bet Shemesh, Rehovot, Lod, Beer Sheva, Arad, Bet Shean, Tiberias, Ashkelon, Ashdod, Gath, Lachish, Ein Gedi, Gilo. These have all been rebuilt, either on the ruins of the former cities or beside them.

The next verse goes on to say:

Aliens will shepherd your flocks;
    foreigners will work your fields and vineyards.

(Isaiah 61:5)

Young people from all over the world – non-Jews – have gone to assist in the restoration of Israel. Even today there are many young people who visit for several months on a working program, in *kibbutzim* where they are paid pocket money, and given accommodation and food, in return for working in the *kibbutz* industries. The industries vary but generally they are agricultural (orchards, flower growing, cotton, date and banana plantations), guesthouse work, quarrying and furniture manufacturing. Kibbutz Lavi exports synagogue furniture all over the world.

Never before in Jewish history has this happened. Never before have Gentile young people wanted to assist the Jewish people in such a way. It is noteworthy that most of the help has been of an agricultural nature.

Another unique prophetic word, that could never have occurred before in Israel's history was spoken by Zephaniah:

> Gaza will be abandoned
>   and Ashkelon left in ruins.
> At midday Ashdod will be emptied
>   and Ekron uprooted . . .
> It will belong to the remnant of the house of Judah;
>   there they will find pasture.
> In the evening they will lie down
>   in the houses of Ashkelon.
> The LORD their God will care for them;
>   he will restore their fortunes.
>
> (Zephaniah 2:4, 7)

Never before have Jewish people settled in Ashkelon. From its foundation until the dispersion of the Jewish people, Ashkelon has been a Gentile city, formerly one of five Philistine cities. Ashkelon became a city in 1955. It was built from money sent from the Jewish community of South Africa and today is an attractive Jewish seaside city.

Costly labor

It was essential for the survival of the first settlers that the land should be quickly made productive. High prices were paid for swamp and stony land:

> "Fields will be bought in this land of which you say, 'It is a desolation, without man or beast; it is given into the hand of the Chaldeans.'"
>
> (Jeremiah 32:43, NASB)

Their task was arduous and the toll upon their life was high. Many returned to their former land. Numbers suffered malarial fever and died. But many persisted and through their sheer hard work saw a dramatic change from thorny wilderness and marshes to a thriving agricultural economy. The following description shows us what was encountered by these pioneers around 1900:

... At the turn of the century, Palestine was no longer the land of milk and honey described by the Bible, but a poor Ottoman province, a semi-desert covered by more thorns than flowers. The Mediterranean coast and all the southern half of the country were sand, and the rare marshy plains were fens of the malaria which decimated the sparse, semi-nomadic population, clinging to slopes and bare hills.[2]

We add to this picture the vivid description of Mark Twain in 1869:

Of all the lands there are for dismal scenery, I think Palestine must be the prince. It sits in sackcloth and ashes. Over it broods the spell of a curse that has withered its fields and fettered its energies. The hills are barren, they are dull of color, they are unpicturesque in shape. The valleys are unsightly deserts, fringed with feeble vegetation. The Dead Sea and Sea of Galilee sleep in the midst of a vast stretch of hill and plain where the eyes rest upon no pleasant tint, no striking object, no soft picture. One may ride ten miles, and not see ten human beings. A blistered, naked, treeless land.[3]

Although the work was hard and most of the Jewish emigrants were not manual laborers but professional men used to clerical and office work, including doctors, lawyers and teachers, the dramatic change in the land in a relatively short time is recorded by Winston Churchill in his comments following his visit to Palestine in 1921:

Anyone who has seen the work of the Jewish colonies which have been established during the past 20 or 30 years in Palestine will be struck by the enormously productive results which have been achieved. I had the opportunity of visiting the colony of Rishon-le-Zion about 12 miles from Jaffa, and there, from the most inhospitable soil, surrounded on every side by barrenness and the most miserable form of cultivation, I was driven into a fertile and thriving country estate. The scanty soil gave place to good crops and good cultivation, then to vineyards and finally to the most beautiful, luxurious orange groves, all created in 20 or 30 years by the Jewish community who live there.[4]

God announced very clearly his earnest desire to take Jewish people home to their land which they would buy and receive the title deeds:

> " 'I will rejoice over them to do them good, and I will faithfully plant them in this land with all My heart and with all My soul ... Men will buy fields for money, sign and seal deeds, and call in witnesses in the land of Benjamin, in the environs of Jerusalem, in the cities of Judah, in the cities of the hill country, in the cities of the lowland and in the cities of the Negev; for I will restore their fortunes,' declares the LORD."
>
> (Jeremiah 32:41, 44, NASB)

I have looked in wonder at the orchards of oranges, plantations of ripening bananas, acres of apples, avocado pears and dates, the long stretches of cotton fields, valleys of wheat and barley, and even at the desert producing lettuce, tomato, cucumber and capsicum all the year round. As well as a large-scale agricultural industry there is also the raising of cattle as healthy as any bred in the West. All of this is packed into a very compact space.

Agricultural exports have grown from $130 million in 1970 to $3.3 billion in 2000 with 20% exported. Relative to the size of her population, Israel has more engineers, and sees more scientific articles published, than any other country in the world (Israel has 135 engineers per 10,000 people; the US has 85). However, the stimulus for the industry's growth has been national survival, both military and economic.

In 2000 there were 160 biotechnology and 400 medical device companies in Israel, compared with 25 in 1988, employing 4,000 people and generating $800 million in turnover. Investment in biotechnology has been growing steadily, reaching a total of $1.7 billion in 2000, including about $200 million in venture capital. In 2000, exports of high-tech products accounted for 55% of all exports, up from 23% in 1991. Exports of electronics communications components, electronic components, medical equipment and software and IT products peaked at over $13 billion.

In 2000, 195,000 people were employed in the various high-tech sectors, compared with 148,870 people a decade earlier. Demand for engineers and technicians is estimated at 2,000–3,000 a year.

National expenditure on civilian research and development (R & D) amounted to NIS 23.9 billion (over $5 billion) in 2001, 4.2% of GDP. Spending on civilian R & D has remained stable despite the recession since 2000, although the focus on research has been shifting from Internet and software to new fields such as biotechnology and nanotechnology. Chemical and chemical products, electronic components, communications components, supervision, monitoring, and medical equipment accounted for 87% of industrial R & D expenditure in 2001.

Israel issues the largest number of companies in the US after the US itself and Canada. According to the Bank of Israel, investment by foreign residents totaled $9.4 billion in 2000, up from $3 billion in 1995. Israeli companies raised $4.2 billion overseas in 2000, mostly on NASDAQ, but also including $800 million raised on European exchanges.

God had decreed this remarkable restoration of the land and growth of productivity:

> "But you, O mountains of Israel, will produce branches and fruit for my people Israel, for they will soon come home. I am concerned for you and will look on you with favor; you will be plowed and sown, and I will multiply the number of people upon you, even the whole house of Israel. The towns will be inhabited and the ruins rebuilt. I will increase the number of men and animals upon you, and they will be fruitful and become numerous. I will settle people on you as in the past and will make you prosper more than before."
>
> (Ezekiel 36:8–11)

The ingathering of the exiles

The Declaration of Independence proclaims: "The State of Israel will be open to Jewish immigration and the Ingathering of the Exiles." Since the rebirth of Israel, the population has grown nearly tenfold, from 650,000 in May 1948 to over 6,276,883 today; almost half the increase came from Jewish people emigrating to Israel, that is, *aliya*.[6] God said, "I will multiply the number of people upon you."

The Reverend David Pawson undertook a study of the rainfall in Israel during the last one hundred years. On graphing the figures he discovered that the periods when larger numbers of Jewish people made *aliya* were marked by greater rainfall and that this was specially pronounced in 1948, the year Israel was reborn.[7]

Through the terraced slopes of the Judean hill country, cropping acres of grapes, the shepherds lead their flocks of sheep and herds of goats to good pasture:

> "Again you will plant vineyards
>   on the hills of Samaria;
> the farmers will plant them
>   and enjoy their fruit . . .
>   they will rejoice in the bounty of the LORD –
> the grain, the new wine and the oil,
>   the young of the flocks and herds.
> They will be like a well-watered garden,
>   and they will sorrow no more."
>
> (Jeremiah 31:5, 12)

This restoration is not yet complete but moves towards total fulfillment. God is in the process of restoring hope:

> "They will come and shout for joy on the heights of Zion."
>
> (Jeremiah 31:12)

This has already happened as oppressed Jews have arrived home, but this is just the beginning.

A restored language for a reborn nation

The traffic officer blew a sharp blast on his whistle. He raced up to me and cautioned me but I didn't understand a word he said; he was speaking in Hebrew.

One of my first impressions of Israel was of hearing the people speaking, shouting and singing in Hebrew. The street signs are in Hebrew. Advertising posters are in Hebrew. Conversation is in Hebrew. Newspapers are printed in Hebrew. Every settlement of any size has a Ben Yehuda street.

Eliezer Ben Yehuda was the man almost solely responsible for the restoration of this ancient language. Born in Lithuania in 1858, he was educated at the Sorbonne in Paris. Eliezer struggled with the

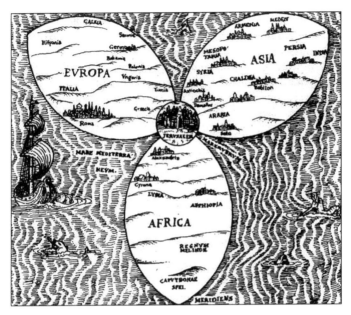

Map showing Jerusalem at the centre of the world: 1580.
"This is what the Sovereign LORD *says: This is Jerusalem, which I have set in the center of nations, with countries all around her"* (Ezekiel 5:5).

question that if freedom could be enjoyed by the population of the Balkan nations, why could the Jewish people not enjoy that freedom?

Ben Yehuda wrote:

> In those days it was as if the heavens had suddenly opened and a clear incandescent light flashed before my eyes, and a mighty inner voice suddenly sounded in my ears – the renaissance of Israel on its own ancestral soil.[8]

In 1880 he wrote to a young lady, who later became his wife:

> I have decided that in order to have our own land and political life, it is also necessary that we have a language to hold us together. That language is Hebrew, but not the Hebrew of the rabbis and scholars. We must have a Hebrew language in which we can conduct the business of life. It will not be easy to revive a language dead for so long a time.[9]

Eliezer's was not an easy task. He was warned against traveling to primitive Palestine leaving the comforts of Europe. His doctor opposed Eliezer's intention because he had contracted tuberculosis. Frail in body but extremely strong in spirit he settled for a mean life in Jerusalem where he began his lifetime's work.

Hebrew had not been spoken for about 2,000 years as an everyday language. It had been preserved and used for worship in the synagogues and for studying the Scriptures, similar to the Roman Catholic practice of using Latin for worship. The task involved a systematic construction of new words from modern vocabulary using linguistic patterns from the ancient language.

As an example to the Jewish State he decided that his children should not hear any language spoken other than Hebrew. Theirs was to be a model Hebrew home. That is exactly what the Ben Yehudas achieved.

Eliezer taught Hebrew as he wrote a dictionary recording the words he constructed and their meaning. He began to publish a newspaper which, in the early years, grew to a circulation of about two hundred. In the newspaper he explained the new Hebrew words he had created as well as writing articles encouraging the formation of a Jewish homeland, giving ideas of how it should be formed and guidelines for the development of the settlements.

Opposition to his work was strong and readily forthcoming. The orthodox Jewish communities were outraged at his progressive views and stoned his office. So angry were they with him that they excommunicated him and refused to bury his wife when she died in 1891, leaving Eliezer to cope with five young children.

Undaunted, Ben Yehuda pressed on with his work. Due to the vision and efforts of this one man, suffering from a then-incurable disease, and assailed on all sides, Jews now spoke, wrote and read a revived national language. There was a Hebrew press and flourishing Hebrew literature. In 1916 the census showed that 40% of the Jewish population spoke Hebrew as their first language.

In 1922 Eliezer Ben Yehuda died. Three days of national mourning were declared. As his body was taken to its last resting place on the Mount of Olives, 30,000 people followed. With the proclamation of the State of Israel in 1948, Hebrew was declared the official language.

No other ancient language has ever been revived, let alone as the everyday language of its people, just as no other people have ever been dispersed around the nations, maintained their identity and been regathered as a nation in their homeland.

> "At that time I will change the speech of my returning people to pure Hebrew so that all can worship the Lord together."
>
> (Zephaniah 3:9, TLB)

Exiled natural life ingathered

When many trees are planted on barren land, not only do they provide shelter, but they also cause increased rainfall. Israel has planted nearly 200 million trees in the past eighty years. The climate has changed and these shady trees have attracted birds and insects.

Lance Lambert gives an excellent account of the natural life in Israel in his book *The Uniqueness of Israel*. Today some 450 species of birds can be found in Israel, including eagles, ravens, storks, sparrows, rooks, gulls, bee-eaters and even pelicans.

Some of these are resident birds while others are migratory. Because Israel links three continents, large flocks of birds travel through in their season. The Hula Valley in north Galilee provides a glorious breeding ground. Flocks of hundreds of birds flying in formation in Israel's clear skies are an awe-inspiring sight.

Although Israel does not today have all the biblical animals, the traveler sees foxes, lynxes, ibex, gazelles, wild goats, jackals, wolves and there are reported sightings of leopards, hyenas and wild boar.

During the past ten years several wild animal farms have been established. Alligators are now ranched on the Golan and ostriches herded on the Golan and in the Negev. Animal husbandry has crossed the wild ibex with the domestic goat, creating the "ya-ez," a hardy source of animal protein.

General Avraham Yoffe, the first Director of Israel's Nature Reserves Authority set about searching the world for animal species that once lived in Israel but have since been wiped out. Wild asses were located in the Copenhagen Zoo. Roe deer were sourced in a Dutch shooting reserve. Addax antelope were found in Chicago. All of these species were acquired and returned to the home of their ancestors.

The Mesopotamian fallow deer, which once inhabited Israel's northern woodlands, were air-lifted out of Iran in December 1978. White oryx antelopes were indirectly acquired from the personal stock of King Faisal of Saudi Arabia.

Many of these animals were brought home to Israel, and released into appropriate reserves – the desert animals to Eilat and the forest animals to Carmel, near Haifa. At these special reserves, the animals were released into protected sections of their natural habitats. They were encouraged to form natural herds, to interact socially, to eat natural foods, to adapt to natural parasites and to be wary of predators.

How long, O Lord, how long?

We could continue to record the remarkable events describing how the people were regathered and taken to Israel, and how they have developed the land of their inheritance. The question on the lips of some Israelis is, "How long will we have this land as our possession? How long are we going to own it this time?"

Until a person has lived in Israel, one does not realize the significance of that question. It is true that many Israelis have the attitude, "Nobody will take it from us again!" An admirable sentiment, often expressed with total conviction. Yet living in a land constantly alerted by the sonic booms of aircraft flying overhead, continually harassed by attacks from surrounding neighbors and an ever-growing incidence of terrorism, the question is well founded, "How long will we have our land?"

To better understand this question we need to know something of the Muslim hatred for the Jewish people and Israel. The hatred of the Jews instilled in the minds of the millions of people populating the surrounding Muslim countries is well summed up in this quotation from an official Egyptian school-book for nine-year olds:

> O mother of Israel! Dry your tears, your children's blood which is being spilled in the desert will produce naught but thorn and wormwood. Wipe off your blood, O mother of Israel, have mercy and spare the desert your filthy blood. Remove your slain, for their flesh has caused the ravens bellyache and their stink causes rheum.

Cry, O mother of Israel, and wail. Let every house be the Wailing Wall of the Jews . . . [10]

Referring to material like this, the Syrian Minister of Education in 1968 said, "The hatred which we indoctrinate into the minds of our children from their birth is sacred."

The reality of this hatred has been suffered by Israel since before its Independence in 1948. Prior to Independence, neighboring Arab nations boycotted trade with Israel and disenfranchised international companies trading with Israel. Upon declaration of Independence, the six neighboring Arab nations attacked with the cry, "We will stop when we have pushed you into the sea!" In their determination they continue to strive for that goal.

The Oslo Peace Process which began in 1993 was supposed to halt the terror that had become part of Israeli life. It resulted in Gaza and Jericho being handed over to the Palestinian Authority (PA); by 1995 the PA had the West Bank and Hebron in 1999. The *intifada* (uprising) which began in September 2000 saw the escalation of terrorism against Israel. Palestinian suicide bombers took the lives of almost seven hundred Israeli civilians in bus bombings, café and hotel bombings and mall bombings. Added to these are the hundreds of maimed civilians.

Israeli troops who had remained to keep stability in Gaza and to protect some 8,200 Israelis living in Gush Katif among 1.3 million Palestinians, withdrew in August 2005. The Israeli civilians were evacuated and re-housed outside the Gaza Strip. This move was interpreted by the fundamentalist Muslims, especially the *Hamas* (an Arabic acronym for "Islamic Resistance Movement" founded by Islamic extremists in the Gaza Strip in 1988), as Israeli weakness.

Lawlessness was soon apparent in the then Palestinian-controlled Gaza, fueled by the illegal importing of arms. The fundamentalist Hamas terrorist group used the opportunity to gather support against the ruling PA Fatah party accused of major corruption. Hamas won the general election in January 2006 by a landslide majority of seventy-six seats.

Hamas ideology combines pan-Arab religious and fundamentalist principles with radical Palestinian aims. It insists that "all of Palestine – from the [Jordan] river to the [Mediterranean] sea is holy Arab territory" and seeks the "liberation" of all of that territory, not just the "West Bank" and Gaza – but all of it, including Tel Aviv and Haifa and, of course, Jerusalem. The immutable aim of the movement is *"that the name of Israel be remembered no more."*

The Psalmist foresaw this hatred:

> O God, do not keep silent;
>> be not quiet, O God, be not still.
> See how your enemies are astir,
>> how your foes rear their heads.
> With cunning they conspire against your people;
>> they plot against those you cherish.
> "Come," they say, "let us destroy them as a nation,
>> that the name of Israel be remembered no more."

(Psalm 83:1–4)

Although this hatred which is expressed towards Israel and the Jewish people is so grievously painful, the hope for Israel and her future lies securely in the God of Israel who declared:

> "I will plant Israel in their own land,
>> never again to be uprooted
>> from the land I have given them,"
>>> says the LORD your God.

(Amos 9:15)

Jubilee

"Each of you shall return to his possession, and each of you shall
return to his family."

(Leviticus 25:10, NKJV)

God means business. He says what he will do and he does it! In what
is probably the most quoted passage concerning Israel's restoration
– Jeremiah 31 – God says that his covenant with Israel and her
descendants could cease only if the laws which govern the sun,
moon, stars and tides ceased to operate according to his design.

To reinforce his point, God says he could reject Israel and her
descendants if it were possible for us to measure the heavens or to
search out the earth's foundations. The fact is clear that God will
not abandon his created order and neither will we search out the
foundations of the earth.

"The apple of his eye"

With such an enduring love for the Jewish people it is little wonder
that God calls them "the apple of his eye" (Deuteronomy 32:10;
Lamentations 2:18, KJV; Zechariah 2:8).

The pupil of the eye which is described as "the apple of the eye"
is the most sensitive external part of the body. Because it is so
precious our Creator has given it special protection. Firstly, the eye
is set in a socket. Rarely is the eyeball damaged by a hit in the face
as this socket protects it. Then, above the eye grows the hairs of
the eyebrow, a hedge to protect the vision from the effects of
perspiration. Eyelashes protect from dust and fine particles and the

eyelids cover our eyes when we blink. However, if fine particles do enter, the eye weeps tears to wash away the foreign matter.

What protection for such an important organ of our body! The Jewish people are equally important to God and similarly have been remarkably protected. As we have seen some of the organized attempts in history to destroy this people, we have to conclude they are "the apple of his eye" – how else could they still exist?

The sign of the fig tree

Once the wiry branches of a fig tree begin to show their green shoots, it is not long before the canopy of the tree is outstretched and life is restored to the once-dormant tree. Birds and insects are attracted and a community has been reborn.

Jesus spoke of this:

> "Look at the fig-tree and all the trees. When they sprout leaves, you
> can see for yourselves and know that summer is near. Even so, when
> you see these things happening, you know that the kingdom of God
> is near. I tell you the truth, this generation [race] will certainly not
> pass away until all these things have happened. Heaven and earth
> will pass away, but my words will never pass away."
>
> (Luke 21:29–33)

On the occasion when Jesus spoke these words, the disciples were admiring the temple stones. They had asked for signs indicating when the destruction of the temple, which Jesus had prophesied, would take place. In his reply, Jesus listed many events, concluding with this reference to the fig tree and the trees. The fig tree coming into leaf is to be a sign of great importance!

Almost throughout Scripture the fig tree has symbolized the nation of Israel. We are instructed to look at the nation of Israel in the setting of the nations of the world. In the nineteenth century, life began to be restored to the land known today as Israel. At last the fig tree was sprouting leaves.

Jesus said that the sign is to announce the imminence of "summer" and "the kingdom of God." The seasons are often referred to in Scripture and summer is known for its precious "summer fruits."

The year of Jubilee

The full harvesting season, of course follows and there is an implication here of a fuller-than-ever manifestation of the power of God – "You know that the kingdom of God is near."

The crowning seventh and final festival of Israel's "feasts of the LORD" is Succot, the feast of Tabernacles, also known as "The Feast of the Ingathering" (Exodus 23:16; Leviticus 23:34–43). Did not Paul underline, "How much greater riches will their [Israel's] fullness bring!" (Romans 11:12)?

To ensure that we do recognize these signs, God has fulfilled them in an unmistakable remarkable way totally in agreement with his Word. At the conclusion of the Basel conference in 1897, Theodore Herzl wrote in his diary:

> At Basel I founded the Jewish State. If I said this aloud, it would be greeted with worldwide derision. In five years, perhaps, and certainly in fifty, everyone will see it.[1]

At this conference of a nation without a land came forth a national flag and a national anthem, *Hatikvah* – the Hope! Of even greater significance is the fact that fifty years from that date, on 29 November, 1947, the United Nations voted on the right of the Jewish people to have a homeland. A few months later, on 14 May, 1948, Israel was proclaimed a State.

The Law of God defines a fifty-year period as a Jubilee:

> Consecrate the fiftieth year and proclaim liberty throughout the land to all its inhabitants. It shall be a jubilee for you; each one of you is to return to his family property and each to his own clan.
> (Leviticus 25:10)

The command of God that people were to return to their land and that families were to be reunited was fulfilled in 1948. In spite of the British restriction on Jewish people returning to their homeland, a great flood of people including at least 700,000 forced out of the Arab lands came home. Family members were reunited in the land of Israel following painful years of separation. The rebirth of the State of Israel was a fulfillment of the law of Jubilee.

O Jerusalem

But that is not all. To be doubly sure that we recognize the sign of the fig tree putting forth its leaves, God fulfilled another Jubilee. This time it concerned Jerusalem. General Edmund Allenby led the allied army into the Ottoman Empire during 1917. With a remarkable dignity and humility he took Jerusalem without a shot being fired.

Menache Eliachar, a witness, described the event:

> Jerusalem was attacked most severely on Saturday, but by Saturday night all was quiet. We managed to see the Turkish soldiers, whose retreat, incidentally was remarkable. The Turkish soldiers did not riot at all – all they asked for as they retreated was *ekmek* – bread.

Jerusalem's Mayor, Hussein Salim al-Husseini, was leaving the city, waving a white flag, when two sergeants met him. There are various stories of why they had strayed and what they were looking for. Eliachar says:

> They were informed that a surrender was taking place, in which the keys of the city were to be handed over to the conquering army. But the first thing they asked us was whether we had any matches. This scene remains engraved in my memory to this day. It was one of the most difficult moments – for ten days, they had cigarettes, but no matches, and they found no way of smoking. To see these two soldiers, ignoring the events around them, just to see them smoking is something I'm unable to forget.[2]

General Allenby reached the Jaffa Gate and dismounted, desiring to enter the Holy City of Jerusalem as a pilgrim, not as a conqueror. He arrived on the first day of Hanukkah and the Jews of Jerusalem were moved to powerful emotion.

Victoria Valero described the arrival of the 60th Division on 9 December, 1917:

> We looked westward and saw a white horse and people applauding. The entire city had already turned out on the sidewalks. General Allenby entered, followed by eight riders on red horses, and behind

them more horses and more officers, greeted by applause and cries
of welcome: Everyone was shouting "Welcome." [3]

Rivka Amdursky-Buxbaum added:

> They were so polite; they shared their rations, biscuits and every-
> thing. It was so joyous and happy. I saw Allenby on a beautiful
> horse ... They told us he was a king. And everyone said: "Let's all
> go out and see the king." It seemed to me that perhaps he was the
> Messiah ... They indeed told us that it was Redemption – not only
> the miracle of Hanukka but Redemption. We knew that it was so
> and hoped that we would be redeemed.

Rivka continues her description as Allenby entered the Jaffa Gate of
the Old City of Jerusalem:

> They opened the great gate for him, which was always closed
> especially during wartime: they'd closed it at night and opened it
> again in the morning. But on that day, it was wide open. When I
> saw him ... I thought perhaps it was the Messiah! So respectable,
> so upright, so handsome. People cheered and applauded. We knew
> the Redemption had come! How we yearned to be redeemed! [4]

Aircraft of the RAF 14 Squadron flew over the city dropping leaflets
commanding the people to surrender. This was written in Arabic.
Allenby's name resembled that of the Islamic deity and many
understood Allah had commanded submission. Some 2,500 years
earlier Isaiah had said:

> As birds flying, so will the LORD of hosts defend Jerusalem;
> defending he will deliver it; and passing over he will preserve it.
>
> (Isaiah 31:5, KJV)

The squadron's motto: "I spread my wings to keep it."

General Allenby accepted the handing over of Jerusalem on
11 December, 1917, the day the Jewish people were commemorating the deliverance of Jerusalem from a previous occupation, that of
Antiochus Epiphanes. It was the festival of Hanukkah, or as named
in the Gospel of John (10:22), the feast of Dedication (*Hanukkah* is

The Lion of Judah is the symbol of Jerusalem, the capital of Israel. This cartoon commemorating the 3,000th anniversary of Jerusalem demonstrates the aggression of various claimants of Jerusalem: Hamas, the Palestinian Authority, Islamic Jihad and the European Community.

"The LORD .... declares: 'I am going to make Jerusalem a cup that sends all the surrounding peoples reeling. Judah will be besieged as well as Jerusalem. On that day, when all the nations of the earth are gathered against her, I will make Jerusalem an immovable rock for all the nations. All who try to move it will injure themselves'" (Zechariah 12:2-3).

the Hebrew for Dedication), a feast of freedom. Many Jews believed Allenby to be the Messiah, so significant was the event.

On 7 June, 1967, during the Six Day War, the ancient city of Jerusalem was restored to Jewish sovereignty. Jerusalem had been under Jordanian occupation from 1948 and no Jewish person was permitted in that area. This meant many were pushed out of their homes and no Jew was able to worship at the Western Wall, the retaining foundation wall of the temple site.

To the Jewish person Jerusalem is the most sacred place in the world. Ever since the destruction of Jerusalem in AD 70, Jewish people have lamented their separation from Jerusalem. This is so vividly presented in Psalm 137 which has been sung often by Jewish people, especially during the last two thousand years:

> By the rivers of Babylon we sat and wept
>   when we remembered Zion...
> How can we sing the songs of the LORD
>   while in a foreign land?
> If I forget you, O Jerusalem,
>   may my right hand forget its skill.
> May my tongue cling to the roof of my mouth
>   if I do not remember you,
> if I do not consider Jerusalem
> my highest joy.
>
> (Psalm 137:1, 4–6)

God commanded:

> Pray for the peace of Jerusalem:
>   "May those who love you be secure.
> May there be peace within your walls
>   and security within your citadels."
>
> (Psalm 122:6–7)

And so they did. They prayed for Jerusalem regularly for two thousand years! The Jewish people scattered around the world concluded the observance of their festivals with the words:

> *Leshana Habaah Biyerushalaim* – "Next year in Jerusalem"

At the celebration of every Jewish marriage the Jewish bridegroom breaks a glass under his foot as an expression of grief for the desolation of Jerusalem and the dispersion of his people.

The yearning to be in Jerusalem was expressed in historic betrothal contracts written in the home of Rabbi Levi Isaac of Berditchev. It was stipulated:

> The wedding will, God willing, take place in the Holy City of Jerusalem. But if, Heaven forbid, because of our sins, the Messiah will not have come by then, the wedding will take place in Berditchev.

Jewish commitment to Jerusalem is portrayed in the words of Rabbi Jacob Emden in 1745:

> Every Jew has to promise himself to go and live in the Land of Israel and to yearn for the privilege of praying there before God's Sanctuary; and even though it is destroyed, the Divine Presence has not left it. So hear me brothers and friends, remember Jerusalem ... and do not, Heaven forbid, think of settling outside the Land. It seems that to us that as soon as we enjoy some tranquility outside the Land of Israel, it is as though we have found another Land of Israel and another Jerusalem, and that is why all these evils have come upon us.

In 1967, while fighting for her life, the Israeli government warned King Hussein of Jordan to keep out of the war. Hussein ignored the advice and it cost him Judea-Samaria, often known as the West Bank, which included the Old City of Jerusalem. The battle for Jerusalem was over! One newspaper reported the event as follows:

Premier, Chief Rabbis Pray at Western Wall
Mr. Levi Eshkol yesterday took part in afternoon prayers at the Western Wall. He was the first leader of a Jewish Government to visit the site of the Temple since its loss 1,897 years ago.

The Prime Minister, robustly cheered by the tired but elated boys and men who had freed the Holy City, was accompanied by the two Chief Rabbis.

Earlier in the day, as soon as the road to the Wall was clear, the Chief Chaplain to the Forces, Aluf Shlomo Goren, came at an eager run, carrying a *Sefer* Torah. He recited a traditional (*sheheheyanu*) blessing, congratulating himself and all Israel, both within the Land and without, on having the privilege of establishing the age-old hope – and without their right hand having lost its cunning, or skill.

The Defence Minister, Rav-Aluf Moshe Dayan, came soon after and there he made his declaration: "We will not give up this place."[5]

The people had been returned to their land and families were reunited. The reunification of Jerusalem fulfilled the law of Jubilee. The God of Israel again put his seal upon this historic event which no man was able to prevent nor to reverse. God spoke through Zechariah concerning Jerusalem:

> This is what the LORD Almighty says, "I am very jealous for Zion; I am burning with jealousy for her ... I will return to Zion and dwell in Jerusalem. Then Jerusalem will be called the City of Truth, and the mountain of the LORD Almighty will be called the Holy Mountain ... Once again men and women of ripe old age will sit in the streets of Jerusalem, each with cane in hand because of his age. The city streets will be filled with boys and girls playing there ... I will save my people from the countries of the east and the west. I will bring them back to live in Jerusalem; they will be my people, and I will be faithful and righteous to them as their God."
>
> (Zechariah 8:2–4, 7–8)

"The fig tree and all the trees"

As the Holy Spirit has accelerated his work in the Jewish people, God's first covenant people, so he is dealing with the nations from whence the Jews have returned. Israel is a specific tree among the trees, or nations.

The fig tree is often linked in the Bible with the vine, both being numbered among the "seven fruits" and symbolizing prosperity and peace. The vine is also used as a symbol of the Church, and the fruit of the vine, grapes, are also among the "seven fruits." Throughout the nations are scattered the other covenant people of God, the Church, and while the Holy Spirit has been touching the hearts of Jewish people he has also been restoring the Church.

Since the turn of the century, as her people are being restored to their inheritance (the Land of Israel), so we have witnessed revivals among the nations. The emergence of evangelistic ministries such as Billy Graham and Oral Roberts emphasizing the need to be born again, has coincided with the rebirth of the State of Israel. Furthermore, there has been an unprecedented move of God in almost all third-world countries. Along with the restoration of Jerusalem to rightful ownership is a parallel deepening of faith within the Church. The fig tree and the vine cannot be separated but the Church cannot produce the fruit that God is requiring from Israel.

Can a fig tree bear olives, or a grape-vine bear figs?

(James 3:12)

These are signs of a move towards a day when the fullness of God's purposes will be known, as both Israel and the Church, the fig tree and the vine, receive their full inheritance.

> The trees are bearing their fruit;
>> the fig tree and the vine yield their riches.
> Be glad, O people of Zion,
>> rejoice in the LORD your God,
> for he has given you
>> the teacher for righteousness.
> He sends you abundant showers,
>> both autumn and spring rains, as before.
> The threshing-floors will be filled with grain;
>> the vats will overflow with new wine and oil.

(Joel 2:22–24)

The Uniqueness of Israel

He [God] has done this for no other nation.

(Psalm 147:20)

Distinguishing achievements

Israel, the 100th smallest country, with less than 1/1000th of the world's population, can lay claim to the following achievements:

- Israel's $100 billion economy is larger than all of its immediate neighbors combined.
- Israel has the highest ratio of university degrees to the population in the world. Israel produces more scientific papers per capita than any other nation by a large margin – 109 per 10,000 people – as well as one of the highest per-capita rates of patents filed. Twenty-four per cent of Israel's workforce holds university degrees, ranking third in the industrialized world, after the United States and Holland and 12 per cent hold advanced degrees. Israel leads the world in the number of scientists and technicians in the workforce, with 145 per 10,000, as opposed to 85 in the US, over 70 in Japan, and less than 60 in Germany. With over 25% of its work force employed in technical professions, Israel places first in this category as well.
- In proportion to its population, Israel has the largest number of startup companies in the world. In absolute terms, Israel has the largest number of startup companies than any other country in the world, except the US (3,500 companies mostly in hi-tech). With more than 3,000 high-tech companies and

startups, Israel has the highest concentration of hi-tech companies in the world – apart from the Silicon Valley, US.

- Israel is ranked number two in the world for venture capital funds right behind the US. Outside the United States and Canada, Israel has the largest number of NASDAQ-listed companies. Israel has the highest average living standard in the Middle East. The per-capita income in 2000 was over $17,500, exceeding that of the UK.

- On a per-capita basis, Israel has the largest number of biotech startups. Israel has the third highest rate of entrepreneurship – and the highest rate among women and among people over fifty-five – in the world. The cell phone was developed in Israel by Israelis working in the Israeli branch of Motorola, which has its largest development center in Israel. Most of the Windows NT and XP operating systems were developed by Microsoft-Israel. The Pentium MMX Chip technology was designed in Israel at Intel. Both the Pentium-4 micro-processor and the Centrino processor were entirely designed, developed and produced in Israel. The Pentium micro-processor in your computer was most likely made in Israel.

- Israel has the highest percentage in the world of home computers per capita.

- Voice mail technology was developed in Israel. Both Microsoft and Cisco built their only R & D facilities outside the US in Israel.

- The technology for the AOL Instant Messenger ICQ was developed in 1996 by four young Israelis.

- Israel has the fourth largest air force in the world (after the US, Russia and China). In addition to a large variety of other aircraft, Israel's air force has an aerial arsenal of over 250 F-16 planes. This is the largest fleet of F-16 aircraft outside of the US.

- According to industry officials, Israel designed the airline industry's most impenetrable flight security. US officials now look (finally) to Israel for advice on how to handle airborne security threats.

- In 1984 and 1991, through Operation Solomon, Israel airlifted a total of 22,000 Ethiopian Jews at risk in Ethiopia, to safety in Israel. Relative to its population, Israel is the largest immigrant-absorbing nation on earth. Hundreds of thousands have emigrated from the former Soviet Union. Immigrants come in search of democracy, religious freedom, and economic opportunity.

- When the US Embassy in Nairobi, Kenya was bombed in 1998, Israeli rescue teams were on the scene within a day – and saved three victims from the rubble.

- Israel was the first nation in the world to adopt the Kimberly process, an international standard that certifies diamonds as "conflict free."

- Israel has the world's second highest per-capita number of new books.

- Israel is the only country in the world that entered the twenty-first century with a net gain in its number of trees, made more remarkable because this was achieved in an area considered mainly desert.

- The Middle East has been growing date palms for centuries. The average tree is about 18–20 feet tall and yields about 38 pounds of dates a year. Israeli date trees are now yielding 400 pounds per year and are short enough to be harvested from the ground or a short ladder.

- Israel has more museums per capita than any other country.

- In medicine, Israeli scientists developed the first fully-computerized, no-radiation, diagnostic instrumentation for breast cancer. Israel's Given Imaging developed the first ingestible video camera, so small it fits inside a pill, which is used to view the small intestine from the inside for cancer and digestive disorders.

- An Israeli company developed a computerized system for ensuring proper administration of medications, thus removing human error from medical treatment. (Every year in US hospitals 7,000 patients die from treatment mistakes.)

- Researchers in Israel developed a new device that directly helps the heart pump blood, an innovation with the potential to save lives among those with heart failure. The new device is synchronized with a camera that helps doctors diagnose the heart's mechanical operations through a sophisticated system of sensors. A new acne treatment developed in Israel, the Clear Light device, produces a high-intensity, ultraviolet-light-free, narrow-band blue light that causes acne bacteria to self-destruct – all without damaging surrounding skin or tissue.

- An Israeli company was the first to develop and install a large-scale solar-powered and fully functional electricity generating plant, in southern California's Mojave Desert.
- Israel is the only liberal democracy in the Middle East.
- When Golda Meir was elected Prime Minister of Israel in 1969, she became the world's second elected female leader in modern times.

All the above achievements occurred while Israel was engaged in regular wars with an implacable enemy that seeks its destruction. Israel has achieved these things despite having an economy continuously under strain by having to spend more per capita on its own protection than any other country on earth.

Exclusive promises by an exclusive God

This is what the Sovereign LORD says

"This is what the Sovereign LORD says to these bones: I will make breath enter you, and you will come to life ... O my people, I am going to open your graves and bring you up from them; I will bring you back to the land of Israel."

(Ezekiel 37:5, 12)

Life from the dead

For if their rejection is the reconciliation of the world, what will their acceptance be but life from the dead?

(Romans 11:15)

Your dead will live;
    their bodies will rise.
You who dwell in the dust,
    wake up and shout for joy.
Your dew is like the dew of the morning;
    the earth will give birth to her dead.

(Isaiah 26:19)

An immovable rock

"On that day, when all the nations of the earth are gathered against her, I will make Jerusalem an immovable rock for all the nations. All who try to move it will injure themselves."

(Zechariah 12:3)

A royal diadem

You will be a crown of splendor in the LORD's hand,
   a royal diadem in the hand of your God.

(Isaiah 62:3)

The ruin restored

"In that day I will restore
   David's fallen tent.
I will repair its broken places,
   restore its ruins,
   and build it as it used to be,
so that they may possess the remnant of Edom
   and all the nations that bear my name,"
            declares the LORD,
               who will do these things.

(Amos 9:11–12)

"I will return to Zion and dwell in Jerusalem. Then Jerusalem will be called the City of Truth, and the mountain of the LORD Almighty will be called the Holy Mountain."

(Zechariah 8:3)

A sign to the nations

"I will give you a new heart and put a new spirit in you; I will remove from you your heart of stone and give you a heart of flesh ... On the day I cleanse you from all your sins, I will resettle your towns, and the ruins will be rebuilt. The desolate land will be cultivated instead of lying desolate in the sight of all who pass through it ... Then the nations around you that remain will know that I the LORD have rebuilt what was destroyed and have replanted what was desolate. I the LORD have spoken, and I will do it."

(Ezekiel 36:26, 33–34, 36)

The Lord is my light

Do not gloat over me, my enemy!
    Though I have fallen, I will rise.
Though I sit in darkness,
    the LORD will be my light.
Because I have sinned against him,
    I will bear the LORD's wrath,
until he pleads my case
    and establishes my right.
He will bring me out into the light;
    I will see his righteousness.

(Micah 7:8–9)

Then your light will break forth like the dawn,
    and your healing will quickly appear;
then your righteousness will go before you,
    and the glory of the LORD will be your rear guard.

(Isaiah 58:8)

In that day

he will swallow up death forever.
The Sovereign LORD will wipe away the tears
    from all faces;
he will remove the disgrace of his people
    from all the earth.
                    The LORD has spoken.

In that day they will say,

"Surely this is our God;
    we trusted in him, and he saved us.
This is the LORD; we trusted in him;
    let us rejoice and be glad in his salvation."

(Isaiah 25:8–9)

Destined for resurrection

Then Simeon blessed them and said to Mary, his mother: "This child is destined to cause the falling and rising of many in Israel, and to be a sign that will be spoken against."

(Luke 2:34)

He shall see of the travail of his soul, and shall be satisfied.

(Isaiah 53:11, KJV)

"As the new heavens and the new earth that I make will endure before me," declares the LORD, "so will your name and descendants endure."

(Isaiah 66:22)

Arise, shine

"Arise, shine, for your light has come,
  and the glory of the LORD rises upon you.
See, darkness covers the earth
  and thick darkness is over the peoples,
but the LORD rises upon you
  and his glory appears over you."

(Isaiah 60:1–2)

Nations will come to you

"Nations will come to your light,
  and kings to the brightness of your dawn.

"Lift up your eyes and look about you:
  All assemble and come to you;
your sons come from afar,
  and your daughters are carried on the arm.
Then you will look and be radiant,
  your heart will throb and swell with joy;
the wealth on the seas will be brought to you;
  to you the riches of the nations will come ...
Your gates will always stand open,
  they will never be shut, day or night,
so that men may bring you the wealth of the nations –
  their kings led in triumphal procession."

(Isaiah 60:3–5, 11)

Praying for Israel

1. We need to repent of any anti-Jewish attitude or behavior in our own lives. We should pray for a repentant attitude from

within our church fellowship. We must pray for a repentant attitude within our own town, city and nation regarding any anti-Jewish behavior.

2. We need to pray for Israel and encourage others to pray. You could collect together a group of people to pray in your home on a regular basis. Remember it does not have to be a large group. Jesus spoke of the power of two agreeing in prayer and of his presence when two or three meet in his name (Matthew 18:19).

   Perhaps you have never committed any anti-Jewish act nor spoken anything anti-Jewish. You simply have been ignorant of anti-Jewish behavior and have never realized God's love for the Jewish people. But, do you pray for the Jewish people? The prophet Samuel said to Israel:

   > "As for me, far be it from me that I should sin against the LORD by failing to pray for you."
   >
   > (1 Samuel 12:23)

3. There is need to educate Christians regarding our responsibility to the Jewish people and Israel. Your understanding can be improved by reading, and by listening to teaching on CD and cassette tape. The sharing with others of literature and tapes are good means of helping others to understand. Have you considered hiring a suitable video tape or DVD on the subject and inviting friends to view it in your home? What about arranging a guest speaker in your home or prayer group and inviting an audience for an evening? Suitable resource people and material are available from the Church's Ministry among Jewish People (PO Box 191, Jerusalem 91001, Israel; *email:* enquiries@cmj.org.uk); Prayer for Israel (PO Box 328, Bromley, Kent BR1 2ZS, England; *email:* pfi@prayer4i.org); Prayer for Israel NZ (PO Box 663, Warkworth 1241, New Zealand); Christian Friends of Israel (PO Box 1813, Jerusalem 91015, Israel; *email:* cfi@cfijerusalem.org).

Our repentant attitude and positive response is promised a fruitful harvest where the years of corruption will be speedily redeemed:

"I will repay you for the years the locusts have eaten –
   the great locust and the young locust,
   the other locusts and the locust swarm –
my great army that I sent among you.
You will have plenty to eat, until you are full,
   and you will praise the name of the LORD your God,
   who has worked wonders for you;
never again will my people be shamed.
Then you will know that I am in Israel,
   that I am the LORD your God,
   and that there is no other;
never again will my people be shamed."

(Joel 2:25–27)

Clearly, there are two barriers to be prayed through. The first is the veil that prevents Christians from understanding God's immutable covenant with Israel and recognizing our debt and responsibility to the Jewish people. Then there is the veil that prevents many Jewish people from recognizing the Messiah and understanding the new covenant, and true biblical Judaism. If we deal with the first veil, we can be God's instruments concerning the second veil.

Postscript: Israel's Enemies Defy Israel's God

On 12 July, 2006, after the manuscript for this book was completed, war again broke out in the Middle East. Near the border with Lebanon, on Israel's soil, two Israeli soldiers were kidnapped and eight soldiers were killed by Hizb'allah guerillas. This was an act of war according to the Geneva Convention on War.

Israel responded with its air force bombing Hizb'allah bases and infrastructure, the airport, the port, roads and bridges in Beirut, Lebanon's capital, then to other areas in Lebanon in an effort to paralyze the Hizb'allah. One commentator declared: "Lebanon is one large launching pad for Hizb'allah." Israel now has a war on two fronts: Gaza in the south and Lebanon in the north.

Hizb'allah, from their well-positioned strongholds along Israel's northern border, consistently barraged Israel with rockets reaching as far south as Haifa, Afula, Hadera, Tiberias and Beit Shean. Over 1,000,000 Israelis either fled to central or southern Israel, or hunkered down in their bomb shelters. Over 500,000 Lebanese fled to Syria and an evacuation of foreign nationals was described as the largest movement of people in a war zone since World War II.

This was déjà vu for both Israelis and Lebanese who recalled the Hizb'allah rocket attacks of northern Israel in April 1996 and the Israeli bombardment of Lebanon in an attempt to neutralize the Hizb'allah forces. That sixteen-day battle came to be known as "Operation Grapes of Wrath."

Our understanding of this war requires us to turn the pages of history back to the early twentieth century.

The birth of the modern Middle East

After a four-hundred-year history, the crumbling Muslim Ottoman Empire that encompassed the Middle East region collapsed as a result of the First World War

Mandates were given by the League of Nations to Britain and France to administer the region. Syria, which had been part of the Ottoman Empire, was truncated to create Lebanon, Palestine, Jordan and Iraq. Syria has constantly striven to recover its former glory: *"Greater Syria."* Lebanon received its independence from France in 1943 as a predominantly Christian state. Part of Palestine was to become the Jewish state of Israel in 1948, and Jordan was also part of mandated Palestine. By 1941 Persia had changed its name to Iran, marking a decision to identify itself as the dominant Shi'ite Muslim nation of the region.

At Israel's birth on 14 May, 1948 (authorized by the UN on 22 November, 1947), the surrounding Muslim Arab nations attacked with the intention of destroying the new state. During that war some 110,000 Arab refugees fled to Lebanon.

From 1970 to 1973, the Palestinian Liberation Organization (PLO) was engaged in the Jordanian Civil War, which routed a large number of Palestinian fighters and refugees into neighboring Lebanon. The numbers were swelled by enraged Syrians, Libyans, Iranians and Egyptians who flocked into Lebanon to fight the "infidel" Lebanese Christians and the "infidel" Israeli Jews.

By 1975, they numbered more than 300,000, creating an informal state-within-a-state in south Lebanon. The PLO became a powerful force and played an important role in the Lebanese Civil War. Continual violence occurred between Israel and the PLO from 1968 in the struggle to protect northern Israel's population.

Extremist Muslims had one vision, to take control of the only Christian country in the Middle East and then to destroy the Jewish state Israel. The next stage would be the reversion of the entire Middle East to Islam.

Syria, with its military already suffocating the Christians, Iran with its militia Hizb'allah, the PLO with their terrorist leader Yasser Arafat, and the other Muslim zealots on a holy mission, were using Lebanon as a terrorist breeding ground. Through it they were exporting terrorism into the rest of the world. Under the auspices of a peacekeeping force in Lebanon, Syria shelled Israel along with Hizb'allah, the Iranian-financed "holy warriors."

On 6 June, 1982, the Israel Defense Forces (IDF) entered southern Lebanon in *Operation Peace for Galilee* to render the north of Israel secure. The IDF remained in south Lebanon at great cost to protect Israel's northern border towns from rocket fire.

The world press, which was getting its information from the Muslim-controlled areas in Beirut, painted a false picture of Israel occupying Lebanon while the Lebanese were fighting back to evict the Israelis from their country. As Israel's continued presence in south Lebanon provided the Syrian-controlled Lebanese government with reasons to continue warring with Israel, and with the escalating number of casualties among Israeli soldiers, Israel withdrew in May 2000.

Syria's controlling influence in Lebanon was not limited to its government but also Syria had a resident army of 140,000. Syria's disparate interest among the various ruling Lebanese clans created fragmentation that was exacerbated by the growing influence of Hizb'allah, mainly a Lebanese militia who had even secured a minor place in the government.

On 2 September 2004, the UN Security Council addressed the situation in Resolution 1559. This was timed to precede the Lebanese presidential elections *"underlining* the importance of free and fair elections according to Lebanese constitutional rules devised without foreign interference."

The resolution called "for the strict respect of the sovereignty, territorial integrity, unity, and political independence of Lebanon under the sole and exclusive authority of the Government of Lebanon throughout Lebanon" and for "all remaining foreign forces to withdraw from Lebanon," and "the disbanding and disarmament of all Lebanese and non-Lebanese militias." The resolution was an unequivocal instruction to the Syrians to leave Lebanon and for the Lebanese government to disband and to disarm Hizb'allah.

Hizb'allah – "Lebanon for allah"

Israel's withdrawal from south Lebanon in 2000 created a vacuum which was rapidly filled by the Hizb'allah. Meaning *Party of allah*, this Lebanese Islamist group was founded in 1982 to fight the Israeli presence in southern Lebanon. Hizb'allah gained international notoriety as a result of their 1983 suicide attack that claimed the lives of 241 US Marines, then stationed in Lebanon. Hizb'allah was also responsible for a series of kidnappings of US and other Western hostages during the 1980s, and attacks against Israeli and Jewish targets in Argentina during the 1990s.

From its beginning Hizb'allah has been engaged in a prolonged fight against Israel and Israel's South Lebanon Army (SLA) ally. It was responsible for the Israeli withdrawal from Lebanon in May 2000 along with the dismantling of the SLA. Hizb'allah continues in a dispute with Israel [and Syria] over the ownership of a small Golan Heights enclave, Shaaba Farms, on the Syrian border. Hizb'allah is a strong supporter of the Palestinian cause.

Hizb'allah's invasion of south Lebanon forced the Lebanese residents, alienated from northern Lebanon by their association through the SLA with Israel, from their homes. Many of these Lebanese refugees were accepted and accommodated in northern Israeli towns where today they live as residents of Israel.

Along with the Amal movement, Hizb'allah is the main political party representing the Shi'ite community, Lebanon's largest religious bloc. Founded with the aid of Iran, it follows the distinctly Shi'ite Islamist ideology. It calls for the establishment of an Islamic state in Lebanon, although recognizing that this could only come about with the consensus of the Lebanese people.

In addition to its military wing, Hizb'allah maintains a civilian arm, which runs hospitals, news services, and educational facilities and participates in the Lebanese Parliament. Its Reconstruction Campaign is responsible for numerous economic and infrastructural development projects in Shi'ite-populated areas of Lebanon. Again a state exists within the state of Lebanon.

A number of Western governments, including that of the United States, have designated Hizb'allah a terrorist organization, while the European Union has designated the party's external security wing, but not the organization as a whole, as a terrorist organization. Hizb'allah has a military branch known as *The Islamic Resistance.''*

Valueless life – the human shield

Fundamentalist Islam views its goals long term, and everything is seen within that goal – no matter how long it takes or what the cost to achieve the goal. Human life is not important in Islamic thinking:

killing, sacrifice and the shedding of blood is acceptable in achieving the goal.

For Muslims, losing life for the extension of Islam earns the distinction of martyrdom (*shahid* in Arabic) and is rewarded with the bliss of instant paradise, while the infidel, especially Jew or Christian, is punished with eternal damnation.

In Israel this attitude has been demonstrated by suicide bombers (since September 2000, 1,120 have been killed). It was witnessed in the Lockerbie airliner bombing (in December 1988, 270 were killed). Suicide pilots flew passenger-filled aircraft into populated buildings in New York and the Pentagon (in September 2001, 2,976 people were killed). Spain experienced human devastation in Madrid's railway bombing (March 2004, when 192 were killed). London witnessed the carnage as underground trains and buses were bombed (in July 2005, 50 were killed).

Islamists have struck India (in July 2006, Mumbai, 200-plus were killed), Egypt (a Muslim Arab country, but in July 2005 in Sharm el-Sheikh, 88 were killed), Turkey (also a Muslim country; in Istanbul, November 2003, 50 were killed), Bali (in October 2002, 202 were killed), and Beslan (in September 2004, 344 were massacred, including 186 children). These figures do not include the thousands of mutilated survivors. No nation is exempt!

The planting of weaponry, rockets and mortars within civilian neighborhoods or under civilian institutions whether they be apartment blocks or hospitals is acceptable practice. This practice scores well for radical Islamic groups as when their enemy bombs those areas to neutralize the radical group's power, the world will cry, "Foul!" That is precisely what happened in Lebanon, especially in Qana, and Israel was accused of excessive bombing.

An example of the human shield practice is provided by the Berlin daily the *Tagesspiegel* in a published letter to the editor on 31 July, 2006, from Dr Mounir Herzallah, a Shiite from the South of Lebanon. Dr Herzallah reports on how Hizb'allah terrorists came to his town, dug a munitions depot and then built a school and a residence directly over it. He writes: "Laughing, a local sheikh explained to me that the Jews lose either way: either because the rockets are fired at them or because, if they attack a munitions depot, they are condemned by world public opinion on account of the dead civilians." Hizb'allah, he says, uses the civilian population "as a human shield and then when they are dead as propaganda."

Just how indifferent the Shiite Islamists are to the lives of their fellow Muslims was already made clear during the Iran–Iraq War, when Khomeini sent thousands of Iranian children into the minefields. Still today, this mass murder is defended as "martyrdom" by people like Ahmadinejad (President of the Islamic Republic of Iran) and Nasrallah (leader of Hizb'allah).

The war is global, the eye of the storm is Israel, and Jerusalem will ultimately be the target – *the "apple of God's eye,"* according to Zechariah 2:8.

Iran – Middle East terror catalyst

In the USA, Iran has been identified as the source of the current wave of violence in and around Israel: both Hamas' kidnap of Corporal Gilead Shalit near Gaza and the abduction of the two soldiers by Hizb'allah near the Lebanon border. This has contributed to Iran establishing its leadership in the Muslim world, and at the same time it drew the world's attention away from Iran's nuclear procrastination at the G8 summit in St Petersburg. According to this theory Syria, which tied its fate to Iran's in a mutual defence treaty, is being used as a pawn in Iran's game, a stepping-stone to Israel.

Syria has an agenda too. Having withdrawn his army from Lebanon, President Basher al-Asad is sitting out the UN investigation into Syria's role in the assassination of Lebanese Prime Minister Rafiq al-Hariri. The inquiry looks likely to continue interminably. Basher has outfaced his French and American critics and now stands tall in the Arab world: a protector of the terrorist groups Hamas, Islamic Jihad and the Popular Front for the Liberation of Palestine, and an implacable enemy of Israel. Moreover, supporting Hizb'allah in Lebanon maintains Syria's influence there too.

Palestinian Authority elections in January 2006 shocked even some Palestinian leaders when Hamas were elected by the people to replace the Fatah leadership of the Palestinian Authority. *Hamas* means "zeal," and it is an acronym for the Islamic Resistance Movement. It was created as the armed wing of the religious revivalist Muslim Brotherhood in Gaza, in 1987.

The Hamas Charter is virulently anti-Semitic and uncompromising in its goal of ridding Palestine of the Jews. Its charter states: *"Israel will exist and will continue to exist until Islam will obliterate it, just as it obliterated others before it."* Consider Hamas' objective with the US-sponsored road map's aim to establish two states: Israel and Palestine. Compare with US Secretary of State Condileeza Rice's statement: "We need to look beyond the war to establishing the road map."

Israel's disengagement, or withdrawal of the Israel Defence Forces (IDF) and Jewish population from Gaza in August 2005, created a vacuum filled with disorder and mayhem. The Hamas government has actively aggravated the situation by their failure to provide law and order. Palestinian factions are warring with, and killing each other. Egyptian security has failed to stop the highway of arms and ammunition, enabling Gaza to become a terror base. For weeks a barrage of rockets has pounded Israeli towns from out of Gaza.

Islam – Restore the region to Islamic rule

For Israel the issue is not simply the Palestinians and their actions, including the rocket fire into Israel. It is the broader problem of radical Islam – of Hamas, as a part of the regional Muslim Brotherhood, and of Iran, a serious regional power with considerable influence on Syria, Hizb'allah, Islamic Jihad and the military wing of Hamas.

While Israel and the United States still hope that Hamas, which is mainly a locally adapted Palestinian branch of the Muslim Brotherhood, will respond to the responsibilities of elected leadership and moderate its rejection of Israel to bring a better life to its people, they have no such hopes for Iran.

Iran's president has denied the Holocaust and made countless provocative statements about Israel. But even before his election, Iran committed itself to undermining any prospect of real peace between Israel and the Palestinians through proxy forces like Hizb'allah in southern Lebanon and the Palestinian group Islamic Jihad.

Iran is also considered to be the main sponsor of the exiled Palestinian leader of Hamas's political bureau, Khaled Meshal. He is the man widely considered to be in charge of Hamas's secretive military wing, instrumental in carrying out the seizure of Corporal Gilad Shalit, touching off the latest explosion.

That seizure came as the Hamas government, led by Prime Minister Ismail Haniya, was finishing negotiations with the more moderate Palestinian Authority president, Mahmoud Abbas, on a political document which might have allowed the renewal of negotiations with Israel.

The expansion of the Gaza crisis into southern Lebanon, confronting Israel with a conflict on its northern and southern borders is not local, nor regional. It is part of the global radical Islamic strategy subjecting the world to terror in its *jihad* to expand the imposition of Sharia law (Islamic law) upon the nations. Hamas and Hizb'allah leaders, supported and abetted by both Iran and Syria, are an integral thread in radical Islam's strategy. The Palestinian Authority, which Hamas controls, and the Lebanese government, in which Hizb'allah is a minority participant, inexcusably failed to prevent or halt these incidents. Iran, which arms Hizb'allah, and Syria, which shelters the most violent wing of Hamas, also share some responsibility.

An Iranian Apocalypse

Professor Moshe Sharon who is an expert in Islamic history at the Hebrew University, spoke at the annual conference of Herzliya's Counter Terrorism Institute on the global Islamic threat and specifically the role of Iran and Israel's security. Sharon made it abundantly clear that Iran is "deadly serious" about procuring and using nuclear weapons in order to bring about its vision of Islamic End Days. "There is no possibility of peace between Israel and the Palestinians whatsoever – *ever*."

> The veteran expert on Islam says that Western officials fail to grasp that the Arab and Islamic world truly see Israel's establishment as a "reversal of history" and are therefore unable to ever accept peaceful relations with it. From the Muslim perspective, "Islamic territory was taken away from Islam by Jews. You know by now that this can never be accepted, not even one meter. So everyone who thinks Tel Aviv is safe is making a grave mistake. Territory

which at one time was dominated by Islamic rule, now has become non-Muslim. Non-Muslims are independent of Islamic rule and Jews have created their own independent state. It is anathema. Worse, Israel, a non-Muslim state, is ruling over Muslims. It is unthinkable that non-Muslims should rule over Muslims."

Sharon dismissed various peace treaties signed by Muslim and Arab officials over the years as "pieces of paper, parts of tactics and strategies . . . with no meaning."

Sharon's assessment focused on the danger posed by Iran. From studying Iranian culture, literature, newspapers, broadcasts and interviews with major players in the Islamic regime, Sharon concludes that a deep belief in a Shi'ite messiah is at the root of Iran's nuclear project. "They truly believe that the Shi'ite messiah, the 12th Imam (also known as the Mahdi), is here, and that he will reveal himself . . . What moves the Iranian government and leadership today is first and foremost the wish to bring about the 12th Imam."

Addressing the theological doctrine of how exactly this Messiah will be revealed, Sharon explained: "How will they bring him? Through an apocalypse. He (the Mahdi) needs a war. He cannot come into this world without an Armageddon. He wants an Armageddon. The earlier we understand this the better. Ahmadinejad wants nuclear weapons for this!"

Sharon has in the past insisted that the Western world was engaging in great folly by differentiating between radical and peaceful Islam. "All of a sudden we see that the greatest interpreters of Islam are politicians in the Western world," he spoke sarcastically. "They know better than all the speakers in the mosques, all those who deliver terrible sermons against anything that is either Christian or Jewish. These Western politicians know that there is good Islam and bad Islam. They know even how to differentiate between the two – except that none of them know how to read a word of Arabic."

"The difference between Judaism, Christianity and Islam is as follows: Judaism speaks about national salvation – namely, that at the end of the story, when the world becomes a better place, Israel will be in its own land, ruled by its own king and serving God. Christianity speaks about the idea that every single person in the world can be saved from his sins, while Islam speaks about ruling the world. I can quote here in Arabic, but there is no point in quoting Arabic, so let me quote a verse in English: 'Allah sent Muhammad with the true religion so that it should rule over all the religions.'

"The idea, then, is not that the whole world would necessarily become Muslim at this time, but that the whole world would be subdued under the rule of Islam."

That, Sharon insists, is the plan, in black-and-white, of the Iranian regime.

"This is why [Iranian President Mahmoud] Ahmadinejad seeks nuclear weapons," he emphasized. "The faster we realize this, the better."[1]

What of the future? – Prophetic words

During this war I received by email a startling news report from CNN's website. While digging in an Irish bog a worker discovered a book of the Psalms which has since been dated between AD 800 and 1000. The director of Ireland's National Museum described it as "really a miracle find."

Three extraordinary facts relate to this find. That in the wet bog any book could survive disintegration over a long period of time is remarkable in itself. The last early medieval document to be found in Ireland was over two hundred years ago. The timing of this find is while Israel is in the midst of a war that could easily develop into a regional war.

The twenty-page book was open at Psalm 83 where Israel's conspirators cry,

> "Come, and let us cut them off from being a nation,
> That the name of Israel be remembered no more."

> (v. 4, NKJV)

It concludes with the prayer:

> O my God, make them like whirling dust,
> Like the chaff before the wind!
> As the fire burns the woods,
> And as the flame sets the mountains on fire,
> So pursue them with Your tempest.

And frighten them with Your storm.
Fill their faces with shame,
That they may seek Your name, O LORD ...
That they may know that You, whose name alone is the LORD,
Are the Most High over all the earth.

(vv. 13–16, 18, NKJV)

Both Isaiah and Jeremiah prophesy into the nations of this region. Isaiah declared of Syria:

"Damascus will cease from being a city,
And it will be a ruinous heap ...
The fortress also will cease from Ephraim,
The kingdom from Damascus,
And the remnant of Syria;
They will be as the glory of the children of Israel,"
Says the LORD of hosts.

(Isaiah 17:1, 3, NKJV)

Not only will Damascus be destroyed but the Lord in his mercy will be glorified through a remnant of Syrian believers. Will this prophetic word be fulfilled as the result of this war?

Isaiah declared of Lebanon:

In a very short time, will not Lebanon be turned into a
        fertile field
    and the fertile field seem like a forest?
In that day the deaf will hear the words of the scroll,
    and out of the gloom and darkness
    the eyes of the blind will see.
Once more the humble will rejoice in the LORD;
    the needy will rejoice in the Holy One of Israel.
The ruthless will vanish,
    the mockers will disappear,
    and all who have an eye for evil will be cut down –
those who with a word make a man out to be guilty,
    who ensnare the defender in the court
    and with false testimony deprive the innocent of justice.

(Isaiah 29:17–21)

Clearly, there is a glorious future ahead for Lebanon as the Spirit of God breathes upon that nation following judgment.

Jeremiah spoke the word of the Lord over ancient Elam, which is modern Iran:

> " 'Behold, I will break the bow of Elam,
> The foremost of their might.
> Against Elam I will bring the four winds
> From the four quarters of heaven,
> And scatter them toward all those winds;
> There shall be no nations where the outcasts of Elam will not go.
> For I will cause Elam to be dismayed before their enemies
> And before those who seek their life.
> I will bring disaster upon them,
> My fierce anger,' says the LORD;
> 'And I will send the sword after them
> Until I have consumed them.
> I will set my throne in Elam,
> And will destroy from there the king and the princes,'
>   says the LORD.
>
> 'But it shall come to pass in the latter days:
> I will bring back the captives of Elam,' says the LORD."
>
> (Jeremiah 49:35–39, NKJV)

UN Resolution 1701 – Cease-fire

On 11 August the UN unanimously passed Resolution 1701 calling for a cease-fire. The Lebanese cabinet unanimously approved the resolution on 12 August and the next day the Israeli cabinet voted twenty-four in favor of the resolution with one abstention. The resolution came into effect at 8:00 am local time, 14 August.

Caroline Glick, deputy managing editor of *The Jerusalem Post* (13 August), assisted by international legal scholar Professor Anne Bayefsky, comments on the resolution that marked the cease-fire and its implications in an article entitled, "An Unmitigated Disaster":

> The resolution represents a near-total victory for Hizb'allah and its state sponsors Iran and Syria, and an unprecedented defeat for

Israel and its ally the United States. This fact is evident both in the text of the resolution and in the very fact that the US decided to sponsor a cease-fire resolution before Israel had dismantled or seriously degraded Hizb'allah's military capabilities...

While the resolution ... does not have the authority of law, in practice it makes it all but impossible for Israel to defend itself against Hizb'allah aggression without being exposed to international condemnation on an unprecedented scale.

This is the case first of all because the resolution places responsibility for determining compliance in the hands of UN Secretary-General Kofi Annan. Annan has distinguished himself as a man capable only of condemning Israel for its acts of self-defense while ignoring the fact that in attacking Israel, its enemies are guilty of war crimes. By empowering Annan to evaluate compliance, the resolution all but ensures that Hizb'allah will not be forced to disarm and that Israel will be forced to give up the right to defend itself.

The resolution makes absolutely no mention of either Syria or Iran, without whose support Hizb'allah could neither exist nor wage an illegal war against Israel. In so ignoring Hizb'allah's sponsors, it ignores the regional aspect of the current war and sends the message to these two states that they may continue to equip terrorist armies in Lebanon, the Palestinian Authority and Iraq with the latest weaponry without paying a price for their aggression.

The resolution presents Hizb'allah with a clear diplomatic victory by placing their erroneous claim of Lebanese sovereignty over the Shaaba Farms, or Mount Dov – a vast area on the Golan Heights that separates the Syrian Golan from the Upper Galilee and is disputed between Israel and Syria – on the negotiating table. In doing so, the resolution rewards Hizb'allah's aggression by giving international legitimacy to its demand for territorial aggrandizement via acts of aggression, in contravention of the laws of nations.

Moreover, by allowing Lebanon to make territorial claims on Israel despite the fact that in 2000 the UN determined that Israel had withdrawn to the international border, the resolution sets a catastrophic precedent for the future. Because Lebanon is receiving international support for legally unsupportable territorial demands on Israel, in the future, the Palestinians, Syrians and indeed the Jordanians and Egyptians will feel empowered to employ aggression to gain territorial concessions from the Jewish state even if they previously signed treaties of peace with Israel. The message of the resolution's stand on Shaaba Farms is that Israel can never expect for the world to recognize any of its borders as final.

By calling in the same paragraph for the "immediate cessation by Hizb'allah of all attacks and the immediate cessation by Israel of all offensive military operations," the resolution treats as equivalent Hizb'allah's illegal aggression against Israel and Israel's legitimate military actions taken in defense of its sovereign territory . . .

Foreign Minister Tzipi Livni had let it be known that Israel's conditions for a cease-fire included the institution of an arms embargo against Hizb'allah. The government also insisted that the international force it wished to have deployed along the border would work to dismantle Hizb'allah.

However, paragraph 8 puts both the question of an arms embargo and Hizb'allah's dismantlement off to some future date when Israel and Lebanon agree to the terms of a "permanent cease-fire." In addition, it places the power to oversee an arms embargo against Hizb'allah in the hands of the Lebanese government, of which Hizb'allah is a member . . .

Finally, the resolution makes no operative call for the release of IDF soldiers Ehud Goldwasser and Eldad Regev now being held hostage by Hizb'allah. By relegating their fate to a paragraph in the preamble, which then immediately turns to Hizb'allah's demand for the release of Lebanese terrorists held in Israeli jails, the resolution all but eliminates any possibility of their returning home . . .

Aside from the resolution's egregious language, the very fact that the US has sponsored a resolution that leaves Hizb'allah intact as a fighting force constitutes a devastating blow to the national security of both Israel and the US . . .

It empowers Iran. Iran emerges as the main victor in the current war. Not only was it not condemned for its sponsorship of Hizb'allah, it is being rewarded for that sponsorship because it is clear to all parties that Iran was the engine behind this war, and that its side has won.

The UN resolution does not strengthen the US hand in future Security Council deliberations regarding Iran's illicit nuclear weapons program because the states that object to any action against Iran – Russia and China – will continue with their refusal to sign on to any substantive action.

Indeed, Russia's behavior regarding the situation in Lebanon, including the fact that a large percentage of Hizb'allah's arsenal of advanced anti-tank missiles was sold by Russia to Syria and Iran, exposes that Moscow's role in the current conflict has been similar to the position taken by the Soviet Union in earlier Middle East wars ...

Many sources in Washington told this writer over the weekend that the US decision to seek a cease-fire was the result of Israel's amateurish bungling of the first three weeks of the war. The Bush administration, they argued, was being blamed for the Olmert government's incompetence and so preferred to cut its losses and sue for a cease-fire.

There is no doubt much truth to this assertion. The government's prosecution of this war has been unforgivably inept. At the same time it should be noted that the short-term political gain accrued by the US by forging the cease-fire agreement will come back to haunt the US, Israel and all forces fighting the forces of global *jihad* in the coming weeks and months.

By handing a victory to Hizb'allah, the resolution strengthens the belief of millions of supporters of *jihad* throughout the world that their side is winning and that they should redouble efforts to achieve their objectives of destroying Israel and running the US out of the Middle East.

A Lebanese Christian's testimony

Transcript of an interview with Brigitte Gabriel

[*Brigitte Gabriel is a survivor of Islam's Jihad against Lebanese Christians. She is now an expert on the Middle East conflict who lectures nationally and internationally on the subject. She's the former news anchor of World News for Middle East Television and the founder of AmericanCongressforTruth.com. The interview was conducted by FrontPageMagazine.com on 11 August, 2005.*]

FP: Brigitte Gabriel, thank you for joining us today.

Gabriel: Thank you for inviting me. I'm delighted to join you.

FP: First things first, tell us a bit about your background.

Gabriel: I was raised in the only Christian country in the Middle East, Lebanon. A lot of people think the Middle East has always been made up of Muslim countries. That is not true. There once were two non-Muslim countries in the Middle East. One is a Jewish state called Israel which is under attack for its existence today and the other was a Christian country called Lebanon now under a Muslim-majority controlling influence.

When Lebanon got its independence from France in the 1940s, the majority of the population was Christian. We didn't have any enemies. We were merchants, descendants of the Phoenicians, strong in commerce in which we prospered. In no time Lebanon became the Paris of the Middle East, the banking capital of the Middle East. We were the only westernized Arabic speaking country in the region.

I was an only child to older parents. My parents were married for twenty-two years before I came into their lives. They were unable to have any children. My mother was fifty-five years old and my father was sixty when I was born. I had the ideal childhood, the love, adoration and attention of two mature adults who looked at me as a miracle in their lives, and were thankful to God for blessing them with a child.

Even though I was raised in a Christian country, it was still an Arabic country trying to please its neighbors, the Arab Muslims. Even the Christian private school I went to was affected. When we studied the Bible, we only studied the New Testament. I never saw the Old Testament or heard anything about it, because it was considered the enemy's Bible. All I heard was, "Israel is Satan, Israel is the devil, Israelis are demons, and they are the source of the problem in the Middle East. The Jews are evil, they are unstoppable and they want to control the world." I heard nothing but hatred toward the Jews.

FP: Can you expand a bit on some of the tragedy that befell your family? I am sorry that this is painful territory.

Gabriel: The Christians in Lebanon always had problems with the Muslims, but we never thought our neighbors would turn on us. That situation was aggravated by the influx of the Palestinians coming from Jordan after King Hussein kicked them out in Black September. That's what tipped the scale in Lebanon. Not only had Muslims become the majority but they now also felt empowered by the presence of the Palestinians and Yasser Arafat wanting to attack the Christians, to take over Lebanon and use it as a base from which to attack Israel.

When the Muslims and Palestinians declared *jihad* on the Christians in 1975 we didn't even know what that word meant. We had taken them into our country, allowed them to study side by side with us, in our schools and universities. We gave them jobs, shared with them our way of life. We didn't realize the depth of their hatred to us as infidels. They looked at us as the enemy, not as neighbors, friends, employers and colleagues.

A lot of Muslims poured in from other Muslim countries like Iran – the founder and supporter of Hizb'allah, one of the leading terrorist organizations in the world today. They came from Somalia, Sudan, Syria, Jordan and Egypt. The Lebanese civil war was not between the Lebanese; it was a "holy war" declared on the Christians by the Muslims of the Middle East.

They started massacring the Christians, city after city: horrific events the western media seldom reported. One of the most ghastly acts was the massacre in the Christian city of Damour where thousands of Christians were slaughtered like sheep. The Muslims would enter a bomb shelter, see a mother and a father hiding with a little baby. They would tie one leg of the baby to the mother and one leg to the father and pulled the parents apart splitting the child in half. A close friend of mine was mentally disturbed because they made her slaughter her own son in a chair. They tied her to a chair, tied a knife to her hand and holding her hand forcing her to cut her own son's throat. They would urinate and defecate on the altars of churches using the pages of the Bible as toilet paper. They did so many things I don't need to go into any more detail. You get the picture.

Americans just don't realize the viciousness of the militant Islamic fundamentalist. I think the biggest disservice for the American people was the denial by the networks to air the beheading video of Daniel Pearl. I think we as a society need to see what type of enemy we are fighting. People have been so sheltered in this country they have not paid attention to what was going on in the last twenty-some years. They were more interested in watching a documentary about Madonna than paying attention to world events.

The majority of the Lebanese army was Muslim. Christians went to universities, not to the military. The Muslims began taking over military bases across Lebanon. They combined their forces with the Palestinians and formed what they called the Arab Lebanese Army and started attacking the Christians. I lived fifty yards below the last military base left in the hands of the Christians. While attempting to bombard the military base their shells missed, landing directly on my home, bringing it down and burying me under the rubble. I was ten years old.

I woke up from a dream life into a nightmare. My eyes were blinded by the bright light of the explosions. But the light faded quickly as a hot liquid started pouring into my eyes, burning and shutting them closed like glue. I was wounded by shrapnel, which cut the artery in my arm that was twisted on top of my face. Blood was pouring over my face and into my mouth. By the time I was rescued by my parents and taken to a hospital the next morning at 8:00 am, I was on my last breath. I was put on a bench in the emergency room and operated on without anesthesia. As the nurses held me down the doctors cut my flesh with scissors and sawed into my bone to get out the embedded shrapnel. As I faded in and out of consciousness, between my screams I prayed to God to stop my torture. I ended up in the hospital for two and half months.

While there, I would ask my parents why this happened to us, they would say because we were Christians and the Muslims want to kill us. So I knew ever since I was ten that I was wanted dead simply because I was born a Christian.

When I returned home my new home was no longer the one that I knew. We ended up living in a bomb shelter underground without electricity, water and very little food. Little did I know that this would become my life for the next seven years. Our bomb shelter was an eight-by-ten foot cinderblock room buried underground, that my father used as a storage room for our restaurant.

FP: What is life like under the threat of Islamic terror?

Gabriel: We borrowed life one day at a time. After sleeping in cardboard boxes for a month that had been stored in the bomb shelter, thinking "This will be over soon," we realized this situation was getting worse and worse. We finally furnished the bomb shelter with two old mattresses from our garage. My Mom and I slept on one and my Dad on the other.

To get food my mother and I would go out and find different

types of grass and dandelions to eat around the shelter in between the bombing. My mother would soak chickpeas, rice, lentils and beans overnight so we could eat something during the day.

My father couldn't get out, because in the bombing of our house, he lost his hearing and he wouldn't hear the snipers' bullets or the bombs coming so he could hide. He had to stay put while my mother and I got out.

To get water we would crawl in a ditch under snipers' bullets to a nearby spring. Every time we'd leave we would say our last goodbyes because we didn't know if we would come back alive. My mother would use her stocking on top of the bottle to filter all the worms and the debris so we could drink it. Then we would crawl back with bullets flying over our heads. Sometimes it would take us hours just to crawl 100 feet back into the bomb shelter.

One day when I was thirteen, one of our soldiers warned us that we were no longer able to fight and we were going to be attacked viciously that night. He wished us a merciful death as he left. Knowing we were going to be slaughtered that night I put on my Easter dress because I wanted to look pretty when I was dead, knowing that there would be nobody to prepare me for burial. I stood in my dress in front of the mirror crying as my mother combed my long hair and tied a white ribbon in it. I told her: "Please, I don't want to die. I'm only thirteen."

FP: Discuss your intellectual journey about your view of Jews and Israelis, from what you were told in your childhood to when you started questioning whether it was true, to what you think today.

Gabriel: My town was two and a half miles from the Israeli border. We in our Christian town were faced with the combined Muslim and Palestinian forces waiting to slaughter us. We knew our fate, knowing what they have done to other Christian towns and cities in the rest of Lebanon. To our back was Israel, the enemy, Satan, the demon-possessed Jews. We had nowhere to turn but one way, to the devil, Israel. After all we knew the Jews wouldn't slaughter us because we had more shared values with them than we had with the Muslims. Under the cover of darkness, few men from our town went to the border, flagged down an Israeli border patrol, explained the situation and begged for help.

Israel agreed to help the Christians. Israel became our lifeline.

The Israeli military would come during the night and bring food and ammunition to the military and milk for the children. They would take the Christian men, anyone from age thirteen to seventy and train them to fight; most of them had never held a rifle before. Most of the Christian men had degrees that decorated their walls, but all the degrees in the world cannot defend you when an enemy is facing you with a gun, wanting to kill you by what your enemy believes is an order from God.

The only reason we stayed alive is because Israel came into Lebanon and drove the Muslims away from the surrounding hills and set up positions in our town to protect us. Things got worse as Syrian, Libyans, Iranians Egyptians became enraged and flocked into Lebanon to fight the infidel Christians and Jews.

The Muslims had one vision, to take control of the only Christian country in the Middle East and then attack Israel. Syria, with its military already suffocating the Christians, Iran with its militia Hizb'allah, the PLO with the number-one world terrorist Yasser Arafat, and all the other Muslim zealots on a holy mission, were using Lebanon as a terrorist breeding ground, exporting terrorism into the rest of the world. Under the auspices of a peacekeeping force in Lebanon, Syria shelled Israel, along with Hizb'allah, the Iranian-financed "holy warriors." The world press, which was getting its information from the Muslim-controlled areas in Beirut, were saying that Israel was occupying Lebanon and the poor Lebanese were fighting back to kick the Israelis out.

By 1982 Israel was fed up with Syria's repeated attacks on its northern border. They invaded Lebanon declaring war on the terrorist infrastructure, going all the way into Beirut. During the first two days of the invasion as the Muslims were retreating they shelled us frantically. In their last artillery barrage, they scored a direct hit on the front of our bomb shelter. My mother was seriously wounded and would die without immediate medical attention. My father was too old and weak to take her to the hospital; the responsibility fell on my shoulders. We had to take her to Israel for treatment. For her it was a life-saving experience. For me it was a life-changing experience. It was my first lesson in the difference between the Arabs and the western world, particularly the Jews.

Before we left my father gave me sixty dollars in case I needed some money since we were going to Israel for treatment. We took her first to the Lebanese hospital in town which was vacant and bombed out. There was an Israeli doctor on duty for first-aid situations. He gave my mother first-aid and we put her in an Israeli ambulance and drove her under the bombs to the border. It was about a ten-minute drive, the driver was a friend of the family. When we got to the border we changed ambulances. The Lebanese driver asked me if I had any money for the ambulance fee. Like an innocent teenager who never handled money, I took it out of my pocket and handed it to him and asked him how much he wanted. He said: "Give me thirty dollars," which was half the money I had. I thanked him for driving us with tears dripping down my face and got in the Israeli ambulance and we drove off.

The drive to the hospital inside Israel was an hour long. The driver was a middle-aged soldier. He treated me like his own daughter with such respect and compassion. He listened to the radio and explained to me how the war was going in Lebanon. I felt alone and afraid. My mother was fading in and out of consciousness and moaning from pain. We got to the hospital and I walked around the ambulance to pay him the fee. I took the money out of my pocket, thinking, "God, I'm sure this is not going to be enough for this man. If the ten-minute drive cost me thirty dollars I'm sure this is going to be much more." I extended my hand with the money, asking him how much I owed him. He looked at me surprised and said: "You don't owe me anything. The ambulance ride is a free service from us to you. Keep your money, I wish everything goes well with you. I wish your mother health and speedy recovery."

I thanked him from the bottom of my heart and thought to myself, "What an honest man! What an ethical man! He could have taken my money and partied all night and I would have not known the difference. Yet he didn't." And all of a sudden I felt this anger towards the Lebanese driver who was supposedly a friend of the family. I realized that he actually stole my money. I didn't have to pay a fee for the ambulance, he basically robbed me. I felt violated. I thanked the Israeli driver from the bottom of my heart for his honesty and help.

We went into the emergency room and I was shocked at such a scene. There were many wounded people lying all over the place. Israeli soldiers, Lebanese Muslims, Christians and even Palestinians brought in from Lebanon! I was stunned at such a scene. I thought to myself, "Why the heck are the Israelis helping the Muslims and the Palestinians? I am a Christian, I am their friend, but why are they helping the Palestinian and the Muslims?" Little did I know about the principles and values of the Israeli people. The doctors treated everyone according to their injury. The doctor treated my mother before he treated the Israeli soldier lying next to her because her injury was more severe. They did not see religion, they didn't see political affiliation, they did not see nationality, they saw people in need and they helped.

They took my mother to the fourth floor of the hospital and put her in a room with two other Lebanese ladies, one Muslim and one Druze. We were in the room for five minutes and we heard this loud commotion outside our balcony. People were walking through our room to go out and look. I went out to see what was going on. Two Israeli helicopters had just landed to deliver wounded Israeli soldiers. I stood at that balcony feeling sick to my stomach. I felt ashamed, humiliated, embarrassed, broken-hearted. After all, these people were wounded because of the war with my country. I didn't even look at any one around me; I kept my eyes down. I was surrounded by mothers, fathers, sisters, brothers and children of wounded soldiers. I felt out of place; I felt uncertain. I didn't want to make eye-contact with anyone because I didn't know how they would react to me.

While I was standing there, I felt someone tapping on my shoulder. I looked up to see a nurse standing next to me. She asked me: "You are new here aren't you?" I said, "Yes they just brought my mother to this room." She put her arm around me and looked into my face and said, "Don't worry, we'll take good care of her. Everything will be fine."

I broke out crying. I never felt such compassion and love. For the first time in my life I experienced a human quality that I know my culture would not have shown to their enemy. I experienced the values of the Israelis who were able to love their enemy in their most trying moments. That nurse didn't even know if I was a Christian, a Muslim or a Palestinian. I spent twenty-two days at that hospital. Those days changed my life and the way I believe information, the way I listen to the radio or to television. I realized I was sold a fabricated lie by my government about the Jews and

Israel that was so far from reality. I knew for fact that if I was a Jew standing in an Arab hospital I would be lynched and thrown over to the crowds amidst shouts of joy of *"Allahu Akbar."* "God is great!" would echo through the hospital and the surrounding streets.

When Israelis heard there were Lebanese wounded in the hospitals they came bringing presents, they brought chocolates; they asked people what they wanted and what they needed. They said, "Our home is your home. If you need anything, let us know." They came extending a peaceful hand. I became friends with Israeli mothers staying at the hospital with their wounded sons.

One in particular was Rina; her only child was wounded in his eyes. One day I was visiting with her and the Israeli army band came to play national songs to lift the spirits of the wounded soldiers. As they surrounded his bed playing a song about Jerusalem, Rina and I started crying. I felt out of place and started walking out of the room, and this mother held my hand and pulled me back in without even looking at me. She held me crying and saying: "It is not your fault." We just stood there crying holding each other's hands. I thought: "What a contrast between her, a mother looking at her deformed nineteen-year-old only child, and still able to love me the Arab, and between a Muslim mother who sends her son to blow himself up to smithereens just to kill a few Jews or Christians."

The Muslim woman who was in the room with my mother stayed in the hospital for about twelve days. And even after ten days when the doctors would come and change her bandages and check on her in their morning tour, as they would be leaving the room she would have an evil look on her face and say: "I hate you all. I wish you were all dead." For the first time in my life I saw evil. I realized that this Muslim couldn't love the Jews even after they saved her life. And when you are unable to be grateful to the people that saved your life there is no hope.

I had to go back to Lebanon because I had to take care of my parents but I vowed that one day I would return to Israel, that one day I would live among these people. These are the types of people I wanted to be like. These are the types of values I wanted to adopt. I knew they had something even I did not. They were able to love the Palestinians and forgive them much more than I was able to, and I was a Christian who was supposed to love like Jesus taught.

FP: What hope is there? I doubt that if the Palestinians get their own state that they will suddenly love the Jews and that the whole Islamic-Arab world will put anti-Semitism on the backburner. What do you think?

Gabriel: Israel is stepping out in "good faith" again to do whatever it takes to achieve peace with its neighbors – as if Hamas is going to appreciate the goodness of the Jews and re-write its charter accepting Israel as neighbor and a friend! Hamas has only one goal, and that is to eradicate Israel one piece at a time until it becomes vulnerable to Arab military aggression and conquest.

As one who knows what's in the hearts and minds of Arabs, let me repeat what seems to be the hardest thing for world opinion to accept: The Arabs have no intention of having peace with the Jews – period, exclamation point, end of discussion. No Jews can exist free and unencumbered in the Middle East. What an outrage. "Jews are *dhimmis*, how dare they come back and live in our midst, make the desert blossom and create a country more advanced than any other in the Middle East. And they don't have any oil?"

So far all territory concessions made by Israel have been an illusion of land for peace. In Egypt, who was given the Sinai Peninsula back in 1979, or Jordan, who signed a peace treaty with Israel, the phone books go from Ireland to Italy as if Israel never existed. What type of peace is this without full acknowledgement of statehood? What type of peace is it when Egyptian government-run and controlled television, airs the *Protocols of the Elders of Zion?*

Intelligence sources say there are plans to create a terrorist state in Gaza where world terrorist operations will be planned and carried out. This is equivalent to Somalia and Afghanistan terrorist-controlled societies, but within striking distance of Israel proper. The mini-Hamas terror state would have an airport and port facilities from which to export terror to the rest of the world.

US security officials have received multiple confirmations of a meeting in March [2003] between al-Qaeda, Hamas, and Hizb'allah figures. Most alarming is Hamas' move towards embracing global *jihad* as evidenced by its publishing the messages of Osama bin Laden's mentor Abdullah Azzam – Palestinian, originally from Jenin. Hamas openly publicizes its support and alliance with al-Qaeda organizations *jihad* action in Chechnya, Kashmir, the Balkans and Afghanistan. As Al Qaeda associate Jordanian terrorist al-Zarqawi firmed up his relationship with bin Laden in Iraq, it is only a matter of time for Hamas to follow suit under the sovereignty of an independent mini-terror state, free from the demands of the weakened Palestinian Authority leadership under Mahmoud Abbas in Ramallah.

They will form an instant terror base from which to attack every corner of Israel bent on *jihad* and revenge for al Nakbah – the catastrophe of their defeat in the 1948 War of Independence. Israel is engaged in an existential crisis of Armageddon-like proportions. Another piece for peace? You have to be kidding, right?

FP: It is interesting that most people think of Hamas as an Israeli problem. Which it is of course. But it is also an American problem. And it will become a great American problem. Can you comment on this?

Gabriel: Many terrorist organizations have already set up shop here in America. The three most threatening ones are Hamas, Al-Qaeda and Islamic Jihad. Some of their operatives and supporters have entered the country illegally using visa fraud.

Of all the Islamic militant groups in the US, Hamas has developed the most sophisticated American infrastructure. Under our liberal un-restrictive environment of the United States these people are operating and were able to set up a whole array of cells that spread across the US from sea to shining sea. According to intelligence information they have cells in the top thirty-one cities in the US. Right in many of our towns and cities. Right in our back yard! And it's our lazy government officials and lax laws that allowed them to come here to plan our destruction. Many are still blind in this country to the threat that we face. When are we going to wake up? Yes, we now have enacted Homeland security but without all Americans supporting the war on terrorism today our success will be limited.

What we need is to know our enemy better. And I'm not just talking about Al Qaeda. How many Americans have read the Hamas charter published August 1988? Excerpts from the charter of the Hamas, the charter of allah, the platform of the Islamic resistance movement Hamas: Article 22: "Our enemies have planned from time immemorial in order to reach the position they've obtained now. They strive to collect enormous material riches to be used in the realization of their dream. With money, they've gained control of the international media beginning with news agencies, newspapers and publishing houses, broadcasting stations. They also used this wealth to stir revolutions in different parts of the world in order to fulfill their interests and reap their fruits. With their money they created secret organizations that spread around the world in order to destroy societies and carry out Zionist interests. Such organizations are: the Freemasons, Rotary clubs, Lions clubs, B'nai B'rith and the like. All of them are destructive espionage organizations. With their money they've taken control of the imperialist states and pushed them to occupy many countries in order to exploit the wealth of those countries and spread corruption there."

How many Rotary club members, Lions club members know they are mentioned in the Hamas charter, the largest militant Muslim infrastructure in the United States, that they are considered the enemy to be destroyed?

We really need to realize, all Americans need to realize, that these people hate us and want nothing but to eliminate us because as far as they are concerned we are the infidels. These are religiously motivated fanatics who you cannot negotiate with. These are people who are convinced that God has ordered them to kill us. Their motivation is tremendous. They believe that the minute they die, at the first drop of blood, a crown of pearls will be placed on their head and they will be carried by the angels to heaven and placed at the right side of God and seventy-two virgins are offered to them. We cannot drop our guard for a minute. We must be more vigilant than ever before. Wake up America!

FP: Brigitte Gabriel, you are an incredible person with an extraordinary, inspiring and vital story to tell. Thank you, it was an honor to speak with you.

Gabriel: Thank you for giving me the opportunity to join you today. Organizations like yours make it possible for people like me to get the word out. Together we can make a difference.

Further information:
www.americancongressfortruth.com and
www.FrontPageMagazine.com

The abdication of Lebanese leaders

[**Editor's note**: This article was originally published by the Metula News Agency, for whom it was translated from the French by Llewellyn Brown, and is reprinted with permission.]

State of denial

The politicians, journalists and intellectuals of Lebanon have, of late, been experiencing the shock of their lives. They knew full well that Hizb'allah had created an independent state in our country, a state including all the ministers and parallel institutions, duplicating those of Lebanon. What they did not know – and are discovering with this war, and what has petrified them with surprise and terror – is the extent of this phagocytosis.

In fact, our country had become an extension of Iran, and our so-called political power also served as a political and military cover for the Islamists of Teheran. We suddenly discovered that Teheran had stocked more than 12,000 missiles, of all types and calibers, on our territory and that they had patiently, systematically, organized a suppletive force, with the help of the Syrians, that took over, day after day, all the rooms in the House of Lebanon. Just imagine it: we stock ground-to-ground missiles, Zilzals, on our territory and that the firing of such devices without our knowledge has the power to spark a regional strategic conflict and, potentially, bring about the annihilation of Lebanon.

We knew that Iran, by means of Hizb'allah, was building a veritable Maginot line in the south but it was the pictures of Maroun el-Ras and Bint J'bail that revealed to us the magnitude of these constructions. This amplitude made us understand several things at once: that we were no longer masters of our destiny; that we do not possess the most basic means necessary to reverse the course of this state of things; and that those who turned our country into an outpost of their Islamic doctrine's combat against Israel did not have the slightest intention of willingly giving up their hold over us.

The national salvation discussions that concerned the application of Resolution 1559, and which included most of the Lebanese political movements, were simply for show. Iran and Syria had not

invested billions of dollars on militarizing Lebanon in order to
wage their war, simply to give in to the desire of the Lebanese and
the international community for them to pack up their hardware
and set it up back home . . .

Of course, our army, reshaped over the years by the Syrian
occupier so it could no longer fulfill its role as protector of the
nation, did not have the capacity to tackle the militiamen of
the Hizb'allah [the party of allah]. Our army . . . [is] a force that is
still largely loyal to its former foreign masters, to the point of being
uncontrollable; to the point of having collaborated with the
Iranians to put *our* coastal radar stations at the disposal of their
missiles, which almost sank an Israeli boat off the shores of Beirut.
As for the non-Hizb'allah elements in the government, they knew
nothing of the existence of land-to-sea missiles on our territory.
That caused the totally justified destruction of all *our* radar stations
by the Israeli army. And even then we are getting off lightly in
these goings-on.

. . . The Security Council's Resolution 1559 – that demanded
that *our* government deploy *our* army on *our* sovereign territory,
along *our* international border with Israel and that it disarm all the
militia on *our* land – was voted on 2 September 2004.

We had two years to implement this resolution and thus
guarantee a peaceful future to our children but we did strictly
nothing. Our greatest crime – which was not the only one! – was
not that we did not succeed but that we did not attempt or
undertake anything. And that was the fault of none else than the
pathetic Lebanese politicians.

Our government, from the very moment the Syrian occupier
left, let ships and truckloads of arms pour into our country without
even bothering to look at their cargo. They jeopardized all chances
for the rebirth of our country by confusing the Cedar Revolution
with the liberation of Beirut [the demonstrations and popular civic
action in Lebanon – mainly Beirut – triggered by the assassination
of former Muslim Prime Minister Rafik Hariri on 14 February,
2005.] In reality, we had just received the chance – a sort of
unhoped-for moratorium – that allowed us to take the future into
our own hands, nothing more . . .

And when I speak of a catastrophe, I do not mean the action
accomplished by Israel in response to the aggression against its

civilians and its army, which was produced from our soil and that we did strictly nothing to avoid, and for which we are consequently responsible. Any avoiding of this responsibility ... means that Lebanon, as a state, does not exist...

Politicians either support this insane idea or keep silent. Those we would expect to speak, to save our image, remain silent like the others. And I am precisely alluding to general Aoun, who could have made a move by proclaiming the truth. Even his enemy, Walid Jumblatt, the Druse leader, has proved to be less vague...

Before the Israeli attack, Lebanon no longer existed; it was no more than a hologram. At Beirut innocent citizens like me were forbidden access to certain areas of their own capital. But our police, our army and our judges were also excluded. That was the case, for example, of Hizb'allah's and the Syrians' command zone in the Haret Hreik quarter (a square measuring a kilometer wide, a capital within the capital), permanently guarded by a Horla army, possessing its own institutions, its schools, its crèches, its tribunals, its radio, its television and, above all its government. A "government" that, alone decided, in the place of the figureheads of the Lebanese government (in which Hizb'allah also had its ministers!) to attack a neighboring state, with which we had no substantial or grounded quarrel, and to plunge *us* into a bloody conflict. And if attacking a sovereign nation on its territory, assassinating eight of its soldiers, kidnapping two others and, simultaneously, launching missiles on nine of its towns does not constitute a *casus belli*, the latter juridical principle will seriously need revising.

Thus almost all of these cowardly politicians, including numerous Shi'ia leaders and religious personalities themselves, are blessing each bomb that falls from a Jewish F-16 turning the insult to our sovereignty that was Haret Hreik, right in the heart of Beirut, into a lunar landscape. Without the Israelis, how could we have received another chance ... to rebuild our country?

With each Irano-Syrian fort that Jerusalem destroys, with each Islamic fighter they eliminate, Lebanon proportionally starts to live again! Once again, the soldiers of Israel are doing our work. Once again, like in 1982, we are watching ... their heroic sacrifice that allows us to keep hoping ... Because, of course, by dint of not giving a damn for southern Lebanon, of letting foreigners take hold of the privileges that belong to us, we no longer had the ability to recover our independence and sovereignty. If, at the end of this war, the Lebanese army retakes control over its territory and gets rid of the state within a state (that tried to suffocate the latter), it will only be thanks to Tsahal [the Israeli Defense Forces]...

As for the destruction caused by the Israelis, that is another imposture ... the parts of my capital that have been destroyed by Israel ... are Haret Hreik – in its totality – and the dwellings of Hizb'allah's leaders, situated in the large Shi'ia suburb of Dayaa.

In addition to these two zones, Tsahal [IDF] has exploded a nine-storied building that housed Hizb'allah's command, in Beirut's city center ... It was Nasrallah's "perch" inside the city, whereby he asserted his presence and domination over us. A depot of Syrian arms in the port, two army radars that the Shi'ite officers had put at the Hizb'allah's disposal and a truck suspected of transporting arms, in the Christian quarter of Ashrafieh.

Moreover the road and airport infrastructures were put out of working order: they served to provide Hizb'allah with arms and munitions. Apart from that, Tsahal (IDF) has neither hit nor deteriorated anything ... Even the houses situated one alley's distance from the targets I mentioned have not been hit, they have not even suffered a scratch; on contemplating these results of this work you understand the meaning of the concept "surgical strikes" and you can admire the dexterity of the Jewish pilots.

Beirut, that is 95% of Beirut, lives and breathes better than a fortnight ago. All those who have not sided with terrorism know they have strictly nothing to fear from the Israeli planes, on the contrary! One example: last night the restaurant where I went to eat was jammed full and I had to wait until 9:30 pm to get a table. Everyone was smiling, relaxed, but no one filmed them: a strange destruction of Beirut, is it not?

Of course, there are some 500,000 refugees from the south who are experiencing a veritable tragedy and who are not smiling. But Jean [Tsadik], who has his eyes fixed on Kfar Kileh, and from whom I have learned to believe each word he says, assures me that practically all the houses of the aforesaid refugees are intact. So they will be able to come back as soon as Hizb'allah is vanquished.

The defeat of the Shi'ia fundamentalists of Iranian allegiance is imminent. The figures communicated by Nasrallah's minions and by the Lebanese Red-Cross are deceiving: firstly, of the 400 dead declared by Lebanon, only 150 are real collateral civilian victims of the war, the others were militiamen without uniform serving Iran. The photographic report "Les Civils des bilans libanais" made by Stéphane Juffa for our agency constitutes, to this day, the unique tangible evidence of this gigantic morbid manipulation, which makes this document eminently important.

Moreover, Hassan Nasrallah's organization has not lost 200 combatants, as Tsahal [IDF] claims. This figure only concerns the combats taking place on the border and even then the Israelis underestimate it, for a reason that escapes me, by about a hundred militiamen eliminated. The real count of Hizb'allah's casualties, that includes those dead in Beirut, the Beka'a Valley, Ba'albek and their other camps, rocket and missile launchers and arms and munition depots amounts to 1,100 supplementary Hizb'allah militiamen who have definitively ceased to terrorize and humiliate my country.

Like the overwhelming majority of Lebanese, I pray that no one puts an end to the Israeli attack before it finishes shattering the terrorists. I pray that the Israeli soldiers will penetrate all the hidden recesses of southern Lebanon and will hunt out, in our stead...

...I wish to express my infinite gratitude to the relatives of the Israeli victims – civilian and military –whose loved ones have fallen so that I can live standing upright in my identity. They should know that I weep with them.

As for the pathetic clique that thrives at the head of my country, it is time for them to understand that after this war, after our natural allies have rid us of those who are hindering us from rebuilding a nation, a cease-fire or an armistice will not suffice. To ensure the future of Lebanon, it is time to make peace with those we have no reason to go to war against. In fact, only peace will ensure peace. Someone must tell them because in this country we have not learnt what a truism is.[2]

The last word

We have endeavored to analyse the Middle East situation from the human perspective. Frequently we do not understand the Lord's purpose in events; he explicitly says we will not understand all things while he also assures us of revealing truth to us:

The secret things belong to the LORD our God, but the things revealed belong to us and to our children forever, that we may follow all the words of this law.

(Deuteronomy 29:29)

In order to pray effectively we need to better understand the situation from the Lord's perspective. We will conclude by giving the Lord the final word, not only concerning the Middle East but globally.

Let us look firstly at the Middle East. There is an amazing prophetic word for Israel at the time when they all know the Lord from the least to the greatest (see Jeremiah 31:34).

"Arise, shine, for your light has come,
    and the glory of the Lord rises upon you.
See, darkness covers the earth
    and thick darkness is over the peoples,
but the LORD rises upon you
    and his glory appears over you.
Nations will come to your light,
    and kings to the brightness of your dawn.

"Lift up your eyes and look about you:
    All assemble and come to you;
your sons come from afar,
    and your daughters are carried on the arm . . .
Herds of camels will cover your land,
    young camels of Midian and Ephah.
And all from Sheba will come,
    bearing gold and incense
    and proclaiming the praise of the Lord.
All Kedar's flocks will be gathered to you,
    the rams of Nebaioth will serve you;
they will be accepted as offerings on my altar,
    and I will adorn my glorious temple."

(Isaiah 60:1–4, 6–7)

Not only is this prophetic of the time when the Jewish people know the Lord and all the nations are coming up to Jerusalem but also when the Arab people know the Lord. Ishmael had many sons, two of them especially famous – one was Nebaioth and the other Kedar. Midian and Ephah are two sons of Abraham from Keturah his wife after the death of Sarah (see Genesis 25:1–4, 13). Collectively they represent the Arab people whom the Lord promises he will draw to worship him, bringing their wealth as gifts to him in the Promised Land. All this will happen after the Lord has broken the power of Islam and set the Arab nations free. The Lord further describes this scene:

> Let the desert and its towns raise their voices;
>   let the settlements where Kedar lives rejoice.
> Let the people of Sela sing for joy;
>   let them shout from the mountain tops.
> Let them give glory to the LORD
>   and proclaim his praise in the islands.

(Isaiah 42:11–12)

God also has a prophetic word for the Palestinians: for Hamas and the Palestinian Authority:

> Ashkelon will see it and fear
>   [how the Lord deals with the Arab countries]
>   Gaza will writhe in agony
>   and Ekron too, for her hope will wither.

(Zechariah 9:5)

Ashkelon, Gaza and Ekron are all cities of the Philistines. In the Arab Bible "Philistia" and "Philistine" are the same word. "Palestinian" today is the same word in Arabic.

Philistia was the Greek name for the land of the Philistines, a people of Aegean origin who occupied Gaza and that region from the twelfth century BC at the time the Israelites also inhabited the region. The Latinised name *Palaestina* was given to Judea by the Emperor Hadrian in AD 135 when he crushed Jewish resistance to Roman rule. After a general massacre he ordered that no Jews could live in Jerusalem, which he renamed *Aelia Capitolina* and consecrated to the cult of Jupiter.

The Eastern Church, then known as the Byzantium Church,

rigorously restored the prohibition of Jews in Jerusalem from about AD 476. Then from the seventh century the new Arab rulers tolerated only a very restricted Jewish presence in Jerusalem.

It is essential to note that Hadrian's exclusion of the Jewish people from Jerusalem was the result of a political war, while the Church prohibition of the Jewish presence in Jerusalem was not political but it was an essential element of their anti-Jewish teaching and replacement theology. This trend continues to this day as an anti-Zionist stand by much of the Church, even influencing Western governments' refusal to acknowledge Jerusalem as the capital of Israel.

God speaks of the Palestinians in Zechariah and he speaks of the changes he plans in them. The Lord has spoken of what he will do with Hamas and the Palestinian Authority:

> Gaza will lose her king [their leaders]
>   and Ashkelon will be deserted.
> Foreigners will occupy Ashdod,
>   and I will cut off the pride of the Philistines.
> I will take the blood from their mouths,
>   the forbidden food from between their teeth.
> Those who are left will belong to our God
>   and become leaders in Judah,
>   and Ekron will be like the Jebusites.
>
> (Zechariah 9:5–7)

The Lord plans an extraordinary transforming work among the Palestinian people, where their violence will cease, their rejection of Israel become acceptance and they will be a redeemed people. It is unbelievable how the Lord plans, not to liquidate the Palestinian people, but to integrate them into Israel. It happened once to the Jebusites, when they were enemies of Israel and the Lord integrated them into the tribe of Judah. He will do it again with the Palestinians, integrating them into the chosen people in the Promised Land.

Then as we survey the nations today, increasingly dragged into fear by global terrorism, we read of God's promises of intervention and transformation as he sovereignly calls the nations into divine order:

Why do the nations conspire
   and the peoples plot in vain?
The kings of the earth take their stand
   and rulers gather together against the LORD
   and against his Anointed One.
"Let us break their chains," they say,
   "and throw off their fetters."

The One enthroned in heaven laughs;
   the LORD scoffs at them.
Then he rebukes them in his anger
   and terrifies them in his wrath, saying,
"I have installed my King
   on Zion, my holy hill."

I will proclaim the decree of the LORD:

He said to me, "You are my Son;
   today I have become your Father.
Ask of me,
   and I will make the nations your inheritance,
   the ends of the earth your possession.
You will rule them with an iron scepter;
   you will dash them to pieces like pottery."

Therefore, you kings, be wise;
   be warned, you rulers of the earth.
Serve the LORD with fear
   and rejoice with trembling.
Kiss the Son, lest he be angry
   and you are destroyed in your way,
for his wrath can flare up in a moment.
   Blessed are all who take refuge in him.

                        (Psalm 2)

The word that Isaiah the son of Amoz saw concerning Judah and Jerusalem.

   Now it shall come to pass in the latter days
   That the mountain of the LORD's house
   Shall be established on the top of the mountains,
   And shall be exalted above the hills;

And all nations shall flow to it.
Many people shall come and say,
"Come, and let us go up to the mountain of the Lord,
To the house of the God of Jacob;
He will teach us His ways,
And we shall walk in His paths."
For out of Zion shall go forth the law,
And the word of the Lord from Jerusalem.
He shall judge between the nations,
And rebuke many people;
They shall beat their swords into plowshares,
And their spears into pruning hooks;
Nation shall not lift up sword against nation,
Neither shall they learn war anymore.

(Isaiah 2:1–4, NKJV)

Appendix 1

Roman Catholic Policy Change

The Second Vatican Council (1962–65), called on the initiative of Pope John XXIII, also dealt with the attitude of the Catholic Church towards Judaism. A declaration, *Nostra aetate* ("In our time"), on the attitude of the Church toward non-Christian religions, was formulated by Cardinal Bea and the Secretariat for Christian Unity, and was promulgated on 28 October, 1965. It reads:

> As this sacred synod searches into the mystery of the Church, it remembers the bond that spiritually ties the people of the New Covenant to Abraham's stock.
>
> Thus the Church of Christ acknowledges that, according to God's saving design, the beginnings of her faith and her election are found already among the Patriarchs, Moses and the prophets. She professes that all who believe in Christ – Abraham's sons according to faith – are included in the same Patriarch's call, and likewise that the salvation of the Church is mysteriously foreshadowed by the chosen people's exodus from the land of bondage. The Church, therefore, cannot forget that she received the revelation of the Old Testament through the people with whom God in his inexpressible mercy concluded the Ancient Covenant. Nor can she forget that she draws sustenance from the root of that well-cultivated olive tree onto which have been grafted the wild shoots, the Gentiles. Indeed, the Church believes that by his cross, Christ our Peace reconciled Jews and Gentiles, making both one in himself.
>
> The Church keeps ever in mind the words of the Apostle about his kinsmen: "Theirs is the sonship and the glory and the covenants and the law and the worship and the promises: theirs are the fathers and from them is the Christ according to the flesh"

(Romans 9:4–5), the Son of the Virgin Mary. She also recalls that the Apostles, the Church's mainstay and pillars, as well as most of the early disciples who proclaimed Christ's Gospel to the world, sprang from the Jewish people.

As Holy Scripture testifies, Jerusalem did not recognize the time of her visitation, nor did the Jews, in large number, accept the Gospel; indeed not a few opposed its spreading.

Nevertheless, God holds the Jews most dear for the sake of their Fathers; he does not repent of the gifts he makes or of the calls he issues – such is the witness of the Apostle. In company with the Prophets and the same Apostle, the Church awaits that day, known to God alone, on which all peoples will address the Lord in a single voice and "serve him shoulder to shoulder" (Zephaniah 3:9).

Since the spiritual patrimony common to Christians and Jews is thus so great, this sacred synod wants to foster and recommend that mutual understanding and respect which is the fruit, above all, of biblical and theological studies as well as of fraternal dialogues.

True, the Jewish authorities and those who followed their lead pressed for the death of Christ; still, what happened in his passion cannot be charged against all Jews, without distinction, then alive, nor against the Jews of today. Although the Church is the new people of God, the Jews should not be presented as rejected or accursed as if this followed from the Holy Scriptures. All should see to it, then, that in catechetical work or in the preaching of the word of God they do not teach anything that does not conform to the truth of the Gospel and the spirit of Christ.

Furthermore, in her rejection of every persecution against any man, the Church, mindful of the patrimony she shares with the Jews and moved not by political reasons but by the Gospel's spiritual love, decries hatred, persecutions, displays of anti-Semitism, directed against Jews at any time and by anyone.

Besides, as the Church has always held and holds now, Christ underwent his passion and death freely, because of the sins of men and out of infinite love, in order that all may reach salvation. It is, therefore, the burden of the Church's preaching to proclaim the cross of Christ as the sign of God's all-embracing love and as the fountain from which every grace flows.

Appendix 2

Profession of faith – renouncing Jewishness

This Profession of faith, from the Church of Constantinople, reflects Christian hatred towards Jews and shows us the impossible situation for Jewish Christians who held precious their Jewishness:

As a preliminary to his acceptance as a catechumen (one undergoing training and instruction before baptism), a Jew, "must confess and denounce verbally the whole Hebrew people, and forthwith declare that with a whole heart and sincere faith he desires to be received among the Christians. Then he must renounce openly in the church all Jewish superstition, the priest saying, and he, or his sponsor if he is a child, replying in these words:

"I renounce all customs, rites, legalisms, unleavened breads and sacrifices of the lambs of the Hebrews, and all the other feasts of the Hebrews, sacrifices, prayers, aspersions, purifications, sanctifications and propitiations, and fasts, and new moons, and Sabbaths, and superstitions, and hymns and chants and observances and synagogues, and the food and drink of the Hebrews; in one word I renounce absolutely everything Jewish, every law, rite and custom, and above all I renounce Antichrist, whom all the Jews await in the figure and form of Christ; and I join myself to the true Christ and God. And I believe in the Father, the Son and the Holy Spirit, the Holy, Consubstantial and Indivisible Trinity, and the dispensation in the flesh and the descent to men of the Word of God, of the one person of the Holy Trinity, and I confess that he was truly made man, and I believe and proclaim that after the flesh in very truth the Blessed Virgin Mary bore him the son of God; and I believe in, receive, venerate and embrace the adorable Cross of Christ, and the holy images; and thus, with my whole heart, and soul, and with a true faith I come to the Christian Faith. But if it be with deceit and with hypocrisy, and not with a sincere and perfect faith and a genuine love of Christ, but with a pretence to be a Christian that I come, and if afterwards I shall wish to deny and return to Jewish superstition, or shall be found eating with Jews or feasting with them, or secretly conversing and condemning the Christian religion instead of openly confuting them and condemning their vain faith, then let the trembling of Cain and the leprosy of Gehazi cleave to me, as well as the legal punishments to which I acknowledge myself liable. And may I be anathema in the world to come, and may my soul be set down with satan and the devils.''

(As quoted in James Parkes, *The Conflict of the Church and the Synagogue*, pp. 397–398.)

Maps

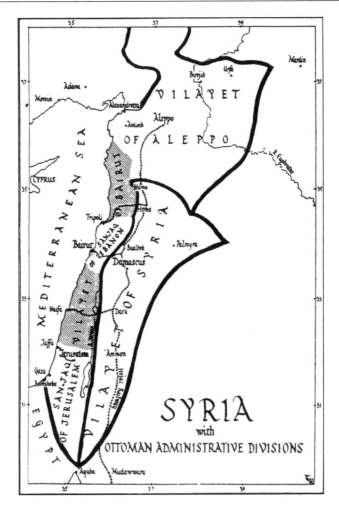

Syria before World War I was a region of the Ottoman Empire.
Note the names of the provinces and sub-provinces ("Villayets"
and "Sanjaks"). After that war, mandates were awarded by the
League of Nations to Britain and France to administer the region.
Syria was truncated to create Lebanon, Palestine, Jordan and Iraq.

Syria has constantly striven to recover its former glory: *Greater
Syria*. Lebanon received its independence from France in 1943 as a
predominantly Christian state. Part of Palestine was to become the
Jewish State of Israel in 1948, and Jordan was also part of
mandated Palestine.

Note: Palestine did not exist during the Ottoman Empire.

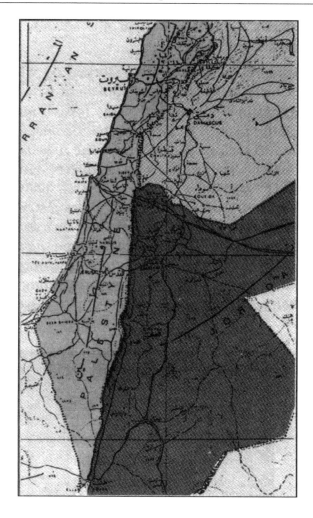

This official map of the Middle East published by the Syrian
Government explains Syria's intention regarding Israel.
Note that "Israel" does not appear, it is replaced with
"Palestyne." Consider this map in the light of Syria's
"peace" overtures and Israel's security. Syrian Defence
Minister Mustafa Tlas spoke on Damascus television on
7 March, 1990: "The conflict between the Arab Nation
and Zionism is over existence, not borders."

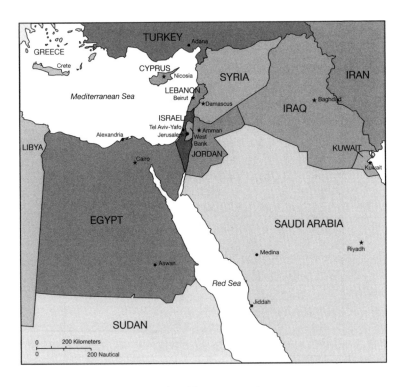

Map of Middle East countries.

Bibliography

Barr, Marius, *The Unholy War*, 1980

Bivin, David and Blizzard, Roy B., *Understanding the Difficult Words of Jesus*, 1983

Burnett, Ken, *Why Pray for Israel?*, 1983

Charif, R. & Raz, S, *Jerusalem the Eternal Bond*, 1977

Cohn, N., *Warrant for Genocide*, 1967

Crombie, Kelvin, *A Jewish Bishop in Jerusalem: Michael Solomon Alexander 1841–1845*, Nicolayson's Ltd, 2006

Crombie, Kelvin, *For the Love of Zion*, Hodder & Stoughton, 1991

Cross, F. L., *The Oxford Dictionary of the Christian Church*, 1963

Dixon, Murray, *Whose Promised Land?*, Heinemann Education, 1991

Edersheim, Alfred, *The Life and Times of Jesus the Messiah*

Edersheim, Alfred, *Sketches of Jewish Social Life*, 1876

Ellison, H. L., *The Mystery of Israel*, 1966

Encyclopedia Judaica, 1972

Eusebius, *The History of the Church*, 1965

Facts about Israel, The Authorized Handbook to Israel 1985

Feinberg, Charles L., *Israel at the Center of History and Revelation*, 1980

Fischer, J., *The Olive Tree Connection*, 1983

Flannery, Edward, *The Anguish of the Jews*

Fruchtenbaum, Arnold G., *Hebrew Christianity: Its Theology, History and Philosophy*, 1983

Gade, Richard E., *A Historical Survey of Anti-Semitism*, 1981

Gartenhaus, Jacob, *Famous Hebrew Christians*, 1979

History until 1880, Keter Books, 1973

Hitler, Adolf, *My Struggle*, 1933

Jocz, Jakob, *The Jewish People and Jesus Christ after Auschwitz*, 1981

Josephus, F., *The Jewish War*

Kjaer-Hansen, Kai, *Joseph Rabinowitz and the Messianic Movement*, 1995

Kjaer-Hansen, Kai, & Skjott, Bodil F., *Facts and Myths about the Messianic Congregations in Israel, 1998–1999*, Mishkan, 1999

Koenig, William, *Eye to Eye: Facing the Consequences of Dividing Israel*, 2004

Laffin, John, *The Israeli Mind*, 1979

Lambert, Lance, *The Uniqueness of Israel*, 1980

Lapide, Pinchas E., *Jesus in Israeli School Books, Journal of Ecumenical Studies*, summer 1973, pp. 515–531

Lapide, Pinchas E., *The Last Three Popes and the Jews*, 1967

Lewis, Bernard, *The Middle East: a Brief History of the Last 2,000 Years*, 1995

Littell, Franklin H., *The Crucifixion of the Jews: the Failure of Christians to Understand the Jewish Experience*, 1975

Lloyd George, David, *Is it Peace?*, 1923

Lossin, Y., *Pillar of Fire*, 1983

MacNaughton, K. A., *The Covenants and the Promises*, 1978

Margolis, Max L., and Marx, Alexander, *A History of the Jewish People*, 1927

Merkley, Paul Charles, *Christian Attitudes towards the State of Israel*, 2001

Morse, A. D., *While Six Million Dies: A Chronicle of American Apathy*, 1967

Mussner, Franz, *Tractate on the Jews: the Significance of Judaism for the Christian Faith*, 1984

Neander, Augustus, *General History of the Christian Religion and Church*, 1871 [5 vols]

Neander, Augustus, *History of the Planting and Training of the Christian Church by the Apostles*, 1851 [2 vols]

Parkes, James, *The Conflict of the Church and the Synagogue*, 1969

Pragai, Michael, J., *Faith and Fulfillment: Christians and the Return to the Promised Land*, 1985

Prince, Derek, *The Last Word on the Middle East*, 1983

Prittie, T. & Nelson, W. H., *The Economic War Against the Jews*, 1979

Rebiai, Marcel, *Islam, Israel and the Church*, 2006

Rupp, E. Gordon, *Martin Luther and the Jews*, 1972

Schonfield, H. J., *The History of Jewish Christianity*,

Shirer, William L., *The Rise and Fall of the Third Reich*, 1960

Sparrow-Simpson, W. J., *Lectures on St Bernard of Clairvaux*, 1895

St John, Robert, *Tongue of the Prophets*, 1952

Trachtenberg, Joshua, *The Devil and the Jews*, 1943

Tuchman, Barbara W., *Bible and Sword*, 1956

Wright, Fred, *Words from the Scroll of Fire*, 1994

Wright, Fred, *The Cross Became a Sword: the Soldiers of Christ and the First Crusade*, 1995

Wright, Fred, *Father Forgive Us: A Christian Response to the Church's Heritage of Jewish Persecution*, 2002

Wright, Fred (editor), *Israel: His People, His Land, His Story*, 2005

Ye'or, Bat, *Eurabia: The Euro-Arab Axis*, 2005

Young, Brad, *The Jewish Background to the Lord's Prayer*, 1984

Notes and Recommended Reading

Chapter 1: "The Truth Will Set You Free"

Notes

1. Jocz, Jakob, *The Jewish People and Jesus Christ after Auschwitz*, pp. 7–8
2. The statement is found in Appendix 1.
3. Stott J., *God's New Society*
4. An example of mistranslation is evidenced in the version authorized by King James I, published in England in 1611. In the New Testament an extraordinary exchange was made. Wherever the name "Jacob" occurred it was replaced by the King's name, "James." "James" is not a Jewish name, it appears nowhere in the Old Testament and there is no mention in the New Testament of the common Jewish name "Jacob" (other than through quotations from the Old Testament).
5. Bivin D. & Blizzard R., *The Difficult Words of Jesus*, p. 38
6. As quoted in *May Your Name Be Inscribed in the Book of Life*, p. iii.
7. Prince D., *Israel and the Church: Parallel Restoration* an address
8. Jewish Christian, a modern current term, is used in this book to denote a Jewish person who has recognized and received the Lord Jesus as Savior and Lord. Many other terms are sometimes used such as Hebrew Christian, Messianic Jew, completed Jew, and fulfilled Jew.

   In Jewish circles, whatever term is used, Jews who have declared such a personal faith in Jesus are usually regarded as "converts" to Christianity. They are generally considered to have forsaken their Jewishness and "gone over to the other side," to the Gentile faith. They are often regarded as traitors.

   This is the complete opposite of scriptural teaching because:
   1. The problem of "who is a Jew?" is only solved through the work of the Holy Spirit as outlined in Romans 2:28–29.
   2. It is the Gentiles who have been converted, and grafted into the Jewish faith (Ephesians 2:12–13).

   It is biblically correct to both call and to regard Jewish believers simply "Jews." Paul said "I am a Jew," subsequent to his transforming encounter with Christ (Acts 21:39 and 22:3).

9. Gartenhaus, J., *Famous Hebrew Christians*, p. 26

10. Ibid, p. 26 footnote

11. Jocz J., *The Jewish People and Jesus Christ*, p. 247

Recommended reading

J. Jocz, *The Jewish People and Jesus Christ after Auschwitz*

David Bivin and Roy Blizzard, *The Difficult Words of Jesus*

Brad Young, *The Jewish Background to the Lord's Prayer*

Chapter 2: The Jewishness of Jesus

Notes

1. Lapide, P. E., *The Last Three Popes and the Jews*, pp. 17–18

2. Ibid

Recommended reading

Arnold Fruchtenbaum, *Jesus was a Jew*

Alfred Edersheim, *The Life and Times of Jesus the Messiah*

Pinchas E. Lapide, *The Last Three Popes and the Jews*

Chapter 3: Members of the Commonwealth of Israel

Notes

1. A. Edersheim, *The Life and Times of Jesus the Messiah, Book 1*, pp. 91–92

2. *Messiah* is the Hebrew word for "anointed One." Most translations of the Bible use the equivalent Greek word "Christ." Jewish people recognize *Messiah* but "Christ" is a Gentile word.

Recommended reading

K. A. McNaughtan, *The Covenants and the Promises*

Dwight Pentecost, *Thy Kingdom Come*

Chapter 4: Mysteries Revealed

Recommended reading

Samuel Schor, *The Everlasting Nation and their Coming King*

Chapter 5: The Synagogue and the Church

Notes

1. Neander, *A History of the Planting and Training of the Christian Church by the Apostles*, volume 1

2. Justin Martyr, *The First Apology* as quoted in *Ante-Nicene Fathers*, vol. 1, pp. 185–186

3. A. Fruchtenbaum, *Hebrew Christianity*, p. 95

4. J. Parkes, *The Conflict of the Church and the Synagogue*, p. 119

Recommended reading

Arnold Fruchtenbaum, *Hebrew Christianity*

James Parkes, *The Conflict of the Church and the Synagogue*

Chapter 6: The Separation of the Synagogue and the Church

Notes

1. Eusebius, *A History of the Church*, p. 231

2. F. L. Cross, *The Oxford Dictionary of the Christian Church*, pp. 1089, 1131

3. H. J. Schonfield, *The History of Jewish Christianity*, p. 54

4. J. Parkes, *The Conflict of the Church and the Synagogue*, p. 92

Recommended reading

A. Fruchtenbaum, *Hebrew Christianity*

J. Jocz, *The Jewish People and Jesus Christ*

J. Parkes, *The Conflict of the Church and the Synagogue*

Chapter 7: The Deluded Church

Notes

1. F. H. Littell, *The Crucifixion of the Jews*, p. 63

2. *Encyclopaedia Judaica*, Volume 10, pp. 21–23

3. P. E. Lapide, *The Last Three Popes and the Jews*, p. 53

4. Ibid., p. 55

5. Pseudo Cyprian, *Adversus Judaeos*, as quoted by Parkes, J., in *The Conflict of the Church and the Synagogue*, pp. 105–106

6. *Chrysostom's Sermons* as quoted by Parkes, J., ibid., pp. 163–164

7. *Eleventh Letter to Theodosius*, as quoted by Parkes, J., ibid., pp. 166–167

8. P. E. Lapide, *The Last Three Popes and the Jews*, pp. 43–44

9. *Encyclopaedia Judaica*, vol. 3, p. 102

Chapter 8: "No Place to Rest and a Despairing Heart"

Notes

1. A. Bridge, *The Crusades*, p. 111

2. W. J. Sparrow-Simpson, *Lectures on St. Bernard of Clairvaux*, pp. 172–174

3. P. E. Lapide, *The Last Three Popes and the Jews*, p. 58

4. L. O. Pike, 1873, as quoted by Lapide, P. I., *The Last Three Popes and The Jews*, p. 55

5. R. E. Gade, *A Historical Survey of Anti-Semitism*, p. 82

6. Ibid. p. 89

7. *Encyclopaedia Judaica*, vol. 4, p. 1121

8. Ibid. p. 1121

9. D. Lloyd George, *Is it Peace?*, pp. 246–247

Recommended reading

R. E. Gade, *A Historical Survey of Anti-Semitism*

B. Tuchman, *A Distant Mirror*, chapter 5

A. Bridge, *The Crusades*

Chapter 9: Preparing the Way for the Holocaust

Notes

1. *Hadashot*, Israeli daily newspaper, 20 March, 1987

2. R.I. Gade, *A Historical Survey of Anti-Semitism*, p. 51

3. M. Barr, *The Unholy War*, p. 121

4. J. Gartenhaus, *Famous Hebrew Christians*, p. 26 footnote

5. W. L. Shirer, *The Rise and Fall of the Third Reich*, p. 294

6. *Christian Jewish Relations*, Vol. 16, No. 4, 1983, article *Hitler on Jesus*, pp. 60–61

7. A. Hitler, *My Struggle*, p. 59

8. *Encyclopaedia Judaica*, vol. 6, p. 582

9. Ibid., p. 582

10. Wikipedia, *The Protocols of the Elders of Zion.*

11. Ibid

12. Ibid

13. A. Foxman, *A Case of Racism* in *Australia/Israel Review*, Vol. 12, No. 8, 11–26 May 1987

14. *Japan's Problem with Israel and Jews* in *The Washington Post*, 21 May, 1987

15. *The Eternal P.L.O.* in *Australia/Israel Review*, Vol. 12, No. 8, 11–26 May, 1987

16. Golda Meir, *My Life*, pp. 152–153, 155–156

17. L. Elliott, "Berlin: 25 Years of the Wall," *Reader's Digest*, August, 1986, p. 89

18. J. Laffin, *The Israeli Mind*, p. 231

19. A. D. Morse, *While Six Million Died*, p. 210

20. Ibid., p. 211

21. Ibid., p. 212

22. Golda Meir, *My Life*, pp. 151–152

23. A. D. Morse, *While Six Million Died*, p. 214

24. *Jerusalem Post*, 21 February, 2006, p. 16: article "Remembering William Temple" by Rafael Medoff, Director of the David S. Wyman Institute of Holocaust Studies
25. E. G. Rupp, *Martin Luther and the Jews*, p. 22

Recommended reading

William Koenig, *Eye to Eye: Facing the Consequences of Dividing Israel*

Chapter 10: "I Will Bless Those Who Bless You"

Notes

1. F. H. Littell, *The Crucifixion of the Jews*, p. 99
2. E. and J. Cartwright, *The Petition of the Jews for the Repealing of the Act of Parliament for their Banishment out of England*, London, 1649 – as quoted by B. Tuchman, *The Bible and the Sword*, p. 121.
3. Ibid, p. 144
4. Ibid, p. 178
5. B. Tuchman, *The Bible and the Sword*, p. 191
6. Ibid, p. 192
7. Ibid, p. 220
8. Ibid, p. 224
9. *Encyclopaedia Judaica*, vol. 4, p. 131
10. B. Tuchman, p. 312
11. C. Sykes, *Orde Wingate*, p. 112, as quoted by M. Pragai in *Faith and Fulfillment*.

Recommended reading

B. Tuchman, *Bible and Sword*
K. Crombie, *For the Sake of Zion*
K. Burnett, *Why Pray for Israel?*

Chapter 11: The Time to Favor Zion Has Come

Notes

1. Comment by the Reverend Wingate about Edersheim as quoted by Gartenhaus, J., *Famous Hebrew Christians*, p. 76
2. Ibid, p. 23
3. A. D. Morse, *While Six Million Died*, p. 218
4. J. Gartenhaus, *Famous Hebrew Christians*, p. 24
5. Ibid, footnote p. 25
6. Ibid, p. 174

7. *Jerusalem Intelligence*, 1843, p. 152 as quoted in *For the Love of Zion*, p. 48

8. Barbara W. Tuchman, *Bible and Sword*, New York 1956, p. 207

9. M. Corey, *From Rabbi to Bishop*, p. 105

10. L. A. Frankel, *Nach Jerusalem* (Leipzig, 1858), p. 70; as quoted in *For the Love of Zion*, p. 3

11. Alfred Sawyer, "The Church that Shouldn't Be" published in *Prayer for Israel NZ*, January–February 1991, No. 55

12. Gershon Nerel, *Israel: His People, His Land, His Story*, chapter "From Death to Life," p. 168

13. Ibid, p. 174

14. Roger Allison, *Journey to Jerusalem*, privately published, p. 45

15. Roger Allison, *Journey to Jerusalem*, pp. 45–46

16. Gershon Nerel, *Israel: His People, His Land, His Story*, chapter "From Death to Life," p. 176

17. Ben Hoekendijk, *Twelve Jews Discover Messiah*, p. 99

18. Kai Kjaer-Hansen and Bodil F. Skjott (editors), *Facts & Myths about the Messianic Congregations in Israel*, pp. 48–49, 229–230

19. Ibid, pp. 50–51

Recommended reading

Jacob Gartenhaus, *Famous Hebrew Christians*

Kelvin Crombie, *For the Love of Zion*

Kelvin Crombie, *A Jewish Bishop in Jerusalem: Michael Solomon Alexander 1841–1845*

Kai Kjaer-Hansen and Bodil F. Skjott, *Facts & Myths About the Messianic Congregations in Israel*

Chapter 12: Israel Regathered by God

Notes

1. *TIME*, 22 June, 1981

2. Keter Publishing, *History of the Land of Israel from 1880*, p. 123

3. See J. Peters, *From Time Immemorial*

4. D. Bivin, *Kesher: The Hebrew Connection in Dispatch from Jerusalem*, 3rd quarter 1987

5. J. Gartenhaus, *Famous Hebrew Christians*, p. 73

6. F. Josephus, *The Jewish War*, p. 292

7. Ibid, p. 303

8. Ibid, p. 323

Recommended reading

Arieh Avneri, *The Claim of Dispossession*

Chapter 13: The Restoration of Israel

Notes

1. BIPAC Publication, *Coming Home*, p. 12
2. *The Jerusalem Post*, 8 January, 1969
3. Mark Twain, *Innocents Abroad*, 1869
4. Winston Churchill, Speech in the House of Commons, 14 June, 1921
5. *Facts about Israel*, 1985, p. 67
6. *Facts about Israel*, 1985, p. 104
7. David Pawson, Speech in Brisbane, 9 October, 1985, *The Meaning of the Feast of Tabernacles*
8. R. St John, *Tongue of the Prophets*
9. Ibid
10. T. Prittie and W. H. Nelson, *The Economic War Against the Jews*, pp. 170–171

Recommended reading

Murray Dixon, *Whose Promised Land?*

Chapter 14: Jubilee

Notes

1. L. Lambert, *The Uniqueness of Israel*, p. 131
2. Y. Lossin, *Pillar of Fire*, p. 55
3. Ibid, p. 57
4. Ibid, p. 61
5. *Jerusalem Post*, 8 June, 1967

Recommended reading

Derek Prince, *The Last Word on the Middle East*
Lance Lambert, *The Uniqueness of Israel*

Postscript

Notes

1. *Arutz Sheva*, News Report, 15 September, 2006
2. Michael Béhé, Beirut, Lebanon (Only at TNR Online; Post date 7 August, 2006)

Recommended reading

Bat Ye'or, *Eurabia: The Euro-Arab Axis*, 2005, Fairleigh Dickinson University Press
Marcel Rebiai, *Islam, Israel and the Church*, 2006, Sovereign World International

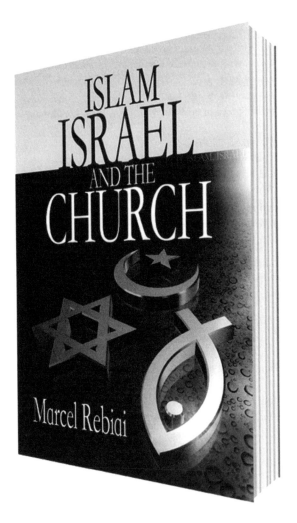

Islam, Israel and the Church
By Marcel Rebiai
£7.99 / PB / 160pp / 978 185240 4536

Operation Exodus
By Gustav Scheller
£7.99 / PB / 160pp / 978 185240 4543

THE CHRISTIAN, ISRAEL
AND THE HOPE OF WORLD REVIVAL

ISRAEL IN
ROMANS 9-11

MICHAEL
EATON

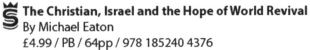

The Christian, Israel and the Hope of World Revival
By Michael Eaton
£4.99 / PB / 64pp / 978 185240 4376

We hope you enjoyed reading this Sovereign World book.
For more details of other Sovereign books and
new releases see our website:

www.sovereignworld.com

If you would like to help us send a copy of this book
and many other titles to needy pastors in the Third World,
please write for further information or send your gift to:

**Sovereign World Trust
PO Box 777
Tonbridge, Kent TN11 0ZS
United Kingdom**

You can also visit **www.sovereignworldtrust.com**.
The Trust is a registered charity.